For Edgar Estes Folk

CONTENTS

FOREWORD

My association with the Baptists began in North Carolina at the height of the Great Depression, when my father, who was a minister but not Baptist, was alienated from the church. "Alienated" may not be the right word. My father, who was Reformed, Nazarene, Advent Christian or Methodist, as the opportunity required, could not get a pastorate, and instead of preaching, which he dearly loved to do, he was walking the backroads of New Hanover County selling trees or Bibles or insurance — none of which moved very fast in those lean years.

We lived, or existed marginally, in a series of shacks on the main approaches to Wilmington, moving every time the past-due rent balance seriously affronted the owner. Uncle Willy Moore, a deacon in Wrightsboro Baptist Church, was the most forbearing, and we stayed in his soot-blackened tenant house on the Atlantic Coast Line Railroad tracks for several years. For me the highlight of every week was Sunday afternoon, when Mrs. George W. Trask — "Miss Emma" — came by in her Buick to pick up the BYPU kids and take them to a testimonial outing at the County Home. For Miss Emma it was an exercise in Christian stewardship, but for the kids, although marvelously subdued by Mrs. Trask's awesome driving, it was a social occasion. For the gift of the joy ride we were willing to make our payment — exacted in the form of a testimony before the old folks about how Jesus Christ had forgiven our transgressions and transformed our lives. To hear us tell it, we had been yanked out of lives of utter degradation by the miracle of conversion, and the old folks, some deaf, some almost blind, some working at a wad of dipped snuff with a sweet-gum brush, were honestly grateful for our entertaining visit; Mrs. Trask, who had strong maternal feelings for all these juvenile elect, was fortified spiritually for another week. Miss Emma took her religion very seriously.

My best friend was Sammy Josenhans, whose family, next to Mrs. Trask's, was the second richest in the church; they were displaced Yankees, but in the generosity of their tithe that misfortune was all but forgiven. Sammy and I had a deep sense of guilt about our Sunday afternoon testimonials, because he and I were not telling the whole truth. Although we honestly felt that we had been washed in the blood of the Lamb — Mrs. Trask said we had — we could not resist telling each other an occasional off-color joke or speculating on the recreational potential of the girls in our crowd. In addition, Sammy had an extensive profane vocabulary which he took joy in exercising. All of this, somehow, did not seem compatible with the trips to the County Home. One time, to please Miss Emma, Sammy dedicated his life to the foreign mission field, an event which greatly disturbed his parents. They had other plans for him, and although they could not openly derogate Mrs. Trask's missions, they tried to pray him out of his pledge. Sammy subsequently was run over by a train on the campus of N. C. State College, where he was studying engineering.

Mrs. Trask ran the church, wielding an influence in direct proportion to the size of her purse. As the principal member, she was often in direct collision with the Rev. J. Linwood Jones, who, like all Baptist ministers, served at the pleasure of the congregation. For his hundred dollars a month Preacher Jones presided at morning and evening worship on Sunday, conducted the mid-week prayer meeting, led the singing, was Master of the Boy Scout troop, oversaw the Sunday School, organized the training unions, encouraged the missionary circles, officiated at all the funerals and performed all the weddings. He was expected to visit the sick, assist the needy (out of his own salary), and play host to every itinerant bum looking for a handout. He was not a profound man, but he was a good one, perfectly situated in a small country church, and most of us were sorry when Mrs. Trask finally disagreed with him on a fine point of theology and ran him out.

I don't mean to imply that Mrs. Trask was vicious. She was the soul of generosity and kindness, with good intentions behind her every act — even the dispatch of the pastor. On the community at large she was surely a civilizing influence, because she kept a lot of us out of mischief and got us started on a quest for our souls. On her own family, a large one, she had very little influence, and the Trask kids were the wildest in the neighborhood. Except under extreme duress they avoided the church as the plague — in doing so following the example of their father. All of us who went with Mrs. Trask, and survived, have grown up to be solid, reasonably sober, respectable citizens. But none of us have come of age more solid, more sober, or more respectable than the Trask young, even though they resisted Miss Emma's spiritual example. And in a way they are the more honorable, because they were honest with their mother, and we were not.

What I have written here is largely of the dead: Sammy is gone, and both his parents, and Miss Emma, and Uncle Willy and Preacher Jones. I have not been back to the Wrightsboro church for thirty years, but it is still there; and a generation has grown up there who never heard of me or Sammy or Miss Emma or the Preacher I knew and loved. It is still Baptist, and I have gone on to other Baptist churches which teach the same things I learned at Wrightsboro. And so my association with the Baptists, which began long ago, has never ended. I attended the Baptist institution at which I now teach; I married a Baptist, who unlike me was born to the faith, and I have since been constantly a member of a Baptist fellowship somewhere. It does not bother me that my own roots are not Baptist; they are spiritual, and Baptists are spiritual. As I said, my father was a minister, and so was my grandfather and my great grandfather.

It has occurred to me over the years that if that tiny country church had so much influence on the Wrightsboro community, then the Baptist Church as a whole must have had a profound impact on American life and institutions. This book is an attempt to explore that relationship. It is not a history in the usual sense, although it contains history; the reader will find here an account of the founding of the Baptist Church in America and of its spread, but he will look in vain for the dates of the establishment of the Sunday School Board and the Woman's Missionary Union. The former movements are pertinent to my purpose, while the latter are not. How have the Baptists influenced American thought, American traditions? How have they been involved in American problems? In seeking the answers to these questions it has been necessary to give a broad overview of the development of the denomination, of its growth, divisions, triumphs and tragedies — and there has been some of all that. In that sense what we have here is the essence of history, shorn of some of its excess baggage.

To those who are offended because their special Baptist interest gets no attention in these pages, I can only apologize: no slight was intended. But, in truth, the diligent Baptist denominational presses have churned out mountains of historical material in which no phase of the life of the church is neglected. This is not an attempt to compete with them. It is conceivable, in fact probable, that some Baptists will be offended at what they find here. In that event the author can only say that he has sought, in love, to present the truth, and the truth is very often painful. But there are truths here, too, almost forgotten truths, that should make the step of every honest Baptist a little more prideful.

To attempt to give credit to all the people who have aided me in the preparation of this volume would be an impossible task, for how does one acknowledge all the influences of forty years? It is necessary, nevertheless, to pay at least passing respect to all those Baptist and non-Baptist historians of years gone by — some exceedingly careful, some unfortunately too jealous of Baptist prestige — who assembled most of the source materials on which I have depended: in particular, Isaac Backus; in particular, Albert Henry Newman; in particular, Davis C. Woolley, who gave so much encouragement in the conception of this work but who did not live to see it completed. It is necessary, too, to thank all those correspondents and interviewees who submitted so graciously to my questions. I am deeply obligated to my wife, through whose eyes I have learned much more about Baptists than I could ever have seen with my own; and I should like to thank the curatorial staff of the Ethel Taylor Crittenden Collection in Baptist History at Wake Forest University for allowing me over so many months to roam at will while examining their treasures.

B. S.

DIVIDED WE STAND

Chapter One: The "Peculiar" Baptists[1]

In almost every community in America, the red-brick church with the white steeple is a sight as commonplace as the town hall. And it is almost as busy. Just before 11 o'clock on a Sunday morning its tolling bell announces the morning worship service, and there may also be bells for Sunday School, before the evening assembly, at mid-week prayer. For weddings, funerals and more routine business, the church is in use almost every day and night of the week, over a surprising range of activities. The church supper and the church "social" endure, and the kitchen and dining tables have been supplemented by skating rinks and basketball courts. This typical church may not be of red brick; it may be of white boards. And if it is relatively new it may float low over the terrain, with large expanses of glass and concrete. Whatever its structure, the chances are about even that it is Baptist — with a name like First or Grace or Calvary or Mt. Gilead.

If it is Baptist, it is probably not the most prestigious church in town. The town fathers, the wealthy, the socially elite, the professional people and the intellectuals tend to be Episcopalian or Presbyterian, perhaps Congregationalist or Methodist, occasionally even Catholic, and their religious groupings are smaller even though more affluent.

The Baptist church is the great middle-class church, and it draws only sparingly from the upper middle class. This is not to say that there are not Baptist doctors and Baptist lawyers; in college towns there are a lot of Baptist professors; but the bulk of the membership is made up of small merchants, shopkeepers, traveling salesmen, minor town functionaries, public school teachers, insurance vendors, clerks, barbers, farmers (although rarely the wealthiest farmers) and their wives. Always the wives, and for them the church is the focal point of the universe. If the church is the second or third Baptist church in town (and therefore even less prestigious), the membership may include a sprinkling of laborers. To be sure, some of the fringe Baptist sects are made up almost exclusively of the lower class, and the minister, running his congregation with an iron fist and a closed mind, may not have attended college and may scoff openly at the idea of theological education. Among the more standard brands of Baptist belief the minister now, almost without exception, is a college graduate, attended a seminary, and often is assisted in his labors by a trained minister of music and other educated staff people. But this upward movement is a modern phenomenon. Baptist origins are among the poor, the class which has always been the most creative — and the most passionate — in launching religious movements.[2]

In the rural South in particular these humble beginnings are still much in evidence. The church may be austere, with a practical sanctuary and little more, perhaps not even a baptismal font. If the membership is less than 400, the pastor is paid, on the average, less than $75 a week, and the Sunday collection is barely adequate to cover that.[3] Nevertheless, this primitive assembly is blood brother to the million-dollar Texas congregation which pays its pastor $25,000 a year and hauls away its Sabbath receipts in an armored truck.

To say "Baptist" is to speak of a particular body of belief rather than a particular church, for there are at least 27 varieties of Baptists in the United States. They have 100,000 churches and nearly 26 million members, making them the largest group of Protestants in the country. (A complete listing and description of

2

the various Baptist branches is carried in Appendix A.) Each separate Baptist denomination is fiercely independent, as is each church within a denomination, and a Southern Baptist would not like to be confused with a Primitive or a Sabbatarian or a footwasher. In the same manner, to speak of National Baptists is to speak of black Baptists — and the Baptists claim more black members than any other church, although not in integrated congregations.

The Baptists are so splintered, in fact, that it is difficult to separate one from the other. What is not difficult is to distinguish the grounds of common belief, for there are certain basic, binding principles upheld by all Baptists, no matter how they may differ on other matters. These bedrock tenets, shared by all who bear the name Baptist, run generally as follows:

1. That the state of every man's spirituality is a matter of the individual conscience, answerable only to God, whom man can approach, through Jesus Christ, without other intermediary.

2. That a Christian church, which is properly both democratic and autonomous, must be made up only of morally regenerated believers in Christ.

3. That the Bible, the inspired Word of God, is the sole rule for faith and practice, and that every man is free to interpret the Scriptures for himself.

4. That the two ordinances of the Christian church are the Lord's Supper and baptism, the latter to be accomplished by immersion and to be accorded only to adult believers on their confession of faith.

5. That any union between the church and the state is repugnant, as is any attempt by the state to direct the religious belief of its citizens; on the other hand, the church has no right to direct the civic activity of its members.[4]

While all of these ideas are important, the area of baptism is the one from which the denomination draws its name and which most truly distinguishes the Baptists from other sects. A number of ideas are related to the baptismal rite. For one thing, Baptists reject the idea of infant baptism. They see baptism as a symbol of one's conscious decision to accept the teachings of Christ and to be converted; since an infant cannot make such a decision, baptism

3

must be reserved for competent adults. But the Baptist does not commit the unbaptized babe to hell; he believes that all babies are saved through God's grace. The Baptist does not believe that any miraculous benefit flows from the ordinance of baptism; it is simply the symbol of his regeneration. And he insists upon immersion, which he holds to be purely biblical, because it connotes one's being "buried with Christ" and "raised to walk in newness of life."[5]

It must be interpolated here that baptism is not a Baptist or a Christian invention. It derives from pagan customs, in which it was a kind of initiatory rite. With Christ it became a sign of the transformation in the life of the believer, and for at least the second and third centuries immersion appears to have been the practiced mode. Sprinkling, as a matter of convenience, was authorized around 250 A. D., and at about that same time the notion was popularized that in the act of baptism itself lay a host of magical virtues.[6] Whether immersion subsequently disappeared altogether is not clear, but by the early days of the Baptist Church, at least, it had been revived in Holland.

All Baptist churches share a preoccupation with baptism (there is a minority movement underway now, which may never be widely accepted, to recognize "alien" baptism — that brought in from another denomination), and they are all organized along the same lines. In church polity the basic idea is that of democracy. The officers, called deacons and trustees, are elected, and all matters of church business are decided by majority vote. The pastor is "called" by vote of the members, and he serves at their pleasure. In some churches this lack of tenure has resulted in a long succession of ministers serving only a short while, but in many churches, particularly in the South, the minister remains for decades. If he is strong, he runs the board of deacons and is the moving force in the church; if he is weak or retiring, the members run him; and if a strong pastor is placed in the midst of a congregation of strong members, clashes grow out of both temperament and theology. As a general rule the real power in Baptist churches lies in the hands of its most generous contributors; that is hardly scriptural, but a basic law of economics is at work. The power thus may reside with a bigot or a fanatic.

4

While the churches are autonomous, they do band together in associations and conventions, at the community, state and national levels. No action taken at these larger meetings, however, is binding upon a local church without its assent. While this spirit of democracy is one of the great strengths of the Baptist church, it is at the same time a great weakness. It is impossible for the Baptists to create a strong or genuinely effective central organization, and what may be ringing policy at the convention level may be no policy at all at the individual church level. For this reason Baptist power, while in certainty it exists, tends to be invisible. One cannot accurately speak, for example, of a Baptist "bloc vote," for at the polls Baptists are first Democrats and Republicans. On a few issues, as on the sale of alcoholic beverages or the licensing of a beer hall, the Baptist position is clear. But one could not with assurance predict that all members of a Baptist church would vote the same even then; otherwise there would not be a wet state in the South. Voting as a solid bloc, Baptists could overturn any proposition there. About the only modern issue on which a fairly unanimous consensus could be achieved among today's Baptists would be one involving an abstract principle as, say, the dispatch of an American ambassabor to the Vatican or Federal aid to parochial schools. Two historic values are imbedded there: the encroachment of civil authority on religion, and the dread hand of the Pope.

If Baptist power, by the nature of the church, is diffuse, it nevertheless is very real. Normally it is expressed through the individual member, governing his life by the rules he has learned starting with the Nursery, the Cradle Roll and the Sunbeams, and continuing on into the adult activities of the church. The hold thus gained on the individual has no comparable power in Protestantism. The Baptist church is strong against sin, and it implants in its members a vivid awareness of earthly vice and carnality and an exceptionally strong sense of guilt over even the most minor transgression. Although as an adult a Baptist may be intellectually liberated from church dogma, the sense of sin he learned as a child never leaves him. This sense is strongest in the areas of sex and alcohol. A Baptist woman may have an affair, but her mental anguish over it will never be entirely relieved; a Baptist man may take a drink, even become a seemingly sophisticated social drinker, but with every glass he will feel a twinge of guilt. And it will happen no matter how long either of them has been away from the church. Baptists take their religion seriously, and for many regular churchgoers life has no more important function. In the generation just passing, in particular, life is in large part dictated by the program of the church, and to suggest to these elders that there are other things worthy of equal attention, as education or government or social problems, would seem impudently offensive.

As individuals, Baptists have nevertheless been distinguished in the history of America. There have been Baptist Presidents (Harry Truman was one) and Baptist lawmakers. Fifty members of the Ninety-Second Congress were Baptists (in numbers fifth in rank behind the Catholics, who had 113; the Methodists, 85; Presbyterians, 83; and Episcopalians, 66),[7] and the denomination is strong in state legislatures, particularly in the South. We have Baptist mayors, state and county officials; they rank high in the operation of the nation's public schools, as board members, administrators and teachers, and in music in particular they have contributed to the American cultural heritage. It was a Baptist pastor, Samuel F. Smith, who wrote "My Country, 'Tis of Thee."[8]

But these individual achievements are not necessarily Baptist achievement. What is distinctively Baptist, as we shall see in this volume, is the position of the Christian church in America, as guaranteed in the basic law, for the separation of church and state, a founding principle of the republic, "was preeminently a Baptist achievement."[9] And there is more than that. John Locke once said that the Baptists "were the first propounders of absolute liberty, just and true liberty, equal and impartial liberty."[10] This idea of liberty, particularly as it involves one's relationship with God, was so woven into the fabric of American life by Baptist craftsmen that it became "the supreme contribution of the new world to the old" and "the chiefest contribution that America has thus far made to civilization."[11] For these historic contributions, if it had done nothing else, the Baptist church would hold an honored place in the annals of the nation.

All Baptists share in these achievements and in this heritage, no matter what they may now call themselves. They call themselves many things, as Appendix A shows, for over the centuries one of the characteristics of the Baptists has been their tendency toward quarrelsomeness, argumentation, Christian brawling and division — at the local church as well as at the convention level. They have not tried to hide this proclivity; how else could they manage, with every man his own interpreter, with no central office handing down the unassailable line by bull or decree? They have, in fact, gloried a little in their cantankerousness and still do. One of their current jokes tells how to make an "instant" Baptist: "Add water and agitate." One of their historians, writing a century ago, said that his people "rejoice in those collisions which produce sparks and flames, and thus illuminate the nations. They have a tendency to produce them."[12] The flaming collisions are still taking place, the inevitable result of Baptist diversity. This diversity is worth examining.

Chapter Two: Baptist Heralds

Baptists of varying stripe may be a little bit hazy about their confusing history in modern times, but they take fierce pride in what they regard as their ancient heritage. For on one historical claim they all agree: Baptists are the true — and probably the only true — descendants of the Jerusalem Church of 26 A. D. In their worship, their beliefs, their doctrine and polity, they believe, they are the only Twentieth Century Christians grouped together in congregations like those established by the Apostles.

In study of the New Testament, Baptists have found four major characteristics of the New Testament churches, and they use this pattern in their own management. Of those early churches they have concluded: (1) that the word of God was their sole rule of faith and the inspiration for their practice; (2) that the church was local in character, with each church entirely independent of all others; (3) that each church chose its own pastor by direct vote of the membership; and (4) that each church was fiercely independent of state authority.[1]

There is hardly a Baptist church anywhere today which does not assert these guiding precepts; they are so actively championed, in fact, that they sound as fresh and alive as last Sunday's sermon.

Baptists have not always been content, however, to claim merely a spiritual identity with the early Christians. They have at times boasted that they were the direct, lineal descendants of the Jerusalem church, through a visible line of succession.[2] Nineteenth Century Baptist historians were fond of cataloguing the links in this chain to antiquity, starting with the Church Fathers and running through a tangled chain of heretical and schismatical groups (Novatians, Donatists, Montanists and Paulicians, to name a few) most of whom in fact had little in common with modern Baptist practice and some of whom were almost heathen.

From some Baptist pulpits, particularly in the South, this old claim is still preached, along with the prideful assertion that because this is true, the Baptist Church is predecessor to, not product of, the Protestant Reformation. The most competent Baptist authorities now discount the succession myth. "It is certain," says Albert Henry Newman, ". . . that the early church, including the first century after the New Testament period, was organized as Baptist churches are now organized and professed the faith that Baptist churches now profess. It is also beyond question that for fully four centuries before the Reformation there were bodies of Christians, under various names stigmatized by the Roman Catholic Church as heretics, who professed nearly — sometimes identically — the faith and practice of modern Baptists and with whom we have a demonstrable historic connection. But a period of a thousand years intervenes, in which the only visible church of unbroken continuity was the Romish church, which had far departed from the early faith."[3]

Sometimes these independents were not so much movements as individuals. "The world is vastly more indebted to a line of individual men who had contended for the truth, each by himself, than to any organic churches which can be traced by visible succession from the Apostles, under any name whatsoever."[4] About most of these individualists and their followers, information is scanty. They were heretics at a time when heresy was a cardinal sin; they opposed the authority of Rome and its bishops; their writings, if any, were suppressed. And such knowledge as has been preserved about them comes from the records of their enemies;

thus colored, the records give up the truth very painfully.

But it seems certain that from about the Eleventh Century onward there were men and movements who opposed the Catholic Church in ways which Baptists, traditionally violent in their antipathy toward Rome, have always appreciated. They wanted the scriptures translated into the languages of the people; they preached that the true church consisted only of believers; they ridiculed rites which utilized holy water, incense, bowing and kneeling and the tolling of bells; they despised the worship of images, refused to confess to priests, declined to address their prayers to saints and challenged the authority of bishops; rank was abhorrent to them; they denied the doctrine of transubstantiation and denounced penances and indulgences, which were then widely abused.[5] It matters little to the Baptist that some of these heretic groups, as the Eleventh Century Cathari and Albigenses, were not wholly Christian.

Christian or not, they took their lives in their hands in opposing the church. In 1179 the Third Lateran Council decreed that heretics should be denied public office; church members were forbidden to trade with them, either as seller or buyer; contracts with them were declared null and void; their houses were destroyed and their lands confiscated, and upon conviction of heresy they were turned over to civil authorities to be burned.[6]

In this heretical agitation of the Middle Ages three religious principles, later fully embraced by the Baptists, emerged from the mists of the past, never to be lost again. These were: (1) reliance upon the scriptures as the sole authority in matters of religion; (2) insistence upon the spiritual nature of Christianity, requiring personal faith and regeneration by the Holy Spirit; and (3) assertion of the right of every person to be his own intercessor with God and to manage his religious life according to his own conscience.[7] In embryo there is the idea of "soul liberty," which was to achieve its fullest expression in a land not yet even discovered by civilized men.

The doctrine of "soul liberty," in fact, is ascribed to Arnold of Brescia, an educated Italian monk born about 1105 who was said to be "the purest, most severe and bold personification of republican democracy, both laical and ecclesiastical, of the century."[8] Baptists also admire him because he agitated for the separation of church and state. In 1155 Arnold was hanged, his body was burned and his ashes were consigned to the Tiber River. From the Baptist point of view only one blot mars his otherwise inspiring history: he never left the Catholic Church.

The first sect which "can honestly be regarded as Baptist in inclination"[9] was that of the Petrobusians of Southern France. They took their name from Peter of Bruys, a converted priest who began his heretical labors about 1104. He is said to have "cast aside all ceremonial mummeries of the Romish hierarchy"[10] and went so far as to advocate even that all churches be pulled down — probably as a protest against the abhorrent rites he saw practiced in them. Peter, most comfortable with the language of the marketplace, once presided at a Good Friday burning of crosses at which all the participants roasted meat in the flames. He was burned at the stake in 1126 at St. Gilles.

At about this same time in Flanders Tenchelyn was preaching that the Bible is the only guide to faith, that Christ is the only head of the church and that neither the mass nor infant baptism has a scriptural basis. These ideas survived him and were circulated widely in the European lowlands by Everwacher. "The later susceptibility of the Netherlands to Baptist principles has some connection with his early sowing."[11] There is a direct connection between the English Baptists, from whom the American branch sprang, and the Seventeenth Century Dutch dissenters. These prenatal stirrings of the faith in Holland are therefore treasured by Baptists everywhere.

Toward the end of the Twelfth Century a man of unusual gifts appeared in Southern France. He is remembered in history as Peter Waldo, more properly Valdez (Latin, Valdesius). His followers were sometimes called Vaudois, after Waldo's birthplace at Vaux, in Dauphine on the Rhone River, but were more commonly known as Waldensians. Waldo, grown rich in the Lyonnaise mercantile trade, gave all his money away, took a vow of poverty and traveled about the Rhone Valley preaching the simple life and faith he found in the teachings of Christ. His converts were known as the Poor Men of Lyons, and although they apparently had no intention of breaking with the Catholic Church at first, Waldo was

11

excommunicated in 1176 for preaching without authority and his converts were condemned by the Council of Verone in 1183, expelled from Lyons and subjected to vigorous persecution. They scattered to the four corners of Europe, spreading their heretical teachings as they went, and by 1233, sixteen years after the death of Waldo, Flanders was full of Waldensians. The story of these harried and hounded people is an incredible chronicle of survival against overwhelming odds and of the nurturing of religious conviction under the most dangerous circumstances. It is unlikely, as J. M. Cramp claims,[12] that many of these Waldensians were "orthodox Baptists," but that there was at least a spiritual tie between them and the Anabaptists, from whom the Baptists were to emerge, is indisputable.[13] On the eve of the Reformation the Waldensians were the largest sect in southern Germany, and they ranged through Prussia, Poland and Austria. An estimated 200,000 worshipped in 400 congregations in Bohemia and Moravia, and 100,000 inhabited the Alpine valleys of Italy.[14] They were responsible for more than 100 editions of the Bible, including 14 in German, 4 in Dutch and 98 in Latin.[15]

The spirit of revolt against the authority and teachings of the Catholic Church found its most studied expression in the England of the Middle Ages with John Wycliffe. Wycliffe is best remembered for giving to the English people the first Bible in their own language, in two editions appearing between 1382 and 1400. The Wycliffe Bible was the only complete version in the vernacular that the English of that time — peasants, commoners and nobles alike — were to know, and it was a powerful instrument in fixing the form of the language.

But it is not only for the Bible that his memory is honored by Baptists. Through study of the scripture alone, apparently insulated from Continental heresies, Wycliffe concluded that every man has an immediate relationship with God and for his salvation requires no temporal intermediary.[16] He denied the authority of the Pope and set up the Bible as the all-sufficient test of Christian conduct. It was this belief in the primacy of Holy Writ itself that led Wycliffe to pioneer the translation of the Vulgate Bible into a language the people could understand.

Born about 1329, probably in the neighborhood of Richmond,

Wycliffe was associated for much of his life with Oxford University, although he also held an appointment as rector at Lutterworth. It was from Oxford that his fame spread, particularly after he began to write his anti-clerical doctrine in English and to preach it from the pulpits of London. Powerful political support, notably that of his patron, John of Gaunt, for a time shielded him from the retaliation of the church. In 1382 Gaunt repudiated his association with Wycliffe and the clergyman's teachings were condemned as heretical. He was banished from Oxford but allowed to spend the last two years of his life at Lutterworth, where he continued to write and to organize the missionary force that was to outlast him, the Lollards. Wycliffe died on December 31, 1384, from a paralytic attack he had suffered while hearing mass. He was allowed burial in consecrated ground, but 44 years later, on the orders of the church, his bones were dug up and burned and his ashes were scattered on the waters of a flowing stream.

K. B. McFarlane, in a rather savage biography, discounts Wycliffe's role as the "Morning Star of the Protestant Reformation" and describes him as a man who showed himself in his writings to be "learned, subtle, ingenious, opinionated, tirelessly argumentative and rather humorless" and whose self-esteem "was excessive and provoked amusement."[17] More moderate historians believe that Wycliffe's writings were carried from Oxford to the University of Prague, in Bohemia, where they strongly influenced John Hus. And Hus, in his turn, was admired by Martin Luther.[18] Baptist historians do not care particularly about that distinction. Cramp says glowingly that "that great man (Wycliffe)... lived and died a priest of the Roman Catholic Church. But... the light he had received would have guided him into Baptist paths had he followed it fully."[19] And Thomas Armitage suggests that "many who carried his (Wycliffe's) principles to their legitimate results became Baptists."[20] That cannot be proven. But it is not beyond reason to suggest that Wycliffe launched in England a spirit of nonconformity which, more than 200 years later, was to see the rise of the Baptist church.

While Lollardy worked its underground leaven in Britain, the principles propagated by the Waldensians were manifested in various forms throughout Continental Europe. In the Fifteenth

Century Peter Chelcicky (c. 1390 — c. 1460), to go down in ecclesiastical history as the spiritual father of the Bohemian Brethren, urged the use of the Bible alone as the basis for Christian faith and practice. God's law, as revealed in His word, was sufficient in every particular, Chelcicky said, and he considered the Catholic union of church and state to be evil. In Chelcicky can also be found ideas which, when enlarged and carried to their logical conclusion, raise questions about the Christian's relationship with the civil government, for he rejected oaths and felt that no true believer could be a king or hold political office.[21] He also was opposed to capital punishment, through which thousands of heretics already had been interrupted in their earthly labors.

In an indirect fashion, Baptists probably owe more to Ulrich Zwingli (1484 — 1531), the Swiss reformer, than to Martin Luther. For it was in Zwingli's bosom, although not by his efforts, that the Anabaptist movement was born. The tie between Anabaptists and Baptists is so close that for many decades the Baptists, even in America, were not distinguished from Anabaptists and were subjected to the same persecutions.

Zwingli was born January 1, 1484, in a Swiss village not far from Lake Constance. He came from an influential family and received excellent schooling at the Universities of Vienna and Basel, both strongly humanist. Ordained a priest in 1506, Zwingli was content at first to try to stamp out ecclesiastical abuses through ridicule.[22] But in 1519, when he was called to take charge of the largest church in Zurich, he began a drive for complete independence from Catholicism. Rejecting fasts, pilgrimages, worship of the saints, Rome's transubstantiation and Luther's consubstantiation, Zwingli established the Swiss Reformed Church, which spread so rapidly and collided so violently with Catholic forces that civil war broke out, resulting in Zwingli's own death — and the scattering of his ashes — in 1531.[23] The movement he founded, however, long survived him, and the cantonal governments ultimately were allowed to choose between the Swiss Reformed and Catholic faiths.

Shortly after Zwingli began his frontal attack on the Roman colossus he won the support of a group of zealous young religious reformers who soon came to be known as the radicals of the Swiss church revolution. For them, Zwingli did not go far enough in his overhaul of theological forms and doctrine; they wanted a return to the pure religion of the New Testament church, and when Zwingli made it clear that he would guide the Swiss Reformed movement in his own way, they broke with him in January, 1525. In the vanguard of the radicals were Conrad Grebel, a young man from a moderately wealthy family in Zurich; a close friend, Felix Manz; George Blaurock, and Wilhelm Reublin, former chief preacher at St. Albans in Basel. They called themselves the Swiss Brethren; but, in mockery, their enemies called them "Anabaptists."

"Anabaptism" means simply "rebaptism." Grebel and his associates believed that the ordinance of baptism is a rite symbolizing one's awareness of his rebirth to Christian principles. Since an infant cannot make such an acknowledgement, they opposed infant baptism; and since most of their converts had been baptized as Catholic babies, they insisted upon a second baptism. This may seem to be an obscure, relatively minor distinction, but it is not to Baptists, and to Anabaptists it was a doctrine so central to genuine Christian experience that many of them gave their lives in defense of it. Rebaptism came to be not just a jailable offense; it came to be punishable by death.

William R. Estep says the rebaptism practiced by the Swiss Brethren "was clearly the most revolutionary act of the Reformation. No other event so completely symbolized the break with Rome. Here, for the first time in the course of the Reformation, a group of Christians dared to form a church after what was conceived to be the New Testament pattern. The Brethren emphasized the absolute necessity of a personal commitment to Christ as essential to salvation and a prerequisite to baptism."[24]

Opposition to infant baptism was not new. Through the centuries purists have argued that the Apostolic Church did not accord this rite to babies, that infant baptism sprang up in North Africa about the year 252, when Christian children were being stolen for sacrifice to heathen gods. With the assent of a Carthaginian council presided over by Cyprian, infants thereafter were baptized to assure their salvation in the event they were kidnapped.[25] Subsequently, the practice was observed throughout the Catholic Church and was accepted as so logical that even Luther did not object to it. But the Anabaptists did, and by their decision to insist upon rebaptism as the test of membership in their fellowship, they alienated both Catholics and Protestants and were hounded and persecuted from both sides.[26]

Rebaptism was, of course, not their only tenet and not the only one their foes found objectionable. As the "true church," they believed they should have no fellowship with other churches or their ministers; they regarded the literal text of the Bible as sufficient guidance for a Christian, without adulteration by theologians; they thought every man who felt the urge should have the right to preach; they doubted whether a true Christian could conscientiously amass rich stores of worldly goods; they felt that Christians should be respectful toward civil authority, but should not themselves hold office; they denied the right of secular authorities to interfere in religion, and abhorred the idea of persecution for one's religious beliefs; they did not swear or take oaths, and they had no use for courts.[27]

How much of this catalog the Anabaptists owed to earlier heretical sects has never been established. With the Waldensians, for example, they held certain beliefs in common. But Estep, a student of the Anabaptist movement, believes that Scriptural influence was far stronger than any historical relationship.[28]

Persecution of the Swiss Brethren was not long in coming. After their break with Zwingli early in 1525 they were denounced, castigated and driven out of Zurich. Conrad Grebel went first to Schaffhausen, there to live and preach underground. On a road near that town he is said to have encountered Wolfgang Wolimann, a citizen of St. Gallen, who had previously preached against infant baptism. Grebel won an easy convert, Wolimann accepting his doctrine with such enthusiasm that "he was not satisfied with having a bowl of water emptied over his head in the usual fashion, but insisted upon undressing and upon his whole body being ducked in the Rhine by Grebel."[29] Claims that this was the origin of baptism by immersion, in the Baptist way, however, ignore a large body of scholarship which indicates that this was the form favored by the Apostolic Church.

16

Grebel thereafter went to Gruningen, near Zurich, where on October 8, 1525, he was arrested on a charge of sedition while preparing to hold a service in an open field. In November he was sentenced to indeterminate imprisonment on a diet of bread and water. At a second trial on March 6, 1526, he was sentenced to spend the remainder of his life in confinement. Fourteen days later he escaped from jail, only to be cut down by plague during the summer.[30] His entire ministry in the new faith had lasted only about a year and a half, and he was only 28 when he died.

Even so, Grebel lived longer than some of his fellows. The first Anabaptist martyr of record was a minister named Eberli Bolt, who was burned at the stake in Schwyz, Switzerland, on May 29, 1525, at the instance of Catholic authorities.[31] Bolt's death began a period of Anabaptist martyrdom that was to extend for three centuries. Some of the killings were particularly fiendish. Two years after Bolt's ordeal by fire an influential Anabaptist minister was put to death in Rottenburg. His sentence read: "Michael Sattler shall be committed to the executioner. The latter shall take him to the square and there first cut out his tongue, and then forge him fast to a wagon and there with glowing iron tongs twice tear pieces from his body, then on the way to the site of the execution five times more as above and then burn his body to powder as an arch-heretic."[32] As Grebel's disciples fanned out across Europe, with the hands of both Catholics and Protestants turned against them, Archduke Ferdinand is said to have remarked that "the third baptism" was the best cure for Anabaptism. He meant drowning, and on August 26, 1527, he issued an edict threatening all followers of that anathematic doctrine with the punishment of death.

At the time of the dispersal of the Swiss Brethren from Zurich, one of Grebel's counselors, Pastor Wilhelm Reublin, took refuge in Waldshut, on the German side of the Rhine River. An extremely effective preacher, Reublin continued his ministry on German soil and by the middle of 1525 had rebaptized about 60 residents of Waldshut in the Anabaptist faith.

His prize convert was Dr. Balthasar Hubmaier, who has gone down in history as possibly the most brilliant Anabaptist theologian and a direct lineal forebear of the Baptist denomination.

At the time of his embracing the new faith, toward which as a Catholic priest he had been struggling for three years, he was 45, and his eloquent tongue and facile pen were to cost him his life before three more years had passed.

Hubmaier is believed to have been born about 1480, of unknown peasant stock, near Augsburg. Even the aspiration to learning was unusual in one from his station, but by dent of pure perseverance he got sufficient educational background to be admitted to the University of Ingolstadt. After a nine-year struggle, he was awarded a doctorate in theology on September 29, 1512. At the time of his ordination to the priesthood he was assigned to a chaplaincy at the University, and in 1515 he became its chief administrative officer. In the January of the following year he was appointed chief preacher at a new cathedral in Regensburg, and upon his arrival there he had no misgivings about joining in an anti-Semitic campaign which had engulfed the city. Its high point came when municipal authorities seized the Regensburg synagogue and converted it into a Catholic chapel. This rude behavior later was defended by Hubmaier, who recorded 54 miracles which took place under the chapel's new auspices.[33]

In 1521, Hubmaier was named pastor at Waldshut, and it was during his early ministry there, in 1522, that he began to entertain serious doubts about Catholic theology and practices. By March of the following year he had been in contact with Zwingli and other leaders of the Swiss reformation, but what he heard from them did not completely satisfy his yearnings for a new faith. Impetuous and outspoken, he made no secret of his growing doubts, and whispers about his revolutionary activities were relayed to Ferdinand. But in the face of a formal demand for Hubmaier's expulsion, the people of Waldshut closed ranks in his support. For his physical protection, they slipped him away to Schaffhausen for a month. He returned in October, 1524, to a hero's welcome and to a bid to resume his old place as chief preacher. By this time, Hubmaier had concluded as a result of his own studies that the baptism of infants had no basis in Scripture, and when a few months later Reublin came through preaching the next most logical step, he found in the priest of Waldshut a receptive audience. In Anabaptism all of Hubmaier's earlier doubts were resolved, and through a steady flow of tracts and zealous preaching he won many adherents to his faith. In one of his most eloquent essays he argued for the right of liberty of conscience, and in another, which was particularly prescient, he warned Anabaptists not to reject the magistracy lest they be looked upon as "enemies of civil government" and "a menace to law and order."[34] In the early days of American colonization, Baptists were to have to contend with this suspicion. Twice before his death Hubmaier, under painful torture, recanted his faith. Each time he regained it, and for doing so, and saying so, he was burned at the stake on March 10, 1528. Three days later his wife was drowned; she, too, had the Anabaptist infection.

By the time of Hubmaier's execution, the campaign to exterminate the Anabaptists was in full swing. The Catholics regarded them as the worst kind of heretics, and the Protestants were equally hostile. In the religious upheaval of the times, mystics, fanatics and religious anarchists of every shade were floating all over Europe, and Anabaptists were regarded as the worst of a sorry lot. By 1530 at least 2,000 Anabaptists had been slaughtered, and the massacre was to continue.

It was given fresh impetus by one of the weirdest projects ever undertaken in the name of God. That was the establishment, in 1524, of a crude kingdom in the Westphalian city of Munster. A fiery Dutch fanatic named Jan Matthys, part Anabaptist and part mumbo-jumbo, had traveled about the Lowlands and the western provinces of Germany preaching that Christ was returning at any minute to deliver His saints and to punish their tormentors. Under his direction, and the co-leadership of John of Leyden and Gerton Gloster, hordes of simple Dutch and German peasants streamed into Munster, which had been "revealed" to Matthys as the site of the New Jerusalem. By mob violence the would-be saints seized the religious institutions of the city, put both Catholics and Lutherans to flight and set up a theocracy with Matthys as king and John of Leyden as a latter-day Enoch. When after a few weeks Matthys was killed, Enoch, claiming divine appointment, succeeded to the throne. Under the influence of another spiritual inspiration he established a system of polygamy and turned it to his own enjoyment by claiming four wives. One of these he later beheaded with his own hand in the city marketplace. The kingdom lasted for more than a year, during which the self-appointed elect worked the most outrageous excesses upon the few city residents who had been unwise enough to stay. In June, 1535, a besieging force directed by the expelled clergymen recaptured the city and put John of Leyden and his chief retainers to death, after appropriate tortures.[35] News of the depravity of the trespassers in Munster spread quickly over Europe, and the already vigorous persecution of the Anabaptists was sharply accelerated. It was a highly unfortunate development, because the Anabaptists who believed in Grebel's principles were gentle people. Cramp says the Munster legions were not Christians but "maniacs."[36] Nevertheless, the identity of those "maniacs" was erroneously fixed in the European mind for generations thereafter. Newman, writing about the affair many years after, said: "The extent to which the Baptist cause has been impeded by the Munster kingdom is incalculable. The Baptist name is odious throughout continental Europe today because of it. In England and America the opponents of the Baptists long urged their extermination on the ground that they might be expected to reenact the horrors of Munster."[37]

The pogrom against the Anabaptists was so successful that they were all but exterminated everywhere except in the Netherlands, where they hung on with particular tenacity. This was the more remarkable since Charles V gave special attention to heresy there. In the 25 years beginning in 1521, around 50,000 persons are said to have been hanged, beheaded or burned in Holland alone, and a very large proportion of these were of the Anabaptist persuasion. Those remaining could easily have drifted off into any of the several fanatic sects which were then mesmerizing dissenters, but they were preserved through the emergence into new faith of a very remarkable man, Menno Simons.[38]

Like most of the other Anabaptist leaders (with the notable exception of Grebel), Menno was converted from the Catholic priesthood. Born in 1496 in the North Sea town of Witmarsum, in Friesland, Menno was consecrated in his childhood to the service of the church. It is probable that he was brought up in the Franciscan monastery at Bolsward, where he no doubt took the usual schooling preparatory to the priestly life. Although he could read and write Latin and knew Greek, he did not read the Bible until two years after his ordination, which took place in March, 1524. In his twelve years as a priest, he wrote later, he took neither his life nor his office seriously. Instead, he and his fellows of the cloth "spent our time emptily in playing (cards) together, drinking, and in diversions as, alas, is the fashion and usage of such useless people."[39] His first church duty was as parish priest in Pingjum, where he remained until 1531 as the second in a rank of three priests. He was then transferred to his home village, and on a visit to Leeuwarden on March 20, 1531, he witnessed an execution that was to change his own life, although not immediately. "A God-fearing, pious hero named Sicke Snijder was, beheaded at Leeuwarden for being rebaptized," he later recalled. "It sounded very strange to me to hear of a second baptism. I examined the Scriptures diligently and pondered them earnestly, but could find no report of infant baptism"[40] He consulted Martin Luther's writings on the subject but found no comfort. He had already privately renounced the doctrine of transubstantiation, and after several years of the first serious and intensive study of his life he concluded that he could no longer be a Catholic.

Concurrently, Obbe Philips, a devout Anabaptist, had begun to organize underground churches in Friesland, and Menno, convinced that these groups represented a restoration of pure, Biblical Christianity, quit the priesthood and joined them. With deep conviction, he threw himself into the affairs of this new religion, wandering from place to place, often with a price on his head, always braving the threat of persecution. With infinite love and patience he imposed upon his devoted brethren in the faith the beginnings of church organization, with regular government and discipline, exercising over them a kind of "apostolic supervision."[41] Not until 1554 did he know relative safety. At that time he found sanctuary at Fresenburg, the vast estate of Baron Bartholomew von Ahlefeldt between Lubeck and Hamburg. The Baron had been impressed by the piety of Menno's people, and at his invitation they flocked to Fresenburg in great numbers, founding settlements and churches. At last Menno had his own printing house, which published and circulated his voluminous writings. He died peacefully on January 31, 1561, and was buried in his own garden in Wirstefelde.

Menno was not unanimously admired. John Calvin, whose stern discipline was to be accepted later by large numbers of Baptists, wrote of him: "Nothing can be more conceited than this donkey, nor more impudent than this dog."[42] But the Mennonite Church, named for this Dutch heretic even though it acknowledges Conrad Grebel as founder, remembers Menno Simons as "the heaven-sent leader who rallied the scattered brethren and gave them the leadership in faith and spirit and doctrine which they needed."[43] Between Baptist and Mennonite today there is little identity, but it was this persecuted Dutchman who in 1539 held up a standard which early Baptists would honor and which remains in the Twentieth Century at the heart of Baptist belief: "Here we have the Lord's commandment concerning baptism, as to when according to the ordinance of God it shall be administered and received; namely, that the Gospel must first be preached, and then those baptized who believe it. . . . Young children are without understanding and unteachable; therefore, baptism cannot be administered to them without perverting the ordinance of the Lord. . . . Faith does not follow from baptism, but baptism follows from faith."[44]

Modern Baptist authorities disagree over the relationship of the Baptists to Menno and the earlier European Anabaptists. Some maintain that Baptist belief is more properly rooted in the Reformation and that from the more orthodox reformers comes Baptist allegiance to believer's baptism. It is historic fact, however, that the basic tenets of Baptist belief were extant among Anabaptists before the establishment of the first Baptist church, and to say that there is no relationship is a misreading of history.

Chapter Three: Rise of the English Baptists

As a formal organization, the Baptist Church was established in England in 1612, during the reign of the sovereign who authorized the translation of the Bible exalted by Baptists today as the King James Version. It is one of the few things Baptists can thank him for, because he was so hostile to them and their ideas that he clapped the pastor of that pioneer church in jail, where he died.

Although 1611 is the logical historical starting point, there is suspicion, but sketchily documented, that believers of the Baptist variety existed in England long before that first church was formed. The expression of dissent runs deep into the history of England, and as early as the Fifteenth Century some of that dissent seems to have had a Baptist flavor; this was augmented in the first quarter of the Sixteenth Century by the arrival in England of Dutch refugees. They undoubtedly brought with them and propagated heretical religious ideas, because in 1534 Henry VIII issued proclamations forbidding the embrace of Anabaptist doctrine and threatening its purveyors with expulsion or death. The following year nineteen Anabaptists were executed, and the purge initiated by Henry (king from 1509 to 1547) was continued without abatement by Edward VI (1547 — 1553), Mary (1553 — 1558) and Elizabeth I (1558 — 1603). Under Elizabeth persecution was particularly severe. Inquisitors sent in the first year of her reign to Essex "with full power to proceed against heretics" found the place teeming. "We have such obstinate heretics, Anabaptists and other unruly persons here as never was heard of," they reported.[1] Many of the "unruly" were foreigners seeking in England the religious liberty they had been denied elsewhere, but the Crown would not allow them to live in peace. On September 2, 1560, a royal proclamation was issued saying that the Queen "willeth and chargeth all manner of persons, born either in foreign parts or in her Majesty's dominions, that have conceived any manner of such heretical opinion as the Anabaptists hold. . . to depart out of this realm within twenty days."[2] The proclamation was honored more in the breach than the observance, although often with painful results.

Thomas Armitage, in a church history written in 1890, said that despite almost unremitting persecution, "since 1535 Baptist witnesses for the truth have stood firmly on British soil, either as individuals or as organized churches."[3] He used the terms "Baptist" and "Anabaptist" almost synonymously, because he believed the English Baptists, as an organized church, grew out of the Anabaptist movement. At odds with his view is that of Henry W. Clark, who wrote in 1911, in *The History of English Nonconformity* that "the Anabaptists are not to be looked upon as being identified with or being ancestors of the great Baptist denomination which has played so great a part in nonconformist history."[4] He felt that English Baptists originated from Wycliffe's time, through generations of "more or less obscure people" who "objected to having their children baptized after the customary rule of the Church."

Both may be right, because the traceable development of the Baptist faith in England proceeded along two independent lines, one influenced strongly by Anabaptist practice, the other more clearly related to English Separatism. The earlier of the two movements was inspired by the leadership of John Smyth, who is acknowledged as "the founder of the modern Baptist churches."[5] Smyth, born in Gainsborough on the River Trent about 1570, was educated at Cambridge University for a career with the Church of England. In 1600 he was elected preacher at Lincoln and subsequently was granted a stipend of 40 pounds a year plus house rent for life. This grant was annulled on October 13, 1602, when he was dismissed as minister for having "approved himself a factious man in this city by personal preaching, and that untruly against divers men of good place."[6] Despite his impulsive nature, Smyth is said to have had a magnetic personality, which won him friends easily. He was "unselfish and charitable; punctilious and courageous; never ashamed to own any wrong in himself which he discovered; a good preacher, and a scholar of considerable acquirements — having, in short, many of the elements of a great and good man. On the other hand, his mind was restless, and perhaps morbidly sensitive to small matters."[7] At the time of his ministerial termination at Lincoln he was also rapidly moving toward nonconformism.

Returning to Gainsborough, about 60 miles north of London, he was attracted to a Congregational Church, organized about 1602, which was to play an important role in American history. The church then was on the verge of a split, apparently less out of a contentious spirit than for the convenience of the congregation. One group, counting among its members John Robinson, William Brewster and William Bradford, withdrew to Scrooby Manor House; later it crossed the English Channel to Amsterdam, moved on to Leyden, and in 1620, with the permission of the English Government, was transplanted across the Atlantic Ocean in the founding of the colony at Plymouth Rock. John Smyth joined the other group, which remained at Gainsborough, and almost immediately became its pastor.

James I was then on the throne, and he was no more tolerant of nonconformists than his predecessors had been. So Smyth and his fellow Christians at Gainsborough resolved to emigrate to Holland, where since 1579 freedom of religion had been guaranteed. Around 1607 a company of about 80 separatists from Yorkshire, Lincolnshire and Nottinghamshire, under the leadership of Smyth and Thomas Helwys, left their homes and resettled in Amsterdam. In that city there was already an English Separatist Church, known as the "Ancient Church," under the direction of

Francis Johnson and Henry Ainsworth, but rather than join with them Smyth organized the "Second Church of Amsterdam." In 1609, having reached the conviction that infant baptism was unscriptural and that the Ancient Church, which practiced it, was a "false church," Smyth and his followers, by then under Mennonite influence, resolved to make a new spiritual beginning by dissolving their church and forming a communion based on rebaptism. So Smyth rebaptized himself and about 40 others. The method used appears to have been affusion — "pouring" — then in vogue among the Mennonites.

In a few weeks Smyth began to doubt the validity of his self-baptism. At the same time he wholeheartedly embraced Mennonite theology and petitioned for membership with the Dutch, along with thirty others inspired by his example. For Thomas Helwys, this was too much. He admired the Mennonites, but he could not agree with them on every doctrinal consideration. As a consequence, Helwys and a minority of eight or ten, including William Piggott, Thomas Seamer and John Murton, excommunicated Smyth's majority. Smyth, incidentally, did not live to see the mortal resolution of his theological travail. He died of consumption in August, 1612; those of his followers surviving were admitted into the Mennonite fellowship in 1615.[8]

By then the Baptist wing of the expatriate church had already returned to England. Sometime in 1611 Helwys and his small company decided that their abandonment of their homeland to escape persecution could be interpreted as an act of cowardice; the place for English Christians, they concluded, was in England, and they resolved to busy themselves there in the propagation of their faith. Accordingly, they returned to England and by the end of 1612 had established the first Baptist Church on English soil at Newgate Street in London. They met surreptitiously, probably celebrating the Lord's Supper every week; it is unlikely that they sang: for centuries hymn-singing, a dead giveaway to inquisitors, was in bad aroma among heretics; and they probably called themselves not "Baptists," a term not generally applied to the denomination until about 1644, but a "baptized church of Christ" or a "baptized congregation gathered according to the primitive pattern."[9] But Baptists they were, and in their basic views they differed very little from modern Baptists. They denied the Biblical validity of the baptism of infants; they insisted that baptism should follow and symbolize conversion; they were devoted to the principles of liberty of conscience in religious matters and democracy in the government of the church. They probably did not practice immersion; that peculiarity of the baptismal rite had not been universally established among Baptists until 1644 — although somewhat earlier some churches were said to have "plunged" their baptismal candidates "over head and ears."[10] There was one other distinguishing mark in that first Baptist church: its doctrine was Arminian in character.

The term "Arminian" derives from the theology of Jacobus Arminius, a Dutch clergyman and theologian, who between the years 1588 and 1609 offered a Christian alternative to John Calvin's rigid doctrine of predestination. The Arminians preached that salvation through grace was available to all who believed, not just to a handful of the elect. Through their Arminianism Helwys's supporters and converts came to be known as General Baptists; the later-springing churches, more rigidly Calvinist, were known as Particular Baptists. Today's Baptist majority would claim to be influenced by Calvinism and therefore Particular in faith — although most Baptists believe in general redemption. The General Baptists have been preserved in a convention still known by that name and in the Free Will Baptist Church.

In Helwys that early church had an able leader. Of good background, he was educated in London for a legal career. He wrote well, convincingly and, as it developed, too bravely. In a series of publications after his return to England he took issue with the predestinarian views of the Calvinists and criticized the Mennonites for their rejection of oaths and the magistracy and their contention that Christians should not involve themselves in civil government. One of his books, *A Short Declaration of the Mystery of Iniquity,* contained the first plea for full religious liberty ever published in England.[11] One copy was unwisely dedicated to James I, with a reminder that "the King is a mortal man and not God, therefore hath no power over the immortall soules of his subjects."[12] His Majesty took offense at this presumptuous Baptist limitation on his royal authority and ordered the author arrested. Helwys died in prison about 1616.

In the pastorate of the London church he was succeeded by John Murton, a furrier who had been with Helwys over the whole route. Conversions were not easy; the Baptist faith was still punishable heresy; a Baptist minister could not legally mount a pulpit; the denial of baptism to infants was widely regarded as a kind of fanatic cruelty to innocent babes. Despite all that, there were by the time of Murton's death in 1626 some 150 enrolled General Baptists in England, loosely assembled in five congregations in London, Lincoln, Sarum, Coventry and Tiverton. Less than twenty years later the number of their churches had grown to 47 — even though none of them had a legal right to exist.[13] The Act of Toleration (1689) was still 45 years in the future.

The precise origin of the Particular Baptists is a little harder to define. It is believed now that they may have existed as individuals possibly well before the General Baptists, either as a pure product of earlier nonconformity or as an offshoot of the orthodox Reformation. The generally accepted opinion as to their origin as a distinctive body of believers traces their emergence to an independent congregation organized covertly at Southwark, London, in 1616, by Henry Jacob, who at one time had been a member of the Scrooby Manor church after it was exported to Holland. Even after the founder's removal to Virginia in 1622,[14] where he died two years later, the Southwark congregation was known as the "Jacob Church." A manuscript attributed to William Kiffin, an early Particular Baptist, tells of the Jacob Church split out of which the Baptists emerged:

"There was a congregation of Protestant Dissenters of the Independent persuasion in London, gathered in the year 1616, whereof Mr. Henry Jacob was the first pastor, and after him succeeded Mr. John Lathrop, who was their minister at this time. In this society several persons, finding that the congregation kept not to their first principles of separation, and being also convinced that baptism was not to be administered to infants, but such only as professed faith in Christ, desired that they might be dismissed from that communion, and allowed to form a distinct congregation, in such order as was agreeable to their own sentiments.

"The (Jacob) church considered that they were now grown very numerous and so more than could in these times of persecution conveniently meet together, and believing also that these persons acted from a principle of conscience, agreed to allow them the liberty they desired, and that they should be constituted a distinct church; which was performed the 12th of Sep. 1633. And as they believed that baptism was not rightly administered to infants, so they looked upon the baptism they had received in that age as invalid; whereupon most or all of them received a new baptism. Their minister was John Spilsbury. What number there were is uncertain, because in the mentioning of the names of about 20 men and women, it is added, with divers other.

"In the year 1638 Mr. William Kiffin, Mr. Thomas Wilson, and others being of the same judgement, were upon their request, dismissed to the said Mr. Spilsbury's congregation."[15]

That would seem to pinpoint exactly the date and origin of the Spilsbury church, uniformly conceded to be the first Particular Baptist congregation in England. But there are some doubts as to the authenticity and reliability of the Kiffin account, not so much as it deals with the rift in the Jacob Church but in a later account of how the Spilsbury church, seeking to authenticate immersion, sent some members to Holland to receive the ordinance from the Mennonites, who by then were immersing. These members are said to have returned to England and thereafter immersed their brethren. A simple chronology, it would seem — but not to all Baptists, many of whom dismiss the Kiffin story as fabricated. As late as 1895 in America, Dr. W. T. Whitsett was dismissed as president of the Southern Baptist Theological Seminary for carelessly asserting that baptism by immersion had been "invented" and introduced among the Particular Baptists about 1641. The Whitsett case set off a round of denominational backbiting which still breaks out intermittently among Baptist history buffs.

Whatever the facts, and they will probably never be established exactly, it is certain that baptism by immersion was the standard mode among the Baptists of England by 1644. For in that year fifteen Particular Baptist ministers, including Spilsbury, Kiffin and Hanserd Knollys, convened to draw up a statement of common principles which is remembered as the London Confession of 1644.

Expressing Calvinistic theology, its fifty articles stipulated that baptism should be by immersion, and it issued a demand for freedom of religion. It also gave assurance that Baptists were eager to live in peace with respect for civil authority: "We desire," the confession said, "to give unto God that which is God's and unto Caesar that which is Caesar's."[16] Seven churches adopted this statement of belief, some of them founded through the efforts of Spilsbury's congregation and others apparently having sprung up independently. In the years after the confession was adopted the Baptist faith spread rapidly, and by 1660 there were about 20,000 members in England.

Not a great deal is known about Spilsbury, the pioneer of the Particularists. He is said to have been a good man and to have enjoyed a long ministry, but even Cathcart's *Baptist Encyclopedia,* the biographical bible of the denomination, sheds little light on his life.

Of two later English Baptist ministers, however, note must be taken. One of these is Benjamin Keach, born in 1640, baptized at the age of 15, a minister from his twenty-eighth year onward. In 1668 he became pastor of the Baptist Church in Horsleydown, London, and "his was the first church amongst the Baptists to introduce singing."[17] This momentous event took place about 1673. A prolific author with 43 volumes to his credit, Keach was often in the pillory or in jail. He had a son who was to make a bizarre entry into the ranks of American Baptists.

Better known than Keach is another author whose fame remains world-wide even though it is not always recognized that he spent much of his life, in pulpit and in jail, as a Baptist minister, either lay or professional. John Bunyan was born in 1628 in Elstow, Bedfordshire, the son of a tinker. In his early years his "love of fun drew him into sin"[18] and he is said to have been addicted to lying and swearing. He had little regard for the Sabbath and went at games with an enthusiasm and vigor which sober Calvinists found reprehensible. His education was minimal, for it was not supposed that he would need much schooling in his chosen craft, that of a brazier. At the age of 16 he was drafted into the Parliamentary Army, in which he served for more than two and one-half years. Upon his release he returned to Elstow, married, and began to study the Bible seriously, and "to it he owes the force, simplicity, rhythm, charm, and other qualities of his own prose."[19] In 1653 Bunyan joined a Baptist church in Bedford, even though it was an illegal conventicle, and in 1655, indulging his natural eloquence, he started preaching. In 1660, under vigorous renewal of the Conventicle Act, Bunyan was sent to Bedford jail for "devilishly" and "perniciously" refusing to attend the established church and for "teaching men to worship contrary to law."[20] His initial sentence of three months was dragged out for six years, and Bunyan found no instruction whatsoever in it. Upon his release he immediately started preaching again and again was jailed, to serve another six-year stretch. In 1672 he was released from prison under a royal declaration of indulgence, and upon his return to Bedford he was elected pastor of the church in which he had so long held absentee membership. Under Anglican pressure the indulgence was withdrawn after three years, and Bunyan was again lodged in jail, this time for only six months. It was at this point in his life that he wrote *Pilgrim's Progress*. In popularity since that time this crowning work has ranked right up next to the Bible. When he finally was allowed to preach in relative safety, Bunyan became the most famous preacher of his day, partly on the strength of his literary reputation but also because of his simple, appealing eloquence. As many as 3,000 persons turned out to hear him on Sunday. Baptists point to him with pride, even though there is some suspicion that he may not have been wholly orthodox in his religious practice. He seems to have favored open communion in his church, which was not then a general Baptist practice and to this day is not universal. And he may even have allowed three of his four children to be baptized as infants.[21]

In 1689, a year after Bunyan's death, the Act of Toleration permitted the Baptists of England to practice and spread their faith unmolested. It did not disestablish the Anglican Church, nor did it permit the free exercise of faith to Catholics or Unitarians. Certain penalties still remained to dissenting Protestants. But practically speaking, the reign of religious terror was over in England, and the Baptist denomination was free to grow and prosper. In the New World across the sea, however, the Act of Toleration was honored

31

neither in principle nor in practice. The religious war there continued unabated, and Baptists were in the thick of it.

Chapter Four: A Beginning In New England

The American schoolboy learns that he has a heritage of religious freedom which originated in the founding days of the republic, and in his first glance back into history he is taught that the English who first settled these shores were in search of a place where they could practice their faith without fear of persecution from a hostile government. All true, as far as it goes. What the schoolboy never comes to understand is that the Puritans and Pilgrims sought freedom only for the exercise of their own religion; they were as intolerant of dissenters from their faith as the established order in England and other parts of Europe had been of them. Of one tenet now regarded as basically American they had no understanding whatsoever. The concept of separation of church and state was both alien and repugnant to them. The great contribution of the Baptists to the American way of life is that they endured two centuries of bitter persecution and against overwhelming odds implanted throughout the land, for the first time on earth, a true understanding of the meaning of soul liberty and honest comprehension of the necessity of total removal of governmental control over religious practice.

Religious intolerance existed in America from the first. The Pilgrims, who established Plymouth colony late in 1620, included that nucleus of dissenters from the Scrooby church who had fled to Holland around 1608. Seeking escape from the control of the Anglican Church, they found the radical religious elements harbored in the Netherlands almost as irritating as England's establishment, and their goal in emigrating to the New World was to find a haven for the cultivation of their Separatist beliefs. They had no interest at all in establishing a community in which all beliefs would be tolerated.

The Puritans, who settled the Massachusetts Bay Colony in 1628, were no better. Non-conformists rather than Separatists, they remained in communion with England's Established Church and believed deeply and sincerely that a union between the church and the state was a necessity for an orderly community. Consequently, they organized Congregational churches and established them by law as the only legal religious institutions. All citizens were required to pay for the support of the church, and political suffrage was limited to members. In a very short time the organization of dissenting congregations was forbidden, and defiance of the order thus established was punished by the withdrawal of citizenship rights, fines, whippings, imprisonment or even banishment. While initially the Pilgrims were not quite as exacting, they came round quickly to the same point of view. Thomas Armitage, quoting "a facetious writer," notes wryly that the Puritans came to America "to worship God according to their own consciences, and to prevent other people from worshipping Him according to theirn."[1] In that observation there is more sober truth than humor.

Throughout the pre-Revolutionary period nine of the American colonies supported an established church.[2] In New England, Massachusetts, Connecticut and New Hampshire made the Puritans' Congregational Church the instrument of the state; the Anglican, or Episcopal, Church was legalized for Virginia, New York, Maryland, North Carolina, South Carolina and Georgia. Only Rhode Island offered full religious liberty to all faiths, including Quakers and Catholics, from the very start, and in 1719 even there the idea was diluted with a prohibition against Catholicism.

34

Enforcement of the establishment was not uniformly rigid; but in Massachusetts and Virginia, where the Congregationalists and Episcopalians reigned supreme, defense of the state church was rabid and unrelenting, and it was in those two colonies that Baptists fought with the greatest determination. They did not fight alone: Presbyterians, Methodists and Quakers were also involved. But over the two centuries of repression the Baptists held out most tenaciously for full religious liberty.

To a full understanding of the rise of the Baptists in New England it is necessary to bring some awareness of the legal barriers they had to surmount. By 1631 the Puritan church had been given an effective monopoly over the colony's religious life through a declaration of the General Court of Massachusetts which "ordered and agreed that, for time to come, no man shall be admitted to the freedom of this body politic, but such as are members of some of the (Congregational) churches within the limits of same."[3] Four years later the members of the churches thus installed were told to "consult and advise of one uniform order of discipline in the churches, agreeable to the Scriptures, and then to consider how far the magistrates are bound to interfere for the preservation of that uniformity and peace of the churches."[4] Involved here was the very critical question of the degree to which civil authority might punish breaches of religious discipline. At about the same time another act made nonconforming groups illegal by providing for the banishment of dissenters – a law which was speedily put to use. In 1638 support of the established church through taxation was made compulsory, and that procedure remained in effect even after dissenting churches were tolerated. In 1644 banishment was prescribed for all those who opposed infant baptism, on whatever ground, and a 1646 law said that for the second offense of scoffing at preaching a delinquent would either be fined five pounds or be required to stand on a block in the town square wearing a sign which branded him A WANTON GOSPELLER. Other laws were to stem from the church protectorate, but these sufficiently set the atmosphere in which Baptists found themselves in the early days of this country.

Among historians there is general agreement that there were colonists of Baptist ideology among the first settlers, but they made no attempt to set up a separate communion. Rather, they seem to have been content to attend the services of the Congregational Church without protest. They may have had reservations about the order of service and some church doctrine, but none of these considerations was given voice. Baptists have always been church-going people, and these, like many to follow, preferred a church with which they disagreed to no church at all. The resident Baptists might have continued in this fashion for years had not a man arrived on the scene who became openly hostile to the suppression of religious belief and who suffered exile rather than yield to principles he could not support. His name was Roger Williams, and through his banishment Baptist beliefs were exported from Massachusetts, later to be reimported with a vigor that eventually would pull down the church-state combine. Most Baptists acknowledge Williams as the founder of the faith in America; actually, had it been left to him, the faith would have been stillborn, because he was a Baptist no more than three months. His great contribution to the Baptist cause lay not in his fatherhood but in his creation of a climate, through the establishment of free Rhode Island, in which the Baptist faith could grow and prosper.[5] And for that contribution he deserves honor not only from Baptists but from all Americans who cherish the principle of religious liberty as we now know it. That concept was slow in emerging in American life; Williams grasped it 150 years before it was written into the Bill of Rights.

Roger Williams was born in London about 1603 to James and Alice Williams, a family of no particular distinction. It was a time of religious ferment, and very early in his life Williams was subjected to the ideas of reformers both moderate and radical. It is probable that he had some early exposure to Baptist thought. While still young he learned shorthand, perhaps with the intention of becoming a clerk or scrivener, and in the use of that skill he came to the attention of Sir Edward Coke, one of the most important jurists in the history of English law. With Coke's support Williams attended Charterhouse School and won a scholarship to Cambridge University, then Puritan in influence. He may have studied some law, but his inclinations were theological and he finally took orders in the Church of England. Early in 1629 he settled at Otes in the parish of High Laver as chaplain to the household of Sir William Masham.[6] While there he had a love affair, apparently somewhat one-sided, with an aristocratic woman named Jane Whalley, and when she spurned his suit he quickly married a maid, Mary Barnard, who was said to be "of a meek and modest spirit"[7] and who had many other wholesome qualities, although proper education was not one of them.

By the time of his marriage, on December 15, 1629, Williams's religious sentiments were becoming increasingly Separatist. William Laud's star, which was to lead him to the archbishopric of Canterbury, was on the rise; he was chief ecclesiastical adviser to Charles I, and his practice was rigidly Anglican. Since Williams was breaking away from the Anglican Church in practice and in doctrine, opposing both its hierarchy and its liturgy, he could see ahead for himself only collision. Although recognized as a brilliant preacher, Williams turned down proffered pastorates in a number of churches and decided to make his future in the new world.

Following that resolve, he and Mrs. Williams departed from Bristol on December 1, 1630, aboard the ship *Lyon* and arrived in Boston February 5, 1631. On his debarkation at the American port of entry, his reputation in the pulpit having preceded him, he was invited to affiliate as teacher with the Boston Congregational Church, largest in the Massachusetts Bay Colony. He announced bluntly that he "durst not officiate to an unseparated people"[8] and somewhat gratuitously spread around Boston his conviction that civil magistrates had no right to punish breaches of the Sabbath or any other violations "of the first table." This meant that he also denied to municipal authority the right to judge transgressions of the Mosaic injunctions against idolatry, blasphemy or heresy, and Williams thereby "in effect was denying the power of the government to compel conformity in matters of faith."[9] This was a rebuke which the Massachusetts Bay authorities neither anticipated nor appreciated, and from that moment Williams was only marking time until his banishment. Both municipal and churchly ears would thenceforth be weighing his every word.

The Congregational Church at Salem fancied itself independent, and Williams was invited to be pastor there. He took up the post on April 12, 1631. Although he was much loved by his parishioners, he was not permitted to preach as openly as he would have liked. So he moved on to Plymouth colony, out of the reach of the Bay Company, and became assistant to the Rev. Ralph Smith, the Pilgrim pastor. In two years at Plymouth Williams gained the high regard of the church not only for his services there but also for missionary work among the Indians.

At midyear in 1633 Williams returned to Salem as assistant to the Rev. Samuel Skelton. He was now somewhat more outspoken, and he lectured the colonists for not buying their lands from the Indians — whom he regarded as the legitimate titleholders. He reiterated his earlier convictions about the limits on the powers of the magistracy and also seems to have written some provocative letters. Although the Salemites were devoted to him, there was agitation against him in the Congregational churches of other towns, and his behavior inevitably became a subject of magisterial interdict. Consequently, on October 19, 1635, a sentence of banishment was pronounced upon Roger Williams. It read:

"Whereas, Mr. Roger Williams, one of the elders of the church at Salem, hath broached and divulged new and dangerous opinions against the authority of magistrates; and also writ letters of defamation, both of the magistrates and churches here, and that before any conviction, and yet maintaineth the same without any retraction: it is therefore ordered that the said Mr. Williams shall depart out of this jurisdiction within six weeks now ensuing, which, if he neglect to perform, it shall be lawful for the Governor and two of the magistrates to send him to some place out of their jurisdiction, not to return any more without license from the court."[10]

Whatever the extent of Mr. William's alleged heresies, one obviously goes deeper than all the rest. Williams was ordered expelled from Massachusetts as a troublemaker, without doubt; he probably was a troublemaker in that Puritan society; but "his denial of the right of the civil magistrates to deal in matters of conscience and religion was certainly one of the reasons why his banishment was decreed."[11] So ingrained in the American fabric is William's belief now that such a question could hardly recur. But it is a belief intrinsically American and is not honored, to this day, on a world-wide scope.

Mary Williams was then expecting their second child (a girl born near the end of October and christened Freeborn) and Roger was recovering from an illness. Before the grace period expired, the deadline for Williams's departure was extended until the following spring. In January it was reported to the Massachusetts Bay authorities that Williams was secretly engaged in winning new converts and the magistrates met in Boston and decided to arrest the heretic and ship him back to England. A marshal, James Penn, was sent to Salem to fetch Williams for his forcible expulsion, but the minister pleaded that he was too sick to travel. With great foreboding, Williams then plunged into the wilderness alone, barely eluding another detachment of the constabulary ordered to carry him off by force, and thus began a period of hardship as famous in American history as Valley Forge. Williams was saved from death only by the attention of friendly Indians, with whom he dwelt in their "filthy smoke holes"[12] for three months. He never recalled that period with any fondness. In his *Hireling Ministry* he wrote of the winter months as a time spent in a "miserable, cold, howling wilderness,"[13] for fourteen weeks without bed or bread, lacking a weapon of any kind, cared for by God alone. His earlier missionary work with the Indians, whose tongue he had learned, paid off in full measure.

In the spring Williams was joined in the wilds by William Harris and Thomas Angell, of Salem; John Smith, a Dorchester miller banished at the same time as Williams, and Francis Weeks, who was traveling in exile with Smith. With these companions Williams crossed to the northern tip of Narragansett Bay with the intention of founding a settlement at Seekonk. The men bought the land from the Indians, pitched a tent and sowed some crops. The life of this first settlement was cut short by a friendly letter from Edward Winslow, governor of Plymouth Colony, warning Williams that he had chosen a spot too near the Plymouth boundary (and thus within reach of the Massachusetts Bay authorities). So Williams pulled up his tent stakes and crossed the Seekonk River to a peninsula reaching down into Narragansett Bay. Once again he bought the land from the Indians, and there he founded Providence Plantations — the birthplace of religious liberty in America. The foundation stone was laid in June, 1636.[14]

The population of Providence in that first year rose to about 30, including Williams's original party of five, and three other men from Salem — John Throckmorton, Joshua Verin and John Greene. Also in residence were the large family of William Arnold, including a son-in-law, William Carpenter, and Mary Williams with her two small children. From the first, Williams wanted to build Providence as "a shelter to persons distressed of conscience,"[15] and he and his fellows based their government on the majority rule of citizens equal before the law, each possessing complete civil liberty, including religious freedom.[16] As word of this bold experiment filtered back to Massachusetts, the Puritans concluded that in Providence there had been established an asylum for the criminally insane. The people there were known outcasts, many of them banished from orderly society, and in the exaltation of liberty of conscience they had proven themselves to be dangerous, fanatic radicals. Freedom of the soul was not then the pleasant commonplace it is now, and the reaction of the Puritans is understandable in the context of their history.

Sometime early in 1639 the worshippers in Providence got into a discussion of baptism, a question apparently broached by Ezekiel Holliman and Catherine Scott. In March about a dozen of the residents decided to form a new church, in which every aspiring member would be rebaptized. Holliman seems to have baptized Williams, and then Williams performed the rite for Holliman and ten others. This church is held to be the first Baptist church on American soil.

Its charter membership has been preserved as including Williams, Holliman, William Arnold, William Carpenter, Robert Cole, John Greene, William Harris, Thomas James, Thomas Olney, Richard Waterman, Stukeley Westcott and Francis Weston.[17] Undoubtedly there were also female communicants, but the names of women were not entered on church rolls at this period. Upon the rebaptism of these Christians, the Congregational Church in Salem, of which Roger Williams had been a member, passed the "censure," which the Providence founder called a "bull of excommunication," against those of its former members who had thus slipped from grace.[18] Its issuance had very little depressing effect on the new communion in Rhode Island.

Assuredly unrelated was the withdrawal from the Providence Baptist church, after three months, of Roger Williams, who had been designated pastor. Always troubled about his religious condition, Williams seems to have concluded that no man then living could administer a proper baptism and that no true church could exist until the apostolic ministry was restored.[19] In that frame of mind he could not honestly affiliate with any organized church, and he withdrew to become, for the rest of his life, a Seeker. This name apparently did not characterize a distinct sect but was applied rather widely at that time to a group of individuals who professed to be serious inquirers after religious truth.

There is a minority school among Baptists which holds that Williams was never an honest member of the faith and that his church was not the first in America. In the 1890 volume *The First Baptist Church in America*, Dr. S. Adlam, one-time pastor of the First Baptist Church in Newport, R.I., claims "there is no shade of evidence that Roger Williams was ever a Baptist one hour of his life."[20] Adlam claims the Newport Church was first and that it was established in 1638. Another historian of more than half a century ago, Dr. Thomas N. Bicknell, declared it "a travesty of history to call Mr. Williams a Baptist, when he did not pass the probationary stages for membership."[21] Whatever the authenticity of William's affiliation, Baptists generally accept the Providence Church as their earliest, though even now the claim can set off a lively dispute among denominational antiquarians.

Although Williams retired from the church, he did not retire from the life of the colony, and his missions to England in quest of a charter and his later endeavors in behalf of religious liberty are valorous, even though they are more properly a part of American than of Baptist history. He was to live to see his banishment from Massachusetts nullified by law, on March 31, 1676 – 41 years after it was invoked. He died in honor in 1683, his place in the birth of the nation secure, without ever again touching the soil of the state which had so cruelly sent him into the cold.

After his withdrawal from the Providence Baptist Church, his place as pastor was taken by Chad Brown, a later arrival in the colony, whom Williams called "a wise and godly soul."[22] The church seems to have met around in the homes of various members, with a succession of pastors, one of whom was Gregory Dexter, a native of London who was one of the first teachers of printing in New England. Dexter was so devoted to his ministerial duties that he could scarcely resist preaching at any group he encountered on the streets. John Callender, the Rhode Island historian, says Dexter was of such sober disposition that he was never seen to laugh, and even a smile rarely relieved his dour mien.[23] The Providence Baptists were without a proper meeting house until 1700, when the Rev. Pardon Tillinghast built one with his own money. This early church, which has not been preserved, was small and crude, and tradition holds that it was "in the shape of a hay cap, with a firplace in the middle, the smoke escaping from a hole in the roof."[24]

Also recorded in its early history is a church split which took place about 1652 over the question of the laying on of hands, which some members believed to be essential to communion.[25]

The Newport church, which may legitimately claim to be the mother church of American Baptists, was organized by Dr. John Clarke, another giant in the development of Rhode Island and, more importantly for our purposes, "a Baptist of the completest and purest type, the most important American Baptist of the century in which he lived."[26] Some research suggests that the Newport church was organized as early as 1638, which would indeed predate the one in Providence, but the Newport records can be traced only to 1648. Which actually came first is one of the open questions of history, but of the fact that the two are the oldest in America there is no doubt at all.

John Clarke,[27] the moving spirit of Newport, was born in Suffolk County, England, in 1609, one of eight children. Four of his brothers and sisters were to join him in America. After a good early education, he studied law, medicine and theology at the University of Leyden, the Dutch hotbed, and returned to London to practice medicine for a time. He appears to have been a Congregationalist in his earlier years. At the age of 28, he arrived in Boston in November, 1637, with his young wife, the former Elizabeth Harges, of Bedfordshire. He was tall, around six feet, with an attractive personality and obvious qualities for leadership.

At the time of his arrival in the New World, Boston was in the middle of an antinomian controversy precipitated by Mrs. Anne Hutchinson (later, in 1643, under banishment for "traducing the ministers and their ministry," to die in an Indian uprising in New York). Very quickly, young Clarke decided to join a group of seventeen settlers who wanted to found a new colony based on genuine civil and religious liberty, and during the winter months the company sailed northward to look over the territory ultimately to be known as New Hampshire. Finding the climate too severe there, Clarke, the already acknowledged leader, took his people back southward. Upon rounding Cape Cod, a delegation headed by Clarke went ashore to seek the advice of Roger Williams at Providence. Williams suggested two possible sites for settlement, one at Sow-wames (now Barrington, R. I.) and the other at Aquidneck Island. After considering both possibilities, and deciding that Sow-wames was too close to Plymouth, Clarke and his advisers chose Aquidneck, an island about fifteen miles long and three miles wide. After Williams's example, they purchased the land from the Indians "for the full payment of forty fathoms of white beads,"[28] worth about a hundred dollars. Portsmouth was established in May, 1638, complete with jail, stocks and whipping post, and a church of some kind, probably of the Congregational pattern, was organized. When a dispute broke out over the ideas of Samuel Gorton, an unorthodox religious zealot who denied the Trinity and the existence of either heaven or hell, a small group including Clarke moved the following April to the southerly end of the island and founded Newport. John and Elizabeth Clarke built their permanent home at the corner of what is now West Broadway and Callender Avenue. All of Aquidneck was called Rhode Island; it was at first a separate entity from Providence Plantations, and the Rhode Islanders tried desperately for years to keep it that way.

The settlers of Aquidneck, unlike the Providence castaways, were a select group, most of them families of some substance. Nearly all of them had had some painful religious experiences in the Massachusetts Bay Colony, but for the most part they journeyed into virgin territory not because they had to but because

43

they wanted to. An exception was Samuel Gorton, later founder of Warwick, R. I., who was nearly always only a jump ahead of the police, and who once, in 1643, did not jump fast enough. Among the other settlers were John Coggleshall, William Coddington, Henry Bull and William Dyer. Coggleshall, who had lived in Boston for six years, had been a selectman, court official and leading churchman there. He was to be elevated to the highest office in Rhode Island. Coddington, a well-to-do merchant, had been an officer of the Massachusetts Bay Company and served the colony as treasurer and assistant governor. Owner of the first brick house in Boston, he fell into popular disfavor when he protested the banishment of Mrs. Hutchinson. Thereafter he became the first signer of the Portsmouth Compact, and as Rhode Island's governor vigorously opposed union with Providence Plantations. Dyer, town clerk of both Portsmouth and Newport, was to become the colony's first attorney general. He had a particular grievance against the Massachusetts Bay authorities: his Quaker wife, Mary, had been hanged on the Boston Common for attempting to propagate "pernicious and dangerous doctrine." Bull was to become governor of the Colony of Rhode Island and Portsmouth Plantations.

By 1640 the estimated population of Aquidneck Island was 1,000, and the religious life of the colony was well-organized. Clarke was minister to congregations in both Portsmouth and Newport, and in the early 1640's the Newport church experienced a doctrinal controversy which sent William Coddington and others out to found a Quaker church. Those who remained, clustering around Clarke, formed a congregation which in about 1644 came to be known as Baptist. It continues to this day and is now known as the United Baptist John Clarke Memorial Church of Newport. The earliest list of members of record was compiled by Samuel Hubbard on the day of his baptism, October 12, 1648. He listed John and Elizabeth Clarke, two of Dr. Clarke's brothers, Thomas and Joseph, Mark Lucer, John Peckham, Nathaniel West, his wife, William Weeden, William Vaughn, John Thorndon, Thomas Winter, Samuel and Tacy Hubbard and Elenor Peckham.[29]

Dr. Clarke was associated with the Newport Church from its founding to his death in 1676, and although he was absent for long periods on colony business, he had an eventful ministry which brought him some suffering. He was a devout, vigorous man, thrice married, so loved by his fellow citizens that he was never allowed to retire from public life. He declined to stand for governor of the colony but twice was deputy governor, holding other important posts as well. He also oversaw division in the Newport Church — a practice of multiplication which has been the rule rather than the exception in Baptist congregations everywhere. In 1656, twenty-one members of the Newport assembly who objected to the singing of psalms during worship and who resisted the "restraints on the liberty of prophesying, particular redemption, and indifference to the laying on of hands"[30] withdrew to form a Six-Principle Church (based on the Scriptural passage, Hebrews 6: 1-2). This congregation came to be known as the Second Baptist Church of Newport. Fifteen years later another group of First Church members, holding Saturday to be the proper Sabbath, withdrew to form the first Seventh-Day Baptist Church in America — thus founding a splinter sect which has persisted into the Twentieth Century, although never with wide acceptance.

Clarke's work as a Baptist minister is overshadowed only by his service, in conjunction with Roger Williams, in the acquisition of a royal charter for Rhode Island. At one time Clarke spent thirteen years in England waiting on the king, mortgaging his Newport property to pay his expenses and supplementing his income abroad by preaching and practicing medicine. After a number of false starts and defective charters, Clarke in 1663 returned from England with the document which for the first time in the history of the world guaranteed religious freedom to the inhabitants of a political subdivision. The key section reads: "No person within the said colony, at any time hereafter, shall be anywise molested, punished, disquieted, or called in question, for any differences of opinion on matters of religion,"[31] Through Williams and Clarke this achievement has a distinctively Baptist foundation, and the Baptists of America prize it as one of the towering triumphs in Christian history. Eighty years ago Thomas Armitage wrote proudly, "These two Baptists shaped the early history of the present state of Rhode Island, and her religious policy has since shaped that of all of the states."[32]

During Clarke's absence from Rhode Island, he was succeeded as pastor at Newport, on an interim basis, by Obadiah Holmes, one of the real firebrands of the early Baptist movement. Born about 1606 in Lancashire, England, Holmes was a glassmaker by trade. He arrived at Salem in the Massachusetts Bay Colony in 1639, joined the Puritan church there and, with Lawrence Southwick, built a glass factory on a two-acre grant of land. He had left England with Baptist leanings, and after a few years of wrangling with the Puritan authorities over religion he was excommunicated from the church and banished from the colony. In 1646 he moved on to Rehoboth, which was then a ward of the colony at Plymouth and somewhat more liberal toward heretics than were the Massachusetts Bay authorities, but his strong religious convictions got him into trouble again. As a member of the Rehoboth church he got into a rather bitter controversy with the pastor, the Rev. Samuel Newman, which resulted in litigation. Holmes sued Newman for slander and won the case, but the majority of the church members seem to have sided with their pastor: they excommunicated the dissenter.

Sometime afterward Dr. John Clarke visited Rehoboth in search of Baptist converts, and after consulting Holmes and other sympathetic souls there he organized a Baptist church in the village with Holmes as pastor. The newly installed minister was forbidden by the Plymouth fathers to hold a Baptist service, however, and when he disregarded the ban he was yanked into court for "the continuing of a meeting upon the Lord's Day, contrary to the order of the court."[33] Clearly, Rhode Island was the only place he would find peace, and in 1650 he took up residence in Newport. Finding favor in Clarke's church, he was chosen to fill in as pastor during the long years of Clarke's absence, and upon the death of the founder he was made full-time pastor until his own passing in 1682.

Holmes had eight children, and one of his daughters became the wife of Chad Brown, the successor to Roger Williams in the Providence Church. His heirs were distinguished, and among his lineal descendants was Abraham Lincoln.

In Rhode Island the Baptist faith was growing. Holmes saw the establishment of three additional congregations — North Kingston in 1665, South Kingston in 1680, and Dartmouth, afterward transferred to Tiverton, in 1685. In Rhode Island there was no hindrance to Baptist expansion, but in Massachusetts the battle for a measure of tolerance was still being waged. Holmes was to discover early in his Rhode Island ministry that a Baptist in Massachusetts was a convincing candidate for the whipping post. What he could do as matter of right in Rhode Island, he could not do without peril across the border. And he was to wear the stripes that proved it.

Chapter Five: In Massachusetts, A Fight For Life

Baptists had gained a foothold in Rhode Island which they were never to relinquish, but not all the Baptists of the New World clustered in the free colony. There were many others of Baptist leaning who for economic or family reasons or out of plain stubbornness declined to move but who were inspired, as an expression of their own faith, to voice objection to Congregational ritual. The protests generally grew out of the baptism of infants, which Baptists opposed, and out of conviction that the true church should consist only of believers baptized as a sign of their regeneration.

It is necessary here to be somewhat charitable. To the New England Puritans, these objections smacked of Anabaptism, for they knew nothing of Baptists, and the word "Anabaptists" struck horror into their hearts. For to them, Anabaptists were associated with outrages like those at Munster, which news had come to them in garbled and exaggerated detail. They were "quite willing to admit that opponents of infant baptism might seem to be quiet and peaceful; but they were convinced that the logic of the Anabaptists led inevitably to the overthrow of the social order, with the denial of the magistracy, oaths, the right of the civil government to censure religious offenses, even to Munster-type outbreaks. So much must be said in order to account for the rancorous hatred of Baptists by the New England theocratic leaders, their lack of judicial fairness in dealing with radical dissidents of all types and their determination, even by the inflicting of the cruelest penalties, if need be, to exterminate heresy."[1]

But hysterical reaction to the Anabaptist threat does not alone account for the treatment Baptists received. Also involved was the theological egocentricity which has characterized almost every religious body thrust into circumstances of ultimate power. The world had seen it in Judaism, which sent Jesus Christ to the cross; it had been manifested for centuries in Catholicism, which left a trail of sacrificial blood and smoke across Europe; the outrages of entrenched Protestantism had been almost as bad, under Zwingli, Luther, Calvin and the Church of England. To the point in history of the founding of America religious toleration was an utterly novel idea, and the Puritans were interested in that kind of novelty only for themselves.

"The fact is," wrote Dr. George W. Paschal, the North Carolina historian, "that the Puritans of New England, having founded a commonwealth in which they might enjoy religious freedom, sought to prevent the intrusion of all who differed from themselves in religion, and for a hundred years did all in their power by employment of fines, cruel whippings, imprisonment and death to keep their communities free from those whose religious views differed from their own."[2]

It naturally followed that upstart Baptists, peculiarly persistent in their heresy, "were driven into the wilderness, were scourged by order of the civil power, were spoiled of their goods, were cast into prison, were pelted by the violence of mobs, were falsely accused, were reviled and defamed and treated as filth and offscouring of mankind; their principles were caricatured, their purposes maligned, their integrity questioned, their petitions slighted, and their hopes deferred; yet trusting in God they were in general true to their Master and their mission, while not a few of them... were distinguished for their moral courage and the:

49

assurance of ultimate deliverance."[3]

The first established case of public censure on the grounds of opposition to infant baptism occurred on December 14, 1642, at the Salem Quarterly Court when the Lady Deborah Moody, a Mrs. King and the wife of John Tilton were charged with heresy. The exact judicial disposition of the case is not clear, but Gov. John Winthrop noted in his journal somewhat later that "the Lady Moody, a wise and anciently religious woman, being taken with the error of denying baptism to infants, was dealt withal by many of the elders and others, and admonished by the Church of Salem (whereof she was a member); but persisting still, and to avoid further trouble, she removed to the Dutch, against the advice of all her friends. Many others infected with Anabaptism removed thither also. She was after excommunicated."[4] Her solution of removing "to the Dutch" meant that she transferred her residence to the colony later to be known as New York.

The next case to reach court involved a neighbor of Lady Moody's in Swampscott, near Lynn, Mass. His name was William Witter, and although he seems to have had very little personal influence, he had a knack for irritating the authorities. He first showed up on the court docket for February 28, 1644, accused of calling infant baptism "a badge of the whore." He was sentenced to make public acknowledgement of his error, which he seems to have done to the court's satisfaction. Apparently his retraction was without conviction, however, because two years later he was back in court for saying that those who stayed in church while a child was being baptized "do worship the devil."[5] He was dealt with lightly, but his house was placed under surveillance for signs of illegal meetings. The watch ultimately was to yield some prize heretics.

While these two cases were the first to reach the court stage, Baptist dissent was sufficiently widespread in Massachusetts to provoke official retaliation. Calling holders of Anabaptist views "incendiaries of commonwealths," "infecters" in religion, and "troublers of churches in all places where they have been," the colonial government on November 13, 1644, "ordered and agreed that if any person or persons shall either openly condemn or oppose the baptism of infants, or go about secretly to seduce others from the approbation or use thereof, or shall purposely depart the congregation at the adminstration of the ordinance, or shall deny the ordinance of magistracy or their lawful right or authority to make war, or to punish the outward breaches of the first table, and shall appear to the court willfully and obstinately to continue therein after due time and means of conviction, every such person or persons shall be sentenced to banishment."[6] This decree must have been aimed at several types of dissenters, for there is no record of a genuine New England Baptist's ever having declined to serve in public office or to carry his full weight in battle. In October, 1645, and again in May, 1646, the General Court was asked to exempt Baptists from the banishment penalty, but it refused on both occasions.

The atmosphere was decidedly hostile to expressions of Baptist belief, and the known troublemakers could worship with impunity only in the sanctity of their own homes. And even their homes were not inviolate. In the summer of 1651, Dr. John Clarke, the by now widely respected minister of the First Baptist Church in Newport, R. I., journeyed to Swampscott, Mass., to visit the aging William Witter, who had taken out non-resident membership in Clarke's church. With the minister were Obadiah Holmes and John Crandall. They arrived on a Saturday afternoon in July, and on the Sunday following they held a worship and baptismal service in Witter's home. At the height of the proceedings two constables entered, broke up the meeting, and arrested the three visiting Rhode Islanders on the ground that they were "erroneous persons, being strangers." In court the three were convicted of "perverting the straight ways of the Lord." Dr. Clarke was ordered to pay a fine of 20 pounds or to be whipped and lodged in jail until the fine was raised; Crandall, whose guilt was largely by association, was given a choice of a five-pound fine or a whipping; and the firebrand Holmes, who had most loudly protested the treatment of God-fearing Christians, was ordered to pay a fine of 30 pounds or "to be well whipt." Friends quickly raised the money to get Dr. Clarke and his friend Crandall out of the clutches of the law, but Holmes refused to be let off so lightly; he insisted on taking the whipping. Accordingly, he was taken to the whipping post at the rear of the Old State House in Boston, at the corner of Devonshire and State streets, and there given 30 lashes with a three-corded whip. As his tormentor finished his exertions, no doubt perspiring in the summer sun, Holmes looked up at him and said, "You struck me as with roses."[7]

While Holmes's sufferings were temporary, the Massachusetts authorities proved themselves capable of sterner action, even to the point of wrecking one's career. Nowhere was this vengeful zeal better illustrated than in the life of Henry Dunster, the first president of Harvard College. Dunster, who "ranks along with Roger Williams and John Clarke as one of the three foremost Baptists in Seventeenth Century America,"[8] was born in Lancashire, England, about 1609. He was educated at Magdalene College of Cambridge University, where he was awarded a master's degree in 1634. Ordained a minister of the Anglican Church, he found himself not wholly in sympathy with its doctrine and decided to emigrate to Massachusetts in hope of finding a more compatible religious atmosphere. He arrived in Boston near the end of the summer of 1640, purchased a piece of property and was almost immediately (August 27) offered the presidency of the newly established Harvard College. In the fourteen years of his service there Dunster formulated the college rules and patterned the procedures of Harvard after the English example. He worked hard to gain needed financial support and once himself, although poor, contributed 100 acres of land to the institution. Widowed in 1641, he remarried the wife of Joseph Glover, a Puritan clergyman who died while bringing America its first press; through Dunster's marriage, Harvard acquired control of the press.

Sometime between 1648 and 1653 Dunster arrived at a pure Baptist conclusion, that "visible believers only should be baptized." He withheld his own child from baptism, leading Cotton Mather to write later that Dunster had "unaccountably fall into the briars" of Baptist heresy.[9] The Boston magistracy could not long ignore the fact that the head of the colony's principal seat of advanced education had begun to show disturbing symptoms. In January, 1654, they addressed a letter to the colony's approved ministers saying that Dunster had "by his practices and opinions against infant baptism rendered himself offensive to this government" and seeking their support of measures for the removal "of that which may tend to the prejudice of the college and scandal to the country." After a lapse of about three months, during which churchmen and politicians sought to present a united front against the Harvard adminstration, the General Court issued the following order: "Forasmuch as it greatly concerns the welfare of this country that the youth thereof be educated not only in good literature, but sound doctrine, this Court doth therefore commend it to the serious consideration and special care of the Overseers of the College, and the selectmen of the several towns, not to admit or suffer any such to be continued in office or place of teaching, educating, or instruction of youth or child, in the college or school, that have manifested themselves unsound in the faith, or scandalous in their lives, and not giving due satisfaction according to the rules of Christ."[10] It was the first American example of heresy-hunting in the realm of education, and from this sorry episode the Baptists did not learn very much: much later they were to become adept at seeking out heresy in their own places of education, and they are still at it.

On June 10, 1654, Dunster offered his resignation as president of Harvard. It was not immediately accepted, and Dunster probably would never have been forced to resign had he been less voluble in espousing his own private principles. While his resignation was pending, he got up in church to denounce the baptism of an infant; that performance was regarded as a violation of the law against disturbance of a public worship service. When he again submitted his resignation, on October 24, 1654, it was accepted, and he was turned out without the payment of salary due him. Dunster rejected an offer of a Baptist pastorate in Dublin, Ireland, and instead moved to Scituate, Mass., which had a reputation as the most liberal settlement in the Massachusetts Bay Colony. Although he probably did a little preaching to Baptist audiences, he spent his last years with his name on the roll of an alien church. When he died on February 27, 1659, he asked to be buried near the school he had helped launch. Harvard University honors his memory.

Such was the suppression of Baptist belief in Massachusetts that through Dunster's time, even though Baptist sentiment was common, there had been no move to organize a Baptist church

53

there. The first attempt was made in 1663 when John Myles, leader of the first Baptist church in Wales, fled to New England to escape religious persecution under Charles II. Settling in Rehoboth, Myles discovered that Baptists had been meeting covertly there for thirteen years, and he boldly organized a church to bring the worshippers out into the open. It struggled along for several years without encountering judicial censure, but in 1667 Myles and one of his members, James Brown, were arraigned "for their breach of order in setting up of a public meeting without the knowledge and approbation of the court, to the disturbance of the peace and order."[11] Myles and Brown were fined five pounds and told to get out of Rehoboth. When they later protested that they had nowhere else to go, the court in October set aside for them a tract of land near the Rhode Island border, in the direction of other fanatics. Myles gathered a company of sympathetic souls, named the new settlement Swansea, and drew up a charter which was not wholly tolerant (it would have excluded Catholics, Lutherans, Anglicans and Quakers, by force, if necessary). The Welshman and his company had not yet grasped a Baptist tenet which was to become cardinal — that if one is to have complete religious freedom for himself, he must see that it is extended to all. Happily, the Swansea charter was never enforced, and the community prospered.

Meanwhile, the Baptists had been kicking up their heels in Boston. They had been meeting in secret for ten years, and in 1665 they formed a church. It met first at Charlestown, near Boston, but later in the year it moved to the city proper. By October its activities had come to the attention of the court, and the pastor, Thomas Gould, and some of his members were hauled before the authorities on a charge of heresy. The General Court showed no sympathy, finding that "the said Gould and company are no orderly church assembly, and that they stand convicted of high presumption against the Lord and his holy appointments, as also the peace of this Government."[12] The offending members were disfranchised and told that if they persisted in meeting they would be jailed. With typical Baptists stubbornness, they persisted, and they accepted the consequences: Gould was imprisoned for a year and upon his release driven out of the jurisdiction of the

Massachusetts Bay Colony. News of the indignities heaped upon this congregation, remembered historically as Boston's first Baptist church, along with reports of religious oppression in other parts of the colony and elsewhere in New England, notably Connecticut, reached London and stirred up immediate reaction. A Congregational Church member in England wrote to a departed Puritan in 1670: "Oh, how it grieves me that New England should persecute!. . . We blush and are filled with shame, when we hear of these things." The reports also surprised Charles II, who wrote to the Massachusetts authorities that it was "a severity the more to be wondered at, whereas liberty of conscience was made a principal motive for your first transportation thither."[13] After Gould's expulsion, this first organization of Baptists in Boston moved to Noddle's Island in the Boston harbor and chose Isaac Hull as pastor. After years of suffering they were let alone as a harmless nuisance.

In 1672 a revised edition of the lawbook of Massachusetts was ordered by the colonial assembly. In it Baptist views were classed as "damnable heresies" and "notorious impieties" and banishment was prescribed for anyone who attempted to propagate them. Fortunately, in that year the religious zealot Richard Bellingham, notorious in his energy at ferreting out dissenters, was succeeded as governor by the more moderate John Leverett, who tended wisely to overlook the supposed transgressions of the Baptists. But Leverett died in 1679, to be succeeded by Simon Bradstreet, and Bradstreet felt it his duty to keep the colony's religious life pure.

One of the first examples of his drive for orthodoxy came in his first months in office in 1679, when Philip Squire and Ellis Callender quietly constructed a plain meeting house in Boston. When it was noised around that the new building was to be used by Baptists, the builders among them, there was a general alarm and the leaders of the aspiring congregation were taken to court. When they argued that there was nothing in colonial law to prohibit the construction of an unorthodox church, the court conceded the point on the spot — and on the spot framed a law to cover the oversight. The church property was ordered forfeited, and the members of the church were ordered not to use the building. With the cunning often found in heretics, the Boston

Baptists obeyed the letter of the ruling: they did not meet in the church, but they held their meetings in the church yard. The exasperated authorities ultimately backed off and permitted the worshippers to enjoy their little sanctuary, but not until a group of English pastors had written: "For one Protestant congregation to persecute another, where there is no pretense to infallibility in the decision of all controversies, seems much more unreasonable than the cruelties of the Church of Rome towards them that depart from their superstitions." The historian Newman, in commenting on the ordeal of Massachusetts Baptists at this time, said: "The sum of their offending had been their refusal to have their children baptized, their refusal to witness the administration of that rite, and in a few cases somewhat demonstrative protestations of dissatisfaction with what they regarded as an utter perversion of an ordinance of Christ."[14] There was no denial that these early American Baptists were Christian; there was no denial that they were earnest; what was denied them was a different interpretation of the very Scriptures the Congregationalists themselves honored.

A new charter issued for Massachusetts in 1692 by William and Mary provided for "liberty of conscience in the worship of God to all Christians, except Papists." This would seem on its face to have cleared up the problems of the Baptists, but as the charter was enforced by colonial authorities, dissenters were little better off then they had been before. "Liberty of conscience" was interpreted by the courts as allowing the government to tax all persons, regardless of their religious preference, for the support of the established church. An implementing law passed in 1693 provided that the eligible voters of a town could choose a minister, who would then be supported by a tax on "all the inhabitants and ratable estates." Since in every town, with the possible exception of Swansea, Baptists were a minority, they found themselves required by law to pay a tax for the support of the elected Congregational minister. At the urging of the court Swansea did designate a Baptist minister as the beneficiary of the tax, but there is no record that property holders ever were assessed to pay him. At this period, in fact, Baptists did not believe in paying the preacher, and their ministers generally were employed gainfully in some other profession, even though the ministry may have been their first interest.

In the case of Boston and a few of the larger towns, Baptists were relieved of the church tax. Things were on such a pleasant footing in Boston by 1714, in fact, that in that year Cotton Mather, previously no friend of dissenters, invited Boston Baptists to participate with other churches in a Thanksgiving service. Four years later, on the occasion of the ordination to the Baptist ministry of Harvard-educated Elisha Callender, son of the church builder, the aging Increase Mather was invited to extend the right hand of fellowship and Cotton Mather was asked to preach the ordination service. Both complied, and the gesture of good will paid off for old Increase in the project dearest to his heart. A wealthy English Baptist, Thomas Hollis, hearing of the Mathers' generosity toward Callender, gave a substantial gift to Harvard College, a precedent later observed by two following generations of Hollises. With the gift Hollis urged Baptists to send their sons to Harvard, of which Increase Mather had been president, and he provided funds for the education of a number of Baptist students there. In the eyes of Massachusetts first families, Hollis was the first Baptist ever to attain honest-to-goodness respectability.

Except in Boston and a few other towns, collection of the church tax proceeded mercilessly. Baptists were indignant at the impost, but when they refused to pay they "oftentimes had their bodies seized upon, and thrown into the common jail, as malefactors, and their cattle, swine, horses, household furniture, and implements of husbandry, forcibly distrained from them, and shamefully sold, many times at not one quarter part of the first value."[15] Appeals to fairness and justice were of no avail. "The fact of their maintaining worship by themselves was not allowed to be a sufficient reason for exempting them from rates to sustain a ministry which in point of conscience they could not hear."[16]

This discriminatory system was in effect until 1728, at which time "persons commonly called Anabaptists, and those called Quakers" were theoretically exempted from the church tax. In various versions over a period of years, the exemption required the presentation of certified lists of church members to local officials, and no penalty was provided should the officials fail to receive or record the names on the list. In practice, the abuse of liberty of conscience continued on a wide scale, with miscreant Baptists continuing to face the threat of jail or the confiscation of such items as spinning wheels, pewter plates or livestock to satisfy tax liens.[17] By the middle of the Eighteenth Century, Massachusetts Baptists were chafing under two burdens they found intolerable: to exercise their faith, they had to deal with political officials, and since the time of Roger Williams a hundred years before, the conviction had been growing that civil authorities had no business meddling in religious affairs; and they had to live in company with an established church, which represented a church-state tie that to them was historically reprehensible.

Baptists have always tended to believe that in times of great trial, God provides a strong leader, and at this point in their history they found the man in Isaac Backus. His is a name little known in American history, and few of today's Baptist laymen are aware of his great contribution to the rescue of their faith from the clutch of state oppression. A clergyman of the first order, he was also historian, lobbyist and tireless worker for the Baptist cause. In a day of primitive transportation, he traveled almost 70,000 miles on religious missions, most of the distance on horseback.

Although identified most closely with the Baptists of Massachusetts, Backus was born in Norwich, Conn., on January 9, 1724. He had slight opportunity for education, and when he was 16 his father, Samuel Backus, died, leaving the widowed mother with eleven children. All his life Isaac was devoted to this noble woman, Elizabeth Tracy Backus, and he saw in her a saintly fortitude which enabled her to accept imprisonment in preference to the dilution of her Christian faith. Backus was a young man in the period when the Great Awakening was sweeping the American colonies in a frenzied outpouring of emotional revivalism, and in 1741 he came under the influence of evangelists inspired by George Whitefield, the English preacher. Whitefield, the Billy Graham of his day, had made an American tour beginning in 1739, and under his exhortation the isolated wellsprings of Christian renewal, first tapped by Theodorus Freylinghuysen and Gilbert Tennent in New Jersey and Jonathan Edwards in New England, flooded the settlements of the Atlantic Seaboard. As it moved across the country the revival movement picked up adherents known as "New Lights" and separated them from the established order, whose defenders were represented as "Old Lights."

The revival spirit came to Norwich in May, 1741, and Isaac Backus was deeply moved. For three months thereafter he underwent the inner anguish of doubt, conviction, self-accusation and surrender which old-time Baptists call "wrestling with the Lord," and his conversion came with the kind of shattering experience that has delighted sawdust-trail evangelists since the day the Apostle Paul walked the road to Damascus. "As I was mowing alone in the field, August 24th, 1741," he later wrote, "all my past life was opened plainly before me, and I saw clearly that it had been filled up with sin. I went and sat down in the shade of a tree, where my prayers and tears, my hearing the Word of God and striving for a better life, with all my other doings, were set before me in such a light that I perceived I could never make myself better, should I live ever so long. Divine justice appeared clear in my condemnation, as I saw that God had a right to do with me as he would. My soul yielded all into His hands, fell at His feet, and was silent and calm before Him. And while I sat there, I was enabled by divine light to see the perfect righteousness of Christ and the freeness and riches of His grace, with such clearness, that my soul was drawn forth to trust in Him for salvation. And I wondered that others did not also come to Him who had enough for all. The Word of God and the promises of His grace appeared firmer than a rock, and I was astonished at my previous unbelief. My heavy burden was gone, tormenting fears were fled, and my joy was unspeakable."[18] Backus wandered around in a daze for some hours afterward. It was two days before he realized what had happened to him: that he had experienced a powerful conversion.

Even so, Backus did not become a member of his mother's assembly, the First Congregational Church of Norwich, until July 11, 1742, and when he did, he was spiritually restive. Among the New Lights, which included Backus and his mother, and the Old Lights there was sharp controversy which raged for more than two years. Early in 1745 thirty dissenting men and a larger number of women withdrew from the church and began to hold separate meetings, and six months later the separatists were "publicly warned of their errors and admonished to return to the church." When they refused, they were suspended. There followed a period of bitter persecution during which Elizabeth Backus was several times jailed, on one occasion for thirteen days.

On September 27, 1746, Backus decided to enter the ministry, and he preached his first sermon to a Separatist congregation the next day. Once committed, he performed zealously as preacher and during the subsequent year rode out on a number of teaching missions. Apparently he spoke with some power and conviction, because on December 28, 1747, the Separatist church at Titicut, Mass., invited him to become its pastor. He was ordained to its ministry on March 31, 1748, and in the second year of his tenure there, on November 29, 1749, he married Susanna Mason, of Rehoboth. At about the same time he began to have second thoughts about baptism, but he was not yet ready to declare himself Baptist. "From the ill behavior charged upon Baptists of former and later times, he was led to fear that some mischief lurked in their principles, and that these were now sent as a delusion in judgement upon them. But he could not exclude the topic utterly from his thoughts."[19] The "topic" was whether "plunging" was the appropriate method for baptism and whether infants are qualified candidates for the ordinance. Despite his reservations, his views became genuinely Baptist over a period of two years, and on August 22, 1751, although continuing in the ministry of the Titicut church, he had himself rebaptized by immersion. Five years later, on June 23, 1756, when a small group of his friends established a Baptist church in Middleborough, he joined it as pastor. It was an association that was to last for more than half a century.

From this point forward, the fortunes of Massachusetts Baptists were closely linked with the activities of Isaac Backus. He helped organize churches (where there had been only six recognized churches in 1740, there were thirty in 1768), assisted in the ordination of ministers, mediated disputes in churches and between churches, corresponded voluminously and was in part responsible for the organization, in 1767, of the Warren Association, the first state-wide Baptist agency in Massachusetts. Although it was created to provide for united denominational action in pressing for full religious liberty, only four churches joined at first. Backus was elected clerk, but his own congregation abstained from membership for three years, fearing associational abrogation of the independence of the individual churches. This has been a long-standing fear of Baptists, who prize the independence of the local church. The principle is as alive today as it ever was, and while it does, indeed, exalt the local church, it also inhibits the formulation of a common denominational front.

While the Warren Association served as a link between scattered churches, provided supplies for the newer or poorer congregations and assisted in preparing young men for the ministry, it took as its first goal a crusade for liberty of conscience in the practice of Christian faith. The association solicited reports from the churches on examples of infringements upon their liberty, and the records for 1769 state that "many letters from the churches mentioned grievous oppressions and persecutions from the standing order; especially the one from Ashfield, where religious tyranny had been carried to great lengths."[20]

In 1769 the Warren Association appointed a committee, consisting of Backus and others, to draft a petition for redress of grievances for presentation to the Massachusetts courts. Another committee was appointed to collect well-authenticated cases of oppression of Baptists, and a third was named to present the petitions and accompanying evidence to the authorities. The material was promptly submitted, but it was brushed aside as a set of complaints of no real consequence. Undaunted, the association tried another approach. To serve the double purpose of collecting facts and to alert the authorities to their intention to attain religious equality, the association ran an advertisement in the Boston *Evening Post* of August 30, 1770. After recounting the persecution of members in the past, the advertisement told Baptists: "You are desired to collect your cases of suffering and have them well-attested — such as the taxes you have paid to build meeting houses, to settle ministers and support them, with all the time, money and labor you have lost in waiting on courts, feeing lawyers, etc., and bring or send such cases to the Baptist Association to be holden at Bellingham; when measures will be resolutely adopted for obtaining redress from another quarter than that to which repeated aplication hath been made unsuccessfully. Nay, complaints, however just and grievous, have been treated with indifference, and scarcely, if at all, credited. We deem this our conduct perfectly justifiable; and hope you will pay particular regard to this desire, and be exact in your accounts."[2 1]

Nothing could have upset the Massachusetts authorities at this time more than an appeal from the Baptists to the British crown — a threat which was inherent in that newspaper advertisement. The Stamp Act, passed in 1765 and repealed the following year, had fanned colonial resentment against the mother country, and "taxation without representation" was a phrase commonly bandied to support the colonial belligerency. The equally repugnant Townshend Acts were enacted in 1767, further eroding relations between the Americans and the British. At a time when sentiment was rising against royal domination, here came the upstart Baptists with the infuriating notice that they were about to seek royal aid in throwing off colonial repression. And they had a good case. The colonists regarded taxation without representation as tyrannical. The Baptists claimed the church taxes they were forced to pay were a form of injustice just as intolerable. It was a tense situation. "That the Baptists should threaten to appeal to a government against which their fellow-colonists were preparing to rebel was looked upon as little better than treason."[2 2]

As a result of the circulation of the newspaper plea, a large number of grievances was presented to the associational meeting that September, and after reviewing the cases of discrimination and unfair taxation the members unanimously voted "to send to the British court for help, if it could not be obtained in America." In that resolution the Baptists were not being disloyal to the Colonial cause. In general they disapproved of the British actions against which the colonists were rebelling, but their church was central to their thinking. Their American neighbors and legislators had denied them the right to worship as they chose, and they could not be blamed for seeking relief from what was then the highest governmental authority. As a matter of practice, Baptists wholeheartedly supported the Revolution. Among Baptist ministers, there was only one avowed Tory (Morgan Edwards), and his political posture lost him favor in the denomination. But in the threatened appeal to the Crown the Baptists had found a way of dramatizing their cause.

At the September meeting John Davis, pastor of the Second Baptist Church in Boston, was appointed to work with a grievance committee in attempting to obtain the remission of church taxes. A petition drawn up by the committee for presentation to the Massachusetts General Court cited the notorious Ashfield case. The facts were these: In 1761 a Baptist church had been established in the frontier settlement of Huntstown, with Ebenezer Smith as pastor. It was the town church — fourteen of the town's nineteen families were members — and under the law it could have collected taxes for the support of its minister. Sometime later the non-Baptists established a Congregational Church and taxed the Baptists for their pastor's support. That action was legalized, through legislative connivance, by passing a law which changed the name of the settlement from Huntstown to Ashfield. In recounting this piece of flim-flammery the Baptist petition said: "In consequence of which law, and by a power granted in the same to the proprietors of Ashfield aforesaid, 398 acres of our land have been sold to build and remove and repair, when moved, a meeting-house in which we have no part, and to settle and support a minister whom we cannot hear. The lands were valued at 363 pounds, 18 shillings. . . and were sold for 19 pounds, three shillings; so that our loss is 344 pounds, 15 shillings. . . Part of the land aforesaid belonged to the Rev. Ebenezer Smith, a regularly ordained Baptist minister, who together with his father and others, their brethren, in the last Indian war, built at their own expense a fort and were a frontier; and they did this without help from any quarter; for which we beg leave to say that they deserve, at least, the common privileges of the subjects of the crown of England. Part of said lands had been laid out for a burying place, and they have taken from us our dead. They have also sold a dwelling house and orchard, and pulled up our apple trees, and thrown down our fences, and made our fields waste places."[23] The petition asked restoration of the lands and "perpetual exemption to all Baptists and their congregations from all ministerial rates whatsoever."

In response the Massachusetts authorities passed a new certification law which gave local officials discretion in exempting dissenters from church taxes. The Baptists found it completely unsatisfactory. Just as the colonists by now would not be satisfied with anything less thaan total independence from Britain, the Baptists would not be satisfied with anything less than a complete annullment of church taxes and the elimination of civil interference in religious worship.

Isaac Backus was appointed the Warren Associations's agent in 1772, and he took over the job with an appeal to all Baptists to refuse to comply with the certification law. "The root of all these difficulties," he said, "and that which has done amazing mischief in our land, is civil rulers assuming a power to make any laws to govern ecclesiastical affairs, or to use any force to support ministers."[24]

Toward the end of 1773, at the behest of Backus, the Baptists published an "Appeal to the Public for Religious Liberty, against the Oppressions of the Present Day." It set forth the basic Baptist demands for absolute liberty of conscience and separation of church and state and said Baptists would refuse to conform to the certificate law "because the very nature of such a practice implies an acknowledgement that the civil power has the right to set one religious sect up above another. . . It is a tacit allowance that they have a right to make laws about such things, which we believe in our consciences they have not."[25]

Throughout the months leading up to the Revolution, Backus remained active in the Baptist cause. He wrote letters, traveled and made speeches urging an end to the church tax, asking for the release of Baptists who had been imprisoned for refusal to pay it and seeking the restoration of their seized property. In September, 1774, he traveled to Philadelphia to join a prominent group of American Baptists who had an audience with national political delegates assembled there for the first meeting of the Continental Congress. Among those the Baptists saw were Thomas Cushing, Samuel Adams, John Adams and R. T. Paine, of Massachusetts; James Kinzie, of New Jersey; Stephen Hopkins and Samuel Ward, of Rhode Island; and Joseph Galloway and Thomas Miflin, of Pennsylvania. Speaking for the Baptists, James Manning, president of Rhode Island College (later Brown University), read a memorial which began: "It has been said by a celebrated writer in politics that but two things were worth contending for — religion and liberty. For the latter we are at present nobly exerting ourselves through all this extensive continent; and surely no one whose bosom feels the patriot glow in behalf of civil liberty can remain torpid to the more ennobling flame of religious freedom. The free exercise of private judgement, and the unalienable right of conscience, are of too high a rank and dignity to be subjected to the decrees of councils, or the imperfect laws of fallible legislators. The merciful Father of mankind is the alone Lord of conscience." After chronicling the difficulties the Baptists of New England had faced over the years, the memorial concluded: "Consistently with the principles of Christianity, and according to the dictates of Protestantism, we claim and expect the liberty of worshiping God according to our consciences, not being obliged to support a ministry we cannot attend, whilst we demean ourselves as faithful subjects."[26] After a four-hour conference the Massachusetts political delegates promised to do what they could to improve the lot of the Baptists, but John Adams is said to have remarked that the Baptists could as easily expect a change in the solar system as to hope Massachusetts would give up its established church.

Backus returned home to renewed charges that the Baptists were trying to undermine the Revolution, but he denied it. In an address to the Massachusetts Provincial Congress on November 22, 1774, he said, "The Baptist churches in this province as heartily unite with their countrymen in this cause as any denomination in the land; and are as ready to exert all their abilities to defend it." After the war he claimed that no denomination had been more unanimous in its support.[27]

With the war won, the Massachusetts General Court of 1780 attempted to sustain the established church by empowering the legislature to make "suitable provision" for the support of ministers. But it also declared that "no subordination of one sect or denomination to another shall ever be established by law." In practice, however, that provision was meaningless. In 1781 a Baptist church in Cambridge was taxed for the support of a Congregational minister, and when its members appealed to the court for relief, they lost. Their only alternative was to hand in certificates of dissent, and in many other Baptist churches in

Massachusetts a similar condition prevailed. Even with the adoption of the Bill of Rights, with its clause forbidding an established church, the Congregationalists remained in a favored position in Massachusetts.

Isaac Backus did not live to see absolute religious freedom in his adopted state. In March, 1806, he suffered a stroke of paralysis, and on April 3, he preached his last sermon. On April 23, his speech failed, and he died November 20. Already in publication then were his history of New England and about 37 pamphlets and tracts, and he left a legacy of Christian perseverance seldom equalled.

It was he who most successfully stirred the currents of religious freedom in Massachusetts, and on any list of Baptist pioneers his name is near the top. Complete religious freedom in Massachusetts, through the final separation of church and state, did not take place until November 11, 1833. It ended 195 years of tribulation for the Baptists in America, not only in New England but also in the South. The two centuries of persecution showed Baptists at their best.

Chapter Six: In Virginia, A Formidable Challenge

If New England was the bulwark of intolerant Puritanism, it had a counterpart equally intolerant in Virginia, where the Anglican Church, known in its American incarnation as Episcopalianism, reigned supreme until the American Revolution. If anything, dissenters were treated more harshly in Colonial Virginia than anywhere else in America, because the religious struggle there was based not just on Christian ideology. There it was also a class struggle. Unlike the Puritans, the settlers of Virginia had not arrived in the New World in search of religious liberty; as Anglicans, they had been free to worship in their fashion in England, and their motivation was entirely different. So was their way of life. The New Englanders, nearly all of them, were artisans, craftsmen, small farmers; the Virginians became big planters, with estates and large holdings, and those favored by the established order supported it. The Episcopal Church was part of the establishment, part of the planters' way of life. When dissent arose, it originated among those who were in large part outside the social elite. They were looked down upon as illiterates, grousers and crackpots, and their religion was regarded as a doctrine intrinsically false. Baptists in particular were prime targets for baitings and beatings; it was little more dishonorable to thrash a peddler of Baptist nonsense than it was to discipline a cantankerous horse. And because the Virginia authorities so carefully protected the favored church, Baptist thought was late in arriving. So were all dissenting religious ideas.

By an act of the first legislature of Colonial Virginia, in 1619, the Church of England was established as the official religious institution, and for almost a century it reigned supreme, so secure that the clergy became lax and indolent, so bolstered by law that no voice was raised in protest against it. Subsequent to 1619 measures were enacted to assure the support of ministers, to induce the conformity of members and to prevent the intrusion of non-believers who might disturb the faith. A 1629 act set up severe penalties for non-adherence to the canons of the Church, and in 1639 and 1642 laws were promulgated against Puritans — not because any had shown up in Virginia but "to prevent the infection from reaching this country."[1]

By mid-century there appears to have been some sub rosa consideration of the legitimacy of infant baptism, because the assemblies of both 1659 and 1662 made it punishable in parents to refuse to have their children baptized. The latter act said: "Whereas, many schismatical persons, out of their averseness to the orthodox established religion, or out of the new fangled conceit of their own heretical inventions, do refuse to have their children baptized; be it therefore enacted by the authority aforesaid, that all persons who in contempt of the divine sacrament of baptism, shall refuse when he may carry their child to a lawful minister of that county to have them baptized, shall be amerced two thousand pounds of tobacco; half to the informer; half to the public."[2] In 1696, the method of paying Episcopal clergymen was changed — an event which later was to cause considerable trouble. At first they had been paid in silver, with the salary fixed at 80 pounds sterling annually. The change, perhaps suggested by a shortage of cash, set the salary at 16,000 pounds of tobacco, to be furnished by the tithable members. At the same time, church fines were converted from cash to tobacco: missing a service on Sunday without a reasonable excuse required a forfeit of a pound of tobacco; missing church for a month running subjected the miscreant to a fine of 50 pounds; anyone who publicly ridiculed a minister, causing his parishioners to lose confidence in him, could be compelled to pay 500 pounds of tobacco and to apologize before the congregation; and no church member was allowed to sell his own tobacco in the fall until he had contributed his share to the church and paid any outstanding fines.

Under the British Toleration Act of 1689, Virginia authorities were required to abandon their policy of excluding dissenters, but they did not advertise the colony as a haven for religious malcontents. By bending the law a little, they could still control the most flagrant offenses to orthodoxy, and as late as 1693 outspoken opponents of infant baptism still were treated as criminals.[3] But when the first Baptists arrived in the colony and settled down quietly and peacefully by themselves they were not disturbed. The initial contingent arrived from England under the leadership of Robert Nordin, an ordained minister, in 1714, and organized a church at Burleigh, in Isle of Wight County. About 1743 another group emigrated from Maryland and settled in Frederick County. Both of these groups were General Baptists, Arminian in doctrine, and they seem to have had no interest in evangelizing activities. When the ardent New Lights, Baptists separate in doctrine and highly vocal in telling about it, began to show up, Cavalier Virginia had to take notice.

This third influx came about through the missionary zeal of Shubal Stearns, a native New Englander who had been set on fire by the Great Awakening. Born in Boston January 28, 1706, Stearns and his parents, Shubal and Rebecca Larriford Stearns, moved to Tolland, Conn., early in his youth and joined the Congregational Church there. Under the preaching of George Whitefield he accepted New Light views in 1745 and joined a separatist church in Tolland. Like Isaac Backus, he found himself drifting toward Baptist views, and in 1751 he was baptized in the new faith by Wait Palmer, a pastor in New Stonington. Stearns's separatists formed a Baptist Church in Tolland, and he was ordained as pastor on May 20 in the year of his baptism. Three years later he was seized with wanderlust and set out for Virginia, settling for a short time at Cacaphon in Hampshire County, about

30 miles from Winchester. He was not happy there, and before long he received a letter from friends in North Carolina telling of a people who were without spiritual leadership but who were "so eager to hear they often came 40 miles each way when they could have an opportunity to hear a sermon."[4] With a brother-in-law, who was also a preacher, Daniel Marshall, Stearns and his entourage packed up again and moved 200 miles to Sandy Creek, N.C., in what is now Randolph County. They founded a church there in 1755 with Stearns as pastor.

Marshall seems to have had some handicaps as a minister; a contemporary historian described him as "a weak man, a stammerer, no schollar."[5] But Stearns was just the opposite. He had a voice that was "musical and strong" and in his sermons he could "fetch tears from the eyes" and "throw the animal system into tumults and perturbations."[6] The tone of his voice was "peculiarly impressive and captivating, and his eyes seem to have had almost magical power over those upon whom they were fixed. Trembling, weeping, screaming and catalepsy were common effects of his highly impassioned exhortations."[7] This soul-shaking impact, preserved to this day in revivals and tent meetings in the rural South, seems to have been a hallmark of the New Light converts, and they had an uncanny ability to transmit it. David Benedict made note of it in his history. The early Baptist preachers, he said, had a "manner of preaching (which) was, if possible, much more novel than their doctrines. The Separates in New England had acquired a very warm and pathetic address, accompanied by strong gestures and a singular tone of voice. Being often deeply affected themselves when preaching, correspondent affections were felt by their pious hearers, which were frequently expressed by tears, trembling, screams, and exclamations of grief and joy... Many mocked, but, the power of God attending them, many also trembled."[8] One characteristic of the ministers' voices has been called the "holy whine," a rising and falling inflection which had a powerful effect upon the audience. Some it hypnotized, or turned into trance. Others it irritated. The historian Morgan Edwards told of one man who said he would "rather go to hell than be obliged to hear a Baptist in order to go to heaven."[9]

Stearns's Sandy Creek congregation was not the first Baptist church in North Carolina. General Baptists had been in the colony since 1727, when Paul Palmer organized a church in Chowan County, near the present town of Cisco. By the time Stearns arrived there were sixteen churches in the State. But in both North Carolina and Virginia, Stearns's Separatists were responsible for the rapidity of the spread of Baptist principles. Out of Sandy Creek came at least 125 ministers over the years, and 42 churches can trace their ancestry back directly to Stearns's settlement of 1755. Its pioneering work reached not only into Virginia but also Tennessee, Kentucky and other distant points.

Stearns and his followers seem not to have been interested at first in the formation of new churches. Rather, their primary goal was to carry the Gospel, as they saw it, to the religiously indifferent who had found no inspiration in formalized Anglicanism. They were itinerants, preaching here in a house and there at a crossroads, as adept at attracting a crowd as were traveling medicine men. And this trumpeting of their message, notwithstanding jeers, bullying and heckling, is what got them into trouble. Under the Toleration Act, Virginia was prepared to allow dissenting ministers to preach if they took out licenses for a particular locality, and those minority preachers who conformed had little trouble. But the Separate Baptists refused to be confined to any specific stump. They roved everywhere, and because of their own excess of enthusiasm in the Lord's work, their meetings sometimes seemed to be disorderly.

Robert B. Semple, commenting a hundred years later on the treatment of Baptists, said that when the Separatists first started their evangelistic activities in Virginia "they were viewed by men in power as beneath their notice; none, said they, but the weak and wicked join them; let them alone, they will soon fall out among themselves and come to nothing. In some places, this maxim was adhered to, and persecution, in a legal shape, was never seen. But in many places, alarmed by the rapid increase of the Baptists, the men in power strained every penal law in the Virginia code to obtain ways and means to put down these disturbers of the peace."[10] At the time of the rise of the Baptists in Virginia there was no law in force which provided for the imprisonment of dissenting ministers. There were laws, however, for the preservation

71

of the peace, and these statutes were so interpreted as to allow the arrest of religious trouble-makers on peace warrants. Because of their low regard for the ministers involved, the authorities had no reluctance to use any means which had faint scent of legitimacy. In *The Great Awakening in Virginia,* Wesley M. Gewehr said that "the Separate Baptists occupied in the popular mind a very definite social status. They had the reputation of being the meanest of the mean — a poor, illiterate, ignorant and awkward set of enthusiasts."[11] The authorities were not alone in that conviction. When Stearns once wrote to a Baptist minister in South Carolina inviting him to participate in the formal ordination of his brother-in-law, Daniel Marshall, at Sandy Creek, the invited divine wrote back that he would have nothing to do with Stearns's Separatists. He believed them to be a disorderly bunch, encouraging noise and confusion at their meetings and allowing any ignorant man who had the urge to preach. And besides, they allowed women to pray in public.[12]

These were harsh judgements, not wholly supported by the facts. The Baptists were, indeed, without learning. James Read, a North Carolinian who was to preach with great success in Virginia, was illiterate at the time of his conversion, and it was only through the patience of his wife that he learned to read the Bible from which he preached. These men were generally very poor; they were without lustre in dress and comportment, and very often their speech was ungrammatical. But they were honest, generally gainfully employed as farmers, and they believed passionately in the truths they had discovered. They felt an obligation to carry the good news to the unconverted, and they were not deterred by threats, jailing or outright violence.

Occasionally their message found a receptive ear not quite so unrefined. Several years after the establishment of the Sandy Creek Church a team of roving preachers held a service in a private home in what is now Pittsylvania County, Va. The sound of their raised voices reached the road, and out of curiosity Col. Samuel Harris, who was passing by, joined the congregation. Harris, a power in the community, had been a warden in the Episcopal Church, sheriff, a justice of the county court, a member of the House of Burgesses and a distinguished military commander in engagements with the Indians. As he listened to the visiting ministers, "the arrow of the Almighty stuck fast in him"[13] and he was converted to Baptist belief. Upon his baptism by Daniel Marshall in 1758, he gave up all his civic duties and converted much of what he had to the propagation of his new-found faith. A new house he was building he converted into a meeting-house, and he served as an evangelist himself for ten years before his ordination as a minister in 1769. He is said to have emitted "streams of celestial lightning from his eyes" and to have been able thereby to "strike down hundreds at once."[14]

Formal organization of Separatist Baptist churches in Virginia began in August, 1760, when Marshall and Philip Mulkey organized 74 converts, eleven of whom were Negroes, into the Dan River Church in Pittsylvania County. One of the converts, the Rev. Dutton Lane, was made pastor, although he was not ordained until 1764. After the establishment of that first church, other bodies of Baptist believers slowly organized, until by 1768 there were ten Baptist churches in the state. The period of greatest Baptist growth coincides exactly with the time of greatest struggle for liberty of conscience, for in the next twenty years, when Baptists were being jailed and otherwise deprived, 200 more churches were formed.

The first attempt to suppress a Separate Baptist minister by legal means, which occurred at about the time of the founding of the first church, involved Lewis Craig, who had gone into Spotsylvania County on a preaching mission. He was arrested as a disturber of the peace, hauled before court and fined. Given an opportunity to address the grand jury that presented him, Craig said: "I thank you, gentlemen, for the honor you did me. While I was wicked and injurious, you took no note of me, but now, having altered my course of life and endeavoring to reform my neighbors, you concern yourselves much about me."[15] On the grand jury that day was a man known as one of the roughest characters in Spotsylvania County, "Swearing Jack" Waller. He was a gambler and carouser with a particular hatred for Baptists, and the prospect of seeing Craig squirm in court had delighted him. However, he was so moved by Craig's conduct and speech that he went into a depression that lasted for seven months. He was brought out of it only by conversion to the faith he had taken such joy in persecuting. "Swearing Jack" became a Baptist minister and was himself often troubled by the authorities. In a long career he ministered to five churches with a combined membership of 1,300.

Naturally, Waller and Craig became good friends, often traveling together on preaching missions, and they were involved in the first Virginia jailing of Baptist ministers. With James Childs they were holding a meeting, again in Spotsylvania County, when they were seized by the sheriff and taken before three magistrates on charges of disturbing the peace. In court two days later one of their prosecutors told the judges, "May it please your worship, these men are great disturbers of the peace; they cannot meet a man upon the road, but they must ram a scripture down his throat."[16] Craig was jailed for four weeks, and Waller and Childs got 43 days. In a letter dated July 16, 1768, Deputy Governor John Blair, from his office in Williamsburg, wrote the Spotsylvania King's Attorney asking that the defendants be dealt with lightly. "I am told," Blair said, "they administer the sacrament of the Lord's Supper, near the manner we do, and differ in nothing, from our church but in that of Baptism, and their renewing the ancient discipline, by which they have reformed some sinners, and brought them to be truly penitent. Nay, if a man of theirs is idle, and neglects to labour and provide for his family as he ought, he incurs their censures, which have good effects. If this be their behavior, it were to be wished we had some of it among us."[17] The court ignored Blair's letter. Even so, the ministers refused to be inhibited. Waller subsequently was jailed in Middlesex for 46 days and in Piscataway for 26 days.

Not all of the sentences were so light. In December, 1770, William Webber and Joseph Anthony, two Baptist ministers laboring in the vicinity of Richmond, crossed the James River into Chesterfield County and were arrested because their preaching "disturbed the peace of the neighborhood." They were sent to jail for four months, but prison bars could not contain their enthusiasm for their faith. They are said to have preached through the cell gratings so effectively that they picked up a number of converts. In all, 30 Baptist ministers were imprisoned between 1768 and 1770, in such widely scattered places as Alexandria,

Warrenton, Culpepper, Fredericksburg, Tappahannock, Urbanna, King and Queen County and Caroline County.[18]

In his 1836 history of the *Rise and Progress of the Protestant Episcopal Church in Virginia,* Francis L. Hawks, no friend to opponents of the establishment, said that "no dissenters in Virginia experienced for a time harsher treatment than did the Baptists. They were beaten and imprisoned; and cruelty taxed its ingenuity to devise new modes of punishment and annoyance. The usual consequences followed; persecution made friends for its victims; and the men who were not permitted to speak in public found willing auditors in the sympathizing crowds who gathered around the prisons to hear them preach from the grated windows. It is not improbable that this very opposition imparted strength in another mode, inasmuch as it at least furnished the Baptists with a common ground on which to make resistance; and such common ground was in a great degree wanting in their creed; for not to speak of their great division into Regulars and Separates, some 'held to predestination, others would have none but the Bible:' and, in fact, the only particular in which there seems to have been unanimity, was in the favorite exclusive opinion of the sect, that none but adult believers are fit subjects of baptism, and that immersion is the only effectual or authorized mode of administering that sacrament."[19] The ingenuity of the Baptists' tormenters was often gross. Mobs broke up their meetings, and threats to the ministers became blows. The Baptist leaders were kicked, stomped, and dragged through the streets by their hair. On one occasion a live rattlesnake was thrown among the worshippers, with near panic the result; at another meeting a nest full of angry hornets was tossed into the crowd. At a service being conducted by the Rev. Robert Ware two neighborhood louts approached him with a whisky bottle, and during his sermon they drank and cursed him. When the final prayer had been said they went to the rostrum and started playing cards, hoping to bait him into rebuke. In Virginia legend these two bullies died insane shortly afterward, each woefully accusing the other "of seducing him into such monstrous behavior."[20]

Baptists were also mocked in print. A notice appearing in the *Virginia Gazette* of October 31, 1771, was entitled, "A Recipe to

Make an Annabaptist Preacher in Two Days Time." Its advice: "Take the Herbs of Hypocrisy and Ambition, of each an Handful, of the Spirit of Pride two Drams, of the Seed of Dissention and Discord one Ounce, of the Flower of Formality three Scruples, of the Roots of Stubbornness and Obstinacy four Pounds; and bruise them altogether in the Mortar of Vain-Glory, with the pestle of Contradiction, putting amongst them one Pint of the Spirit of Self-Conceitedness. When it is luke-warm let the Dissenting Brother take two or three Spoonfuls of it, Morning and Evening before Exercise, and whilst his mouth is full of the Elestuary he will make a wry Face, wink with his Eyes, and squeeze out some Tears of Dissimulation. Then let him speak as the Spirit of Giddiness gives him utterance. This will make the Schismatic endeavor to maintain his Doctrine, wound the Church, delude the People, justify their proceedings of Illusions, foment Rebellion, and call it by the name of Liberty of Conscience."[21]

But nothing daunted the Baptists. In their rude churches, in private homes, in groves of trees or shaded arbors, they went about preaching repentance, conversion to God and justification by faith. As the temper of the times changed, their attacks on the Established Church became bolder and bolder. And circumstances conspired to sweep converts in large numbers into the Baptist fold. One was the Baptist insistence upon religious independence, a theme which struck an answering chord in the hearts of Virginians rapidly becoming inspired to seek political independence. The other was the highly vulnerable position of the Episcopal clergy. By 1770 a class of ministers had arisen in the established church who catered to a single Cavalier class and even over them had little influence. The ministers, guaranteed tax support, for the most part owed their appointments to British influence, and almost as one they were vocal opponents of colonial rights. And there was a further damning condition, according to Gewehr: "The evidence is overwhelming," he wrote, "that, as a class, the Virginia (Episcopal) clergy were sadly deficient in the attributes of scund morals and good character. . .Immorality, card-playing, drunkenness, profanity, avariciousness, quarrelsomeness were common enough among the Eighteenth Century parsons to bring almost the entire body into disrepute."[22] Coupled with that, the church tax itself, still payable in tobacco, had become burdensome even to those who were willing to pay it. In several years of crop failure, the clergy had declined to accept a reduced rate. When the Virginia Assembly made all tobacco debts payable at the rate of two pence to the pound of tobacco, the church so opposed the change that the intervention of the Crown was sought to compel parishioners to pay off at market prices. In this procedure, according to Newman, "they signed the death warrant of their special privilege. The action of the King in council in declaring the law passed by the Assembly void was one of the most irritating of all the measures that led to the Revolution."[23] This was one more of the grievances piling up against the church. The result, not alone by Baptist efforts, was that by the time the war broke out, two-thirds of the people of Virginia had become dissenters — according to the estimate of Thomas Jefferson.[24] Many of the dissenters were Baptists, by now gathered in churches and with a State-wide organization which was to prove more potent than the Warren Association of New England.

As the Baptists grew in number, they began to pelt the Colonial Assembly with demands for religious freedom and for an end to the distinction between the establishment and the dissenter, and the leaders of political thought, who controlled the machinery of Colonial government, were forced to yield. It was the price they had to pay for popular support of the brewing rebellion. That Baptists were leaders in the assault on the Episcopal Church there can be no doubt. Hawks candidly admits that "the Baptists were the principal promoters of this work and in truth aided more than any other denomination in its accomplishment."[25]

From whatever source, the petitions from individual churches and the associations of rural areas, where the Baptists were strongest, sounded much the same. They said the Baptists were denied the equal rights of citizenship because they had to pay taxes for the support of a church they could not attend; this discriminatory practice, they argued, was most keenly felt on the Virginia frontier, populated mostly by dissenters who were required to acquire land (glebes) for churches which were attended by but few settlers; the best interests of the colony, they argued, would be served by declaring every man free to worship God as he pleased, without the intervention of civil authority. As clearly in Virginia as in Massachusetts, the Baptists had laid hold of two basic principles: liberty of conscience and separation of church and state.

In order to present a united church front, the Virginia General Association of Baptists in 1775 voted to collect signatures on petitions asking the General. Assembly to do away with the tie between the government and the Episcopal Church and to guarantee freedom to all religious societies willing to worship peacefully. They also asked that Baptists be given the right to preach in the Revolutionary Army. Jeremiah Walker, John Williams and George Roberts were appointed to present the petitions to the legislature, and the denomination at that time won a foothold which was eventually to topple the edifice of the state church: the Assembly took no action on the body of the petitions, but Baptists were granted the privilege of preaching to the troops. Hawks wrote that this acceptance of Baptists into the chaplaincy "was the first step towards placing the clergy, of all denominations, upon an equal footing in Virginia."[26]

The Baptists were not dismayed by the slighting of their chief petition, and they continued to popularize their cause. In June, 1776, when a delegation of Virginia political leaders met at Williamsburg to frame the Virginia Declaration of Rights, one of the articles included specified that "all men are equally entitled to the free exercise of religion, according to the dictates of conscience."[27] The declaration did not have the force of law, and a new constitution adopted for Virginia seventeen days later contained no concurring religious guarantee. Back the Baptists went to the petition business, for one document collecting 10,000 signatures asking the new Assembly for full freedom for the churches. Other petitions again asked for the disestablishment of the Episcopal Church. (The Methodists of Virginia at that time, strangely enough, opposed the Baptist initiative. In a petition to the House of Delegates they described themselves as a religious society "in communion with the Church of England" and felt that disestablishment might have unhealthy results.[28] Three years later, however, they were to side with the Baptists.)

Prior to the meeting of the Virginia General Assembly in

October, 1776, the Baptists appointed a committee to "inquire whether any grievances existed in the civil laws, that were oppressive to the Baptists."[29] After a survey, the committee reported that the marriage law was "partial and oppressive" because it allowed only Episcopal clergymen to officiate at weddings. So among the religious petitions presented to the Assembly was one which asked that ordained ministers of every denomination be placed on an equal footing before the law. The marriage restriction was not eliminated until 1785, by which time Baptist ministers had been joining couples illegally for years. But the 1776 Assembly did make some important concessions, largely at the insistence of Thomas Jefferson. It passed laws suspending the payment of clerical stipends, partly a blow at all things English, and "exempting the different societies of dissenters from contributing to the support and maintenance of the church, as by law established, and its ministers."[30] Thus was ended the hated church tax on those who did not wish to pay it. Complete religious equality had not yet been attained; the Anglican Church was still "by law established," but that affiliation was not to last much longer.

The leading Baptist spokesman at this period, particularly in the area of freedom of religion, was John Leland, a pastor in Culpeper County, whose church Jefferson occasionally visited. (Leland's admiration for Jefferson was lifelong. In 1801, during Jefferson's presidency, a Baptist church at Cheshire, Mass., made a cheese weighing 1,450 pounds as a gift for the Chief Executive. It was taken to Washington by John Leland, who had become the pastor of the New England church.) Born in Massachusetts in 1754, Leland took up his ministry in Virginia in 1775, staying there for fifteen years before returning to Massachusetts. During his Virginia pastorate he was credited with baptizing 700 members. He traveled a great deal in conference with other church and political leaders, and although regarded as somewhat eccentric he came to be very influential.

About 1784, by which time Virginia Baptists had 14,960 members in 151 churches, there was a renewal of interest in Virginia in a general church assessment. Baptists worked hard to defeat the idea, and the battle culminated in the passage, in

January, 1786, of the Virginia Bill of Rights, which Jefferson considered one of the greatest achievements of his life. It provided, in part, "that no man shall be compelled to frequent or support any religious worship, place or ministry whatsoever, nor shall be enforced, restrained, molested, or burthened in his body or goods, nor shall otherwise suffer on account of his religious opinion or belief; but that all men shall be free to profess, and by argument to maintain, their opinions in matters of religion, and that the same shall in no wise diminish, enlarge or affect their civil capacities."[31] This novel statement, bold for its time, fell sweetly upon Baptist ears, but it was not universally hailed as a pristine achievement. Hawks, the Episcopal historian, says the Virginia Bill of Rights "was viewed by many as utterly subversive, in its declarations, of the Christian religion," a blow "aimed at Christianity itself."[32]

Joy over the Virginia document yielded to concern two years later when the question of ratification of the Federal Constitution was put up to the states. No Baptist had been among the framers of that document. Among them were nineteen Episcopalians and eight Congregationalists, to whom an established church was perfectly acceptable, seven Presbyterians, two Catholics, two Quakers, one Methodist, one Dutch Reformed and a deist (Edmund Randolph) who later became an Episcopalian. The only reference in the original Constitution to religion is a clause barring a religious test for office-holders.

Baptists generally were luke-warm to the Constitution, because they felt, and many of them very strongly, that it did not sufficiently provide for religious freedom. The Baptists of Virginia pointed out that deficiency by resolution, and they expressed those fears to George Washington. In a letter to him, drafted by Leland, they said: "When the Constitution first made its appearance in Virginia, we, as a society, feared that liberty of conscience, dearer to us than property or life, was not sufficiently secured. Perhaps our jealousies were heightened by the usage we received in Virginia, under the regal government, when mobs, fines, bonds, and prisons were our frequent repast."[33] In a reply, General Washington was both complimentary and conciliatory. He said: "If I could have entertained the slightest apprehension that the Constitution framed by the Convention where I had the honor to preside might possibly endanger the religious rights of any ecclesiastical society, certainly I would never have placed my signature to it... I recollect with satisfaction that the religious society of which you are members have been, throughout America, uniformly and almost unanimously the firm friends to civil liberty, and the persevering promoters of our glorious revolution."[34]

At the moment of Virginia's decision — by convention — on ratification of the Constitution, eight states had already acted favorably — Delaware, Pennsylvania, New Jersey, Connecticut, Massachusetts, Georgia, Maryland and South Carolina. A ninth state was required for ratification, and in Virginia sentiment was evenly divided between Federalists and Anti-Federalists. The Baptists, resolving to oppose ratification, had decided to send John Leland to the Convention as delegate from Orange County. They had the votes Leland needed. On the day of the election, Leland had some private conversations with his opponent, and on the strength of those conversations, he withdrew in favor of the other man — James Madison. Without Madison, the Virginia Convention probably would have failed to ratify, and without Virginia, the whole constitutional scheme might have failed. Leland, out of his great admiration for Madison and out of respect for the assurances obtained from him, had played a key role in the adoption of the American Constitution.[35]

What were those assurances? There is no record, but it is significant that subsequently the Baptists, under the persuasion of John Leland, rose up in support of James Madison in his election to a seat in the House of Representatives, after he had been defeated in an unwilling candidacy for the Senate. And it was from that House seat that Madison submitted the original drafts of the first ten amendments to the Constitution, subsequently to be known as the Bill of Rights. In August, 1789, the House gave its approval, and a month later the Senate concurred. On December 15, 1791, the requisite number of states (not including Massachusetts or Connecticut) having ratified, the Bill of Rights became part of the basic law of this land. In the very first amendment, what the Baptists had sought for so many generations was spelled out with crystal clarity: *"Congress shall make no law respecting an establishment of religion, or prohibiting the free exercise thereof. . . "*

Of the Baptist role in the shaping of the First Amendment William Cathcart, a revered Baptist historian, has said: "Denominationally, no community asked for this change in the Constitution but the Baptists. The Quakers would probably have petitioned for it, if they had thought of it, but they did not. John Adams and the Congregationalists did not desire it; the Episcopalians did not wish for it; it went too far for most Presbyterians in Revolutionary times. . . To the Baptists, beyond a doubt, belongs the glory of engrafting its best article on the noblest Constitution ever framed for the government of mankind."[36]

And Thomas Armitage put it in a way which Baptists appreciate even more: "Thus the contemned, spurned and hated old Baptist doctrine of soul liberty, for which blood has been shed for centuries, was not only engrafted into the organic law of the United States, but for the first time in the formation of a great nation was made its chief cornerstone."[37]

Chapter Seven: The Spread of Baptist Principles

While some Baptists were fighting for their existence in New England, others, through dispersal or the happier choice of a home, were raising churches to the south, and well before Massachusetts finally relented in its persecution, Baptists were firmly entrenched all along the Atlantic Seaboard. In numbers they were at first few, but in the religious fervor stirred up by the Great Awakening in 1740, the Baptist church was the chief beneficiary. Even before that, however, Baptists had shown that they were here to stay.

In 1682 William Screven had attempted to establish a Baptist church in Kittery, Me., but he found himself there so harassed by the protectors of Congregationalism that he and his followers sailed to a more receptive environment near Charleston, S. C. There he met Lady Blake, wife of Joseph Blake, and her mother, Lady Axtell, members of a party fresh from England. They were both Baptists, and with Screven as pastor they founded a church which met in private homes until 1700, when a meeting-house was erected in Charleston.

Meanwhile, arriving Baptists had found a cordial reception in Pennsylvania and New Jersey. William Penn's announced policy of religious freedom encouraged a rapid influx of churchmen regarded in Europe and other parts of America as dangerous radicals, including Quakers, Mennonites, Dunkards and Baptists. In Pennsylvania the Quakers were numerous and wealthy, but in them there was no arrogance or intolerance. Members of minor sects were free to worship openly, without dissipating their energies in a constant fight for existence, and one of the consequences was that they could tend to their businesses and farms with a mind at peace. The first Baptist Church in that colony was organized by Thomas Dungan, an Irish minister said to have been "an ancient disciple and teacher,"[1] at Cold Spring, in Bucks County, about 1684. The second church in Pennsylvania, that at Pennepek, was founded in 1688 by one of the most famous imposters in Baptist church history. His name was Elias Keach, and he was a wild, devilish son of the famous British minister and Baptist writer, Benjamin Keach. The roguish son arrived in the New World in 1686 and, as a lark, got off the boat wearing a dark suit and an armband which he hoped would identify him as a minister — which he was not. As Morgan Edwards, a contemporary historian, tells the story, "the project succeeded to his wishes, and many people gathered to hear the young London divine. He performed well enough till he had advanced pretty far in his sermon; then, stopping short, he looked like a man astonished. The audience concluded he had been seized with a sudden disorder; but, on asking what the matter was, received from him a confession of the imposture, with tears in his eyes and much trembling."[2] It changed the young man's whole life. He was converted to his father's faith, which earlier he had scorned; he was ordained a minister and became an itinerant evangelist, with great influence. The one time he settled down was after his establishment of the church at Pennepek, from which he resigned in his second year in a controversy over the laying on of hands.

New Jersey had an equally amiable climate, perhaps exceeded in its religious benevolence only by Rhode Island. Henry C. Vedder, in his study of the Baptists of the Middle Atlantic region, says that the New Jersey proprietors "promised only toleration, but they gave liberty. Not only was there never any persecution in the colony, but the power of the Assembly to create and maintain an established church was never used."[3] As early as 1660 there were in Jersey a few settlers of Baptist inclination, but not until 1688 did they form the Middletown Church. Its first pastor was John Bowne, not an ordained minister but a Baptist of particular distinction. In his time he became Speaker of the House of Deputies, was judge of the court of Monmouth County and held other positions of trust. In 1689 a Baptist Church was formed at Piscataway (then Piscatagua) under the leadership of Thomas Killingsworth, who also served as a county judge. Two years later a group of Baptist settlers from Tipperary, Ireland, founded a church at Cohansey.

The Piscataway Church also had troubles with an imposter, but unfortunately, unlike the impish Keach, he was a pretty thorough-going scoundrel. In 1730 the church's regular pastor, John Drake, was old and needed an assistant. The church then had almost 100 members, and it seemed like divine providence when a young man with credentials identifying him as Henry Loveall showed up with what was thought to be a letter of recommendation from the Rev. John Comer, well-known pastor of the church at Newport, R. I. In the letter Comer said Loveall was a recent convert who showed promise, and to Piscataway that was sufficient reason to designate the stranger assistant pastor. In the meantime, Comer had done a little checking and discovered that Loveall's real name was Desolate Baker, that he had served time in prison and since his release had been living with another man's wife. In a classic letter beginning, "Brethren, I am in a straight what or how to write to you. . . ," Comer broke the news to the good people of Piscataway. He also upbraided them as "persons infatuated" for ordaining Loveall-Baker without a little closer check into his background.[4]

(Comer's diary, from which this rebuke is taken, is a rich source of commentary on the mores and peculiarities of New England during the early Eighteenth Century. Typical of his earnest observations is this entry for May 31, 1728: "About 3 P.M. one Deborah Grinman was killed with thunder at Narragansett. There were some things remarkable in her death. Two nights before she dreamed that a woman lay dead in the same spot she was struck down in. She told her sister of it in great surprise, and that she was kill'd with thunder. In the morning of the day in which she was kill'd 'twas very clear, but she apprehended it would be a fatal day. And when the cloud arose she said *there is that which will do the business.* Accordingly she was kill'd in the same spot. She was burnt on the side of her face, and her instep was broke. At that time she had a child in her arms, which was stunned, but soon recovered." On October 8, 1730, he wrote of a scandal in a Congregational church: "About this time I heard of this sad and terrible story. One------Barter,. . . who was a member of the New North Church in Boston,. . . had lately fallen into the prevailing sin of drunkenness; he was improved (employed?) by the church to take care of the meeting house and to ring the bell, having once been suspended communion for said sin, but upon acknowledgement and repentance was restored to his place. About a month ago the deacons of said church having set the sacramental vessels on the table in the meeting house for communion, between the ringing of the first and second bell, before the congregation came together he went to the vessels and drank so excessively that he with difficulty got into the belfry, but was incapacitated upon the operation of the drink to perform his office, and lay there dead drunk all sermon and sacrament time. The church next day call'd a meeting and suspended him out of his office. Oh, terrible and almost unheard-of wicked action.")[5]

Norman H. Maring, who made a study of the early Baptists of New Jersey, found that they were "a sturdy farming folk, most of whom owned lands and were entitled to vote."[6] Most of them had farms of at least 100 acres, to judge from wills, and some had more substantial holdings. A James Grover owned 500 acres, and Richard Stout held more than 2,500 acres. Very often the property of the Baptists, even that of their pastors, included slaves.

By 1707 there were nine churches in Pennsylvania and New Jersey, and in that year they banded together in the Philadelphia Association, the first union of Baptists in the New World. Its history has been adorned with intelligent leadership, and for more than 250 years it has been one of the most influential and respected agencies in the American church.

The next colony to have a Baptist church was Delaware, where one was founded in 1703 at Welsh Tract. Its sixteen members had emigrated from Wales as a body in 1701, and two years later they moved into Delaware. Thomas Griffith, one of the original emigrants, was the first pastor.

In southeastern Connecticut a group of scattered Baptists petitioned the General Court in 1704 for permission to hold meetings and organize a church, notwithstanding the fact that Congregationalism was the colony's prescribed religion. When the petition was ignored, its signers took silence for consent and in 1705 imported the Rev. Valentine Wightman from Rhode Island to preside over the congregation formed at Groton. Five years later, when a second Baptist church sprang up at Waterford, the legislature passed a law forbidding private religious meetings and any baptismal ceremony not supervised by the regular minister of a licensed church. Baptists took no notice of the law, and at one time all the members of one congregation and their pastor were confined in New London County jail for holding a worship service "contrary to law on the Sabbath Day."[7] There are other recorded cases of ministerial floggings, and in this period Connecticut Baptists were generally harassed because of their religious sentiments. By 1729 dissenters had become so numerous that provision for them had to be made in the law, and Connecticut passed an act exempting Baptists and Quakers from church taxes on presentation of acceptable certificates of membership in a non-conforming church. In the Massachusetts pattern, Connecticut's certificate system broke down in its administration, to the disadvantage of minority churchmen. The elimination of all barriers to complete freedom of religion did not take place in that state until 1818, when a new constitution was approved. The article securing liberty of conscience was drafted by a Baptist minister, the Rev. Asahel Morse, of Suffield.

Although some of the persecuted Baptists of New England took refuge among the Dutch in New Amsterdam, they apparently kept their religion to themselves. Under the Dutch there was no real religious freedom, and a Baptist minister who went on an evangelical crusade there, William Wickenden, of Providence, R. I., was clapped in jail for four months. Even after the British took over the colony and renamed it for James, Duke of York, Baptists were slow to organize. That was not the fault of the British. The

87

Charter of Liberties of the Colony of New York provided explicitly for liberty of conscience, guaranteeing "that no person or persons, which proffesse ffaith in God by Jesus Christ shall, at any time, be any wayes molested, punished, disquieted, or called in question for any difference in opinion or matter of religious concernment, who do nott actually disturbe the civill peace of the province, butt thatt all and every person or persons, may, from time, and at all times freely have and fully enjoy his or her judgments or consciences in matters of religion throughout all the province, they behaving themselves peaceably and quietly, and nott using this liberty to lycenciousness, nor to the civil injury or outward disturbance of others."[8]

The Duke of York approved the charter, but after he ascended to the throne, to be known as James II, he repealed it and promulgated "instructions" for New York which were no less liberal. They directed the authorities to "permit all persons of what Religion soever quietly to inhabit within your Government without giving them any disturbance or disquiet whatsoever for or by reason of their differing Opinions in matters of Religion, Provided they give noe disturbance to the publick peace, nor doe molest or disquiet others in the free Exercise of their Religion."[9] Conceivably, the New York government could have acted against minority religious groups under the peace provisions, as Virginia was later to do, but in fact dissenters found themselves free to worship as they pleased. In the early 1720's a group of Baptists began holding meetings in New York in the home of Nicholas Eyres, a Wiltshiremen who was "a brewer by occupation, a business in which Christian men in that day did not scruple to engage for their own profit and the glory of God."[10] They did not formally constitute a church until September, 1724, and it was four more years before they built a church, on what is now Cliff Street, near John Street. In 1731, Eyres resigned as minister to go to the Second Church of Newport as associate pastor, and a year later the church he left behind disbanded, "having lost its house of worship by the action of one of the trustees who is said to have sold it without the knowledge or consent of the congregation."[11] A highly successful church later constituted as the First Baptist Church of New York was organized June 19, 1762, with the Rev.

John Gano, one of the leading Baptists of his time, as pastor. The church building, on Gold Street, was used during the Revolutionary War as a cavalry stable by British troops occupying New York. Prior to that time the church had split in a controversy over the purchase of some hymnbooks, which some members regarded as a needless extravagance. The disgruntled parties withdrew to form the Second Baptist Church of New York, later to be known as Bethel Baptist. Gano served the church for 26 years before moving to Kentucky.

As has already been set forth in Chapter Six, Baptists first organized in North Carolina in 1727, with the more evangelical group, that of Shubal Stearns, arriving in 1775. William Tryon, whose unpopular Colonial governorship began there in 1765, was an ardent supporter of the established Episcopal Church and as a defender of the faith railed against the Baptists. He called them "the avowed enemies of the mother church" and "a scandal to common sense."[12] Their pastors he dismissed as "rascally fellows." But the Episcopal Church never had the position in North Carolina which it enjoyed in Virginia, and North Carolina was the first Southern state to provide for disestablishment. That occurred in the Constitution of 1776, which guaranteed liberty of conscience and gave parity to all churches. The latter idea was set forth in an article which said: "There shall be no establishment of any one religious church or denomination in this State in preference to any other, neither shall any person, on any pretence whatsoever, be compelled to attend any place of worship contrary to his own faith or judgment, or be obliged to pay for the purchase of any glebe, or the building of any house of worship, or the maintenance of any minister or ministry, contrary to what he believes right, or has voluntarily and personally engaged to perform, but all persons shall be at liberty to exercise their own mode of worship." That article, which provided in one sweep what the Baptists of New England and Virginia had to fight years to achieve, was the work of a Baptist minister, Henry Abbott, of Pasquotank County.[13] For some strange reason ministers were barred from serving in the Legislature while "in the exercise of the pastoral function," and for many years North Carolina denied itself the legislative services of some of its best men.

Although the colony of Maryland was dominated by Catholics, it provided very early for the peaceful coexistence of Christians of differing belief. An act of the Assembly of 1649 said "that no persons professing to believe in Jesus Christ shall be molested in the respect of their religion, or the free exercise thereof, or be compelled to the belief or practice of any other religion against their consent." Non-believers there were required to be discreet, however, because the act provided that "anyone speaking reproachfully against the Blessed Virgin, or the Apostles, shall forfeit five pounds, but blasphemy against God shall be punished with death."[14] Not until almost a hundred years after the passage of that act, however, did the Baptists of Maryland organize a church. It came about then through the instance of Henry Sater, who for several years had been inviting Baptist ministers to preach at his home at Chestnut Ridge, about ten miles north of Baltimore. Sater, an Englishman who had emigrated to America in 1709, was instrumental in the founding of a church in 1742. Not until January 15, 1785, was a church organized in Baltimore.

In the meantime the first Baptist churches had been established in the states of New Hampshire, at Newtown in 1755, and Vermont, at Shaftesbury in 1768. In Georgia the Kiokee Church was organized in 1772. Seventeen years later it was officially recognized in an act of incorporation which described it as "the Anabaptist Church on the Kioka," which was said to have been meeting "for many years past."[15]

This was the extent of Baptist expansion prior to the Revolutionary War. In all of America, as the country went down the road to rebellion, there were probably no more than 100 congregations of Baptists. Their influence was out of all proportion to their numbers and organization. Many of these churches were small, without a regular pastor, dependent for preaching on itinerant ministers or ministers who had several churches. Services for some of the assemblies were so infrequent that the members were known facetiously as "Thirty-Day Baptists."[16] It is probable that in the entire Baptist ministry there were only a handful of college-trained men, and most of them were in New England. Virginia had none, and the level of ministerial education to the south remained low. Yet as a body the Baptists were almost unanimous in their support of the aims of the Revolution, and they threw themselves whole-heartedly into the cause of independence. For most of them the ideas of religious and political liberty were inseparable. Of the Baptists at this time Thomas Armitage wrote, "Scarcely was the first shot fired at Lexington when every Baptist on the continent sprang to his feet and hailed its echo as the pledge of deliverance, as well from domestic as foreign oppressors. They were amongst the first to suffer and sacrifice, and where the British triumphed Baptist pastors were obliged to flee, their meeting houses were destroyed and they were hated of all men."[17]

In 1776, John Hart, a deacon in the Baptist church at Hopewell, N. J., was one of the signers of the Declaration of Independence. A farmer with interests in grist and fulling mills, he had been elected to the Colonial legislature in 1761. Subsequently, he voted against the Stamp Act and for the withholding of supplies from British troops. He was a thoroughgoing patriot.[18]

To the South, New York-born Richard Furman, just 21 at the outbreak of the war but already a Baptist minister at the High Hills of Santee for two years, rushed to volunteer for military service and only retired from the ranks when he was convinced he could be more useful in the pulpit than on the battlefield. He was so successful in whipping up Patriot enthusiasm that Lord Cornwallis at one time offered a reward for his apprehension. Furman became the foremost Baptist of the South and was a leader of the denomination nationally at the time of his death in 1825. Furman University bears his name.

There is no record of the number of Baptists who served in the American Army, but of the 23 Revolutionary chaplains whose names are remembered, eight were Baptists. Best known was the Rev. Hezekiah Smith, a Princeton graduate who had been a pastor at Haverhill, Mass. He was an intimate of George Washington and is said to have repeatedly exposed himself to fire in battle while comforting wounded soldiers. The others were John Gano, who started out with George Clinton's New York Brigade; David Jones, of Pennsylvania, who proved so effective at inspiring men that Gen. William Howe offered a reward for his capture; William Vanhorn, also of Pennsylvania and later pastor at Scotch Plains, N.

91

J.; Charles Thompson, of New Jersey, who was captured and imprisoned on a Newport guard ship; William Rogers, of Philadelphia, a brigade chaplain; Nicholas Cox, of the Wantage Church in New Jersey's Sussex County, who served for four years; and William Worth, who entered the chaplaincy from the Pittsgrove Baptist Church in Salem County, New Jersey.[19]

When on October 23, 1781, the news of the American Army's entry into Yorktown reached Philadelphia, it caught the Philadelphia Association in session. In his *The Baptists and The American Revolution,* William Cathcart says that "the oldest Baptist Association in the land got up by sunrise to celebrate the best news that had reached them for six long years — tidings for which their inmost soul blessed God. And this was the spirit of the whole Baptist people all over this broad land."[20]

One remarkable transformation occurred in the social image of the Baptists between 1770 and 1790, particularly in the most populous states. Baptists had gone into the Revolutionary period as small, persecuted groups, identified in large part with the lower social class. Cultured people, in fact, believed that Baptists were freakish both intellectually and physically. In *Fifty Years Among the Baptists,* David Benedict tells of a conversation he had with an elderly woman who knew Baptists from a distance at about the time of the Revolution. "Your society," the lady told Benedict, "are much more like other folks now than they were when I was young. Then there was a company of them in the back part of our town, and an outlandish set of people they certainly were. You yourself would say so, if you had seen them. As it was told to me, you could hardly find one among them but what was deformed in some way or other. Some of them were hair-lipped *(sic)* others were blear-eyed, or hump-backed, or bow-legged, or clump-footed; hardly any of them looked like other people. But they were all strong for plunging, and let their poor ignorant children run wild, and never had the seal of the convenant put on them."[21]

With the close of the Revolutionary period, however, the Baptists had gained great respectability along the Atlantic Seaboard. Particularly in Virginia the planter class which had forsaken Episcopalianism and all things British began to identify with the Baptists, in large part because Baptists had so vigorously championed individual liberty. In all of the great centers of population wealthy and influential citizens had become Baptists, and the respectability of the denomination was at least equal to that of any other body of Christians. The Revolution had also paid off in a great increase in Baptist numbers. By 1790 there 688 Baptist churches in the country, with 710 ordained ministers and a total membership of around 65,000.[22]

Not all of these, to be sure, were gentle, cultured people. By this time hardy pioneers had started moving into the wilds in the opening of the frontier. They were not burdened by social niceties and they had little regard for educational attainment. They had high respect, however, for the Baptist farmer-preacher, uneducated, working in the fields six days a week, serving his Christian flock without pay, but bringing the gentling virtues of salvation to a wild land. As the population moved to the westward, so did the Baptists. Tennessee and Kentucky were the first to attract large groups of settlers, and Baptists, particularly from Virginia and North Carolina, were thick among the migrating peoples. So many Carolinians were in this move to the West that in seventeen years the membership of the Sandy Creek Baptist Church declined from 606 to 14.[23] Before the end of the century one-fourth of the Baptists of Virginia had moved to Kentucky[24] (but without seriously weakening the Baptists in the Old Dominion: in the churches left behind, new converts quickly took the places of those who had departed, and the 151 churches of 1784, which had 14,960 members, grew to 218 in 1792, with 20,443 members[25]).

There had been Baptists in East Tennessee soon after 1765 and two churches were said to have been organized, but in 1774 they were driven out by Indians. Among the large numbers of Carolina and Virginia Baptists settling Tennessee about 1780 were eight or ten ministers, and in a year they had established half a dozen churches. Squire Boone, brother of Daniel Boone, was a Baptist, and there was at least some Baptist sentiment in the founding of Boonesborough, Ky., in 1775. Early in 1776 two Baptist ministers, Thomas Tinsley and William Hickman, settled at Harrodsburg and began holding services. In 1779 John Taylor, a Virginia Baptist minister, spent the winter in Kentucky on a religious tour of the frontier, but he came back crestfallen over the low estate of

Christian worship in the wilds. Joseph Redding, another Virginia preacher, had a similar experience the following year. William Marshall was among the first Baptist ministers to stick it out in Kentucky, and he was followed by Joseph Barnett, John Whitaker, James Skaggs, Benjamin Lynn and John Gerrard, all ministers although not all ordained. On June 18, 1781, Barnett, Whitaker and Gerrard founded the Severns Valley Baptist Church, representing the first formal congregation of Baptists west of the Allegheny Mountains.[26] The location was about 40 miles south of Louisville at what is now Elizabethtown. Gerrard, appointed the first pastor, subsequently was slain by Indians. In a concurrent development of 1781 Lewis Craig, the Virginia minister who had been jailed and beaten for his faith, decided to give up the pastorate of the Upper Spottsylvania Church in Virginia in order to move to Kentucky. When he made his intentions known to his congregation, many of them, deeply devoted to the pastor, decided to go with him. They became the first "travelling church" of record. Through the cold and deprivation of a Kentucky winter they traveled, finally establishing Craig's Station on Gilbert's Creek and forming the Gilbert Creek Baptist Church.[27]

By 1784 there were six Baptist churches in Kentucky with 400 members. In eight years the number of churches had grown to 42 and the number of members to 3,095.

The Baptists of Ohio organized their first church in 1790, in what is now Cincinnati, and Illinois got its first, called New Design, in 1796. Two years later Indiana saw the founding of the Silver Creek Church. One of the most famous of the early Indiana churches was that at Pigeon Creek, organized in 1819. The building was a log rectangle 26 feet wide and 30 feet long, and it had a brick chimney and fireplace. The window frames, door casings and pulpit were made by Thomas Lincoln, an itinerant carpenter in whose household lived a ten-year-old boy, Abraham Lincoln. Missouri saw its first Baptist church, that at Tywappity Bottom, set up in 1805 and dying almost immediately. Bethel, which dates from 1806, prospered. The first church in Louisiana, at Bayou Chicot, was brought together in 1812 through the efforts of Joseph Willis, a mulatto.

Mississippi had been strongly Catholic from its beginnings, but members of the first Baptist church, founded in 1780 on Cole's Creek, southeast of Natchez, and called the Salem Church, were not molested until about 1783, when some of the members thoughtlessly denounced Catholicism. The minister, Richard Curtis, Jr., was haled before the Spanish commandant and threatened with deportation to the Spanish mines in Mexico if he persisted in making trouble. A 1795 law said that "if nine persons were found worshipping together, except according to the form of the Catholic Church, they should suffer imprisonment."[28] Curtis had to flee to escape jail, but in 1797 the territory was ceded to the United States and Baptists suffered no further harassment.

To the simple people on the American frontier around the turn of the Nineteenth Century religion was a way of life rather than an adornment. In the mild seasons of the early days, shaded groves were sufficient as temples, and when it was rainy or cold the cabin of one of the members, of logs, generally unfloored, was made to serve. When the people were affluent enough to erect a meeting house, it need be only a large room without fancy trimmings of any kind. It was a long time before any Baptist church invested in a stained-glass window, and Baptists were among the last of the popular denominations to install pipe organs. Such niceties were unheard of on the frontier.

Central to church life was the frontier farmer-preacher. In his *Winning of the West,* Theodore Roosevelt paid tribute to these pious men. "These Baptist preachers," he said, "lived and worked exactly as did their flocks: their dwellings were little cabins with dirt floors and, instead of bedsteads, skin-covered pole bunks; they cleared the ground, split rails, planted corn, and raised hogs on equal terms with their parishioners."[29] They took it for granted that they would work without regular payment from their congregations. Just as they were hostile to education — a hostility they had learned from the abuses of established clergymen — the early Baptists also were suspicious of a paid ministry. Richard Furman said Baptists of this period had a philosophy about the clergy: "The Lord keep thee humble, and we'll keep thee poor." And John Leland remarked that Baptists "loved the Gospel, and they loved its ministers, but the sound of money drove all the good feelings from their heart."[30] As the years went by, a few of the ministers got a little support. It was not enough to sustain them, and some of the subscriptions would have shocked many of today's churchgoers. William Warren Sweet, in his *Religion on the American Frontier,* dug up the pledge sheet of the South Elkhorn, Ky., Baptist Church for the year 1798. Fourteen names appear on the list, and the pastor, John Shackleford, got a little cash, 12½ pounds of salt, 12½ barrels of corn, 3 bushels of wheat, 363 pounds of pork, 100 pounds of "flower," and 100 pounds of "beaf." In addition, John Young by his "X" pledged 5 gallons of whisky, Ahijah Wood 4 gallons plus cash, and Abraham Hedo, apparently the biggest distiller in the church, 27 gallons.[31] In spirits the parson was pretty well supplied, with about 3½ fifths a week if he nursed it along.

Preachers could be created without a great deal of stir. If a brother felt called of God to preach the Word, he let his brethren know it. He was then allowed to preach a trial sermon. If the church thought his "gifts" were sufficient, it could issue him a license, which would allow him to preach but not to administer the sacraments. The latter he could perform upon ordination as a full-fledged minister. The success of these "raised up" brethren at soul-winning was so remarkable that the frontier Baptists came to a logically simple conclusion: learning was not only not a prerequisite for the ministry; it could be downright harmful, inducing men to place their faith in human rather than in spiritual resources.[32] "Under such circumstances," Newman says, "emotional excitement was often mistaken for spiritual quickening."[33]

Regardless of the condition of the clergy, these frontier Baptist churches in many communities represented the only force for moral and spiritual order. Through the discipline of the church, which was rigorous, the standards for personal conduct were set, and the church was not only the inspirer to a better life but the judge of the life one lived. Once a month, usually on a Saturday, the churches met for a business session at which church discipline was enforced. Attendance was mandatory, and generally much of the session was given over to handing out punishment or dealing out reprimands. The most common offense was drunkenness. There seemed to be no objection to the use of alcohol, to its manufacture or sale (except on the Sabbath). But "drinking too much" was forbidden. Other offenses which could bring about punishment ranging from public apology to expulsion included lying, stealing, gambling, gossipping, adultery, swearing, or defiling the Sabbath. Other recorded offenses were "frolicking and dancing," "selling an unsound mare," removing cornerstones, calling another member a liar, abusing one's wife, threatening a slave or improper respect for worship services.[34]

Even ministers were subject to discipline, and in his *History of the Rise and Progress of the Baptists in Virginia,* Robert Baylor Semple lists 20 ministers who went astray before 1810. They included Aaron Bledsoe, "fraudulent dealing"; Thomas Bridges, "horse stealing"; a Rev. Cary, "imposter"; Dr. Thos. Chrisman, "yielding to temptations of the most diabolical sort"; Benjamin Coleman, "misconduct"; Samuel Counsel, "bad life"; Obadiah Echols, "gross immorality"; Joseph Flood, "bigamy"; Moses Foley, "misconduct"; Philip Hughes, "his candle went out in darkness"; John McLeroy, "wretched traitor to the cause"; William Moorman, "neglected to keep his body under"; George Morris, "charged with crimes of the deepest die"; Younger Pitts, "disorderly"; James Reed, "downfall"; James Tompkins, "malconduct;" Jeremiah Walker, "criminal intrigue"; and the pastor of the Fork Church, "misconduct."[25]

These instances are worth mentioning because examples of pastoral downfall actually were rare. Baptist ministers as a rule were respected and honored, in New England, in the South and on the frontier. Baptists by this time had splintered into a variety of sub-types, among them General, Particular, Regular, Separate, United, Primitive, Free Will and Two-Seed-in-the-Spirit Baptists. But on five principles they were united and identifiable; these had not changed, and they have not changed yet: adult baptism and conversion as a condition of church membership; immersion as the most truly Scriptural form of baptism; the advisory nature of church associations, which were not to supplant the primacy of the individual church; one's direct responsibility to his Maker, without the necessity of intermediary; and separation of church and state. Some Baptists may have believed other things in addition; there was still controversy over the laying on of hands. But these were the identifiable beliefs of the Baptist, whatever category he might place himself in.

By 1800 there were 80,000 Baptists in the country, and by 1812 their number had grown to 172,972 members, affiliated with 2,164 churches and served by 1,605 ministers. Virginia, with 35,665 Baptists, was most saturated. Kentucky was in second place with 22,694. New York had 18,499, Georgia 14,761. North Carolina, its ranks most decimated by emigration, had 12,567. In all of New England there were 32,272 Baptists, and the Middle Atlantic states counted 26,155.[36] It was a growing church, and it was ready for a giant step forward.

Chapter Eight: The Great (?) Commission

There are few Baptist children today, from orthodox Baptist families, who cannot cite chapter and verse for the Great Commission. It was one of the last commandments given by Jesus Christ to the eleven faithful Disciples after His resurrection, and it is found at Matthew 28: 19-20: "Go ye therefore, and teach all nations, baptizing them in the name of the Father, and of the Son, and of the Holy Ghost: Teaching them to observe all things whatsoever I have commanded you." That, the fledgling Baptist will tell you, is the basis for Christian missionary work and the inspiration for the thousands of Baptist medical and ministerial emissaries laboring among heathen tribes in Africa, the Far East, the Middle East, South America and other remote parts of the globe. The Baptist missionary endeavor also reaches into Indian tribes, Mexican villages and urban ghettoes here in the United States through home mission activities. To assume that American Baptists have always been missionary minded, or that they have unanimously supported the conversion of the heathen, however, is erroneous. They were late in arriving in the field of missions, and the undertaking so alienated some members of the denomination that in modern times there are churches known as Missionary Baptists and churches referred to as Anti-Missionary Baptists. The latter are also called Primitives, Old School or Hard-Shell Baptists. This schism took place in the first quarter of the Nineteenth Century.

English Baptist missionary work by that time had already begun, and the work of William Carey, tireless scholar and minister in faraway India, was an inspiration to young American students itching to carry the Gospel abroad. Carey had not had an easy time of it. He was born August 17, 1761, at Paulersprung, Northamptonshire, where his father, Edmund Carey, operated a small free school and through it supervised the education of his son. When he was 14, Carey was apprenticed to a shoemaker, but his life was completely changed in 1783 when he was converted to the Baptist faith. When he was 25 he was made pastor of the Baptist Church at Moulton, and even though so poor he could not eat properly, he schooled himself in Greek, Latin and Hebrew. In the process he found that he had a remarkable gift for mastering languages. From a subsequent ministry at Leicester in 1789 Carey joined in a movement aimed at establishing Baptist missions abroad, and against some vigorous opposition he pleaded with the English Baptists to honor the Great Commission. On one occasion he was told by a fellow Baptist, "Sit down, young man; when the Lord gets ready to convert the heathen he will do it without your help or mine."[1] Nevertheless, his agitation resulted in the founding of the Baptist Missionary Society and his own appointment as its first export to India. He and his family arrived in Bengal in 1794 and promptly discovered that living in Calcutta would plunge them into bankruptcy. In desperation, Carey sought a place to settle. His funds depleted, he took employment as overseer of an indigo factory at Maldah, and for five years he had to work at a job which frustrated his aspirations as an envoy of the church. But in 1799 he moved to Serampore, then a colony of the hospitable Danes, and his missionary career from that point forward was an inspiring story of Christian accomplishment. He established a school and a press and became so proficient at the Indian tongues that he was a part-time university lecturer. From his press rolled Bibles in 26 languages, which he and his staff had translated, and

100

by 1814 he had 20 mission stations across India despite the opposition of British commercial representatives.[2]

The tales of Carey's romantic employment, along with stories of other missionaries, reached the American centers of theological learning, and two young men on whose ears they fell resolved at all costs to join in this most fascinating of Christian enterprises — but not as Baptists. Their paths crossed in 1810 at Andover Theological Seminary, and in Baptist history their names were to be inextricably interwoven: Adoniram Judson and Luther Rice. They represent not just missions; they also are responsible for welding the Baptists into a national organization. For if the support of missions alienated a Baptist minority, it also brought the remainder, by far the majority, into a body unified for a specific purpose for the first time in the history of the denomination in America. In the fight for religious freedom and separation of church and state the Baptists had been unified in spirit; but through missions they became united in fact.

Judson was born August 9, 1788, in Malden, Mass., to Adoniram and Abigail Brown Judson. The father was a Congregational minister who held successive pastorates at Wenham, Braintree and Plymouth. Young Judson graduated from Brown University in 1807 as class valedictorian. For a year afterward he taught school at Plymouth, at the same time publishing two textbooks, *Elements of English Grammar* and *The Young Lady's Arithmetic.* Although something of a skeptic, Judson decided to follow in the footsteps of his father and enrolled in Andover seminary. It was there that he got fired up about missions, and it was there that he met Rice.

Luther Rice was five years older than Judson. He was born March 25, 1783, in Northborough, Mass., the son of Captain Amos and Sarah Rice. The mother was a woman of considerable intellectual attainments and was an inspiration to her son all his life. Luther attended the public schools, and at the age of 16 he showed a roving disposition: he contracted with the state of Georgia to assist in obtaining lumber for shipbuilding. It was a short-lived enterprise, however, and Luther soon returned home. At the age of 19 he joined the Northborough Congregational church, of which his parents were members, and he subsequently paid his way through Leicester Academy by teaching during his vacations and giving singing lessons at night. After the academy, Rice attended Williams College, and in 1810 he enrolled in Andover Theological Seminary. The missionary bug got to him there, and he sat for hours listening to Judson, for whom "the Orient's teeming millions and ancient cultures represented the ultimate challenge."[3] Rice left the seminary in 1811 without graduating, but his purpose was fixed. In a letter written to a friend on March 18, 1811, he said, "I have deliberately made up my mind to preach the gospel to the heathen."[4]

Judson and his group of missionary zealots, Rice among them, presented a petition to a convention of evangelical ministers then meeting at Bradford, and through their cooperation, and largely with Congregational sponsorship, the American Board of Commissioners for Foreign Missions was formed. After an abortive trip to London in quest of British support (on which trip Judson was taken prisoner aboard a French privateer and lodged briefly in prison at Bayonne), Judson was appointed by the American Board as one of four missionaries to Burma, or such other Oriental fields as might open, on September 19, 1811. Rice failed to get an appointment, but was told he could represent the board if he could raise money for his own passage and outfit. On February 5, 1812, Judson married Ann Hasseltine, a highly refined and dedicated woman who was the first of Judson's three remarkable wives (William Carey was also married three times). Rice's fiancee, Rebecca Eaton, refused to be a missionary's wife, and he never married at all. On February 6, Judson was ordained to the Congregational ministry, and thirteen days later he embarked with Ann from Salem, bound for Calcutta. Rice, who had raised his money by frantic effort, had sailed the day before from Philadelphia.

Judson and Rice left America as Congregationalists, but they arrived at the mission field as Baptists. With Judson it came about through study of the Bible on the ocean passage; he knew that he would be dealing with English Baptist colleagues in missionary work in India, and he wanted to be able to defend his own beliefs about baptism. The study led to a conviction that infant baptism was wrong, and soon after his arrival in India, on September 6,

1812, he and Ann Judson were rebaptized by an English missionary in Calcutta, the Rev. William Ward. With Rice the process of conversion took a little longer. He was not a Baptist when he stepped ashore in Calcutta, but the news of Judson's defection so unsettled him that he undertook his own private study of the Biblical treatment of baptism. This led to a "conviction, that those persons only, who give credible evidence of piety, are proper subjects (for baptism); and that immersion is the only proper mode. . . ."[5] He submitted to baptism by Ward on November 1, 1812.

For the two missionaries the change of persuasion, however comforting spiritually, was embarrassingly awkward from a professional standpoint. They had been dispatched from their homeland with the sponsorship and blessing of Congregational churchmen; to accept the support of the American Board of Commissioners for Foreign Missions would be somehow fraudulent; and yet there was no American Baptist missionary agency to which they could turn for support. They were, in effect, destitute in a foreign land. As might be expected from men of such honest conviction, they did the honorable thing. Judson wrote to his sponsors explaining his change of heart, and he also sent letters to Thomas Baldwin, of Boston, and Lucius Bolles, of Salem, influential Baptist acquaintances, suggesting the establishment of a missionary organization within that denomination. The two young ministers held a strategy session and agreed that Rice would return to America to inspire the Baptists in the performance of the Great Commission, and Adoniram and Ann Judson would try to set up a mission station somewhere. The Judsons struck out for Burma, where they were to encounter extreme hardship but were also to become effective religious pioneers; Rice set sail on the return trip to America.

September 7, 1813, is a red-letter date in the history of American Baptists, for it marks the return of Luther Rice to his homeland and the beginning of the conversion of the denomination to important new forms of evangelization. Prof. William H. Whitsett, years later president of the Southern Baptist Theological Seminary, assessed Rice's return as "the most important event in Baptist history in the nineteenth century."[6] After first checking in

103

with his Congregational sponsors, and being rather rudely discharged, Rice approached the Baptists, and what he found was rather disconcerting. Aside from a few powerless state conventions, the Baptists had no organization whatsoever. There was no central authority, no established channel of intercommunication, not a single national Baptist publication. Judson needed help immediately; it could not wait for the convening of delegates from distant states. So with the organizing drive of Boston's Dr. Baldwin, to whom Judson had written, the interim Baptist Society for Propagating the Gospel in India and Other Foreign Parts was organized in Massachusetts. Rice took to the road, soliciting mission support in New York, Philadelphia, Washington, Richmond, Charleston and other centers. His visits were followed by the formation of state mission societies, and on May 18, 1814, thirty-three delegates from eleven states met to form the General Convention of the Baptist Denomination in the United States of America for Foreign Missions. Since the agency was to hold meetings every three years, this cumbersome title was quickly shortened popularly to the Triennial Convention. Richard Furman, by now pastor of the First Baptist Church of Charleston, S. C., and the most influential Baptist minister in America, was named president of the Convention, and Dr. Baldwin was elected secretary. Luther Rice was designated Convention Agent, with the responsibility of visiting the churches to raise money for the missionary endeavor.

At last the Baptists of America had established a national base. It was a base dedicated to a single purpose, but it was to prove that churches united could accomplish more in some large areas of Christianity than they could hope to accomplish alone. Other denomination-wide enterprises were to be modeled after the agency for foreign missions. Newman, in his church history, wrote that "the bringing of the denomination together in so noble a cause constitutes one of the great events in the history of the Baptists. Such a union had been for years an object of endeavor on the part of a few foreseeing leaders of the denomination but to bring about a realization of such aspirations required the enthusiasm awakened by the accession of Judson and Rice to the Baptist ranks and the providential opening up of Baptist foreign mission work."[7]

Philadelphia was chosen as the first headquarters city for the Convention; in 1822 the offices were moved to Washington, and in 1826 they were transferred to Boston.

As might be expected, Judson, already at work in Burma, was named the Convention's first missionary, and Rice stayed on the road soliciting financial support. In the Convention's first year the churches gave $1,239.29 to missions, but within two years when Rice got organized, the annual amount rose to $12,236.84. Rice and Furman also whipped up support for the establishment in Washington of a seminary for the training of missionaries. It graduated its first class in 1821. Cooperation in the mission program also hastened the formation of state Baptist conventions. South Carolina formed one in 1821 which was to be "a bond of union, a center of intelligence, and a means of vigorous, united exertion in the cause of God, for the promotion of truth and righteousness."[8] Although there were in some places signs of strong resistance, particularly from those Baptists who feared central organizations might rob the local churches of their treasured autonomy, other states followed suit, in this order: Georgia, 1822; Connecticut and Virginia, 1823; Maine, 1824; New York and Vermont, 1825; New Hampshire, 1826; Pennsylvania, 1827; New Jersey and, over fierce opposition, North Carolina, 1830; Tennessee, 1832; Missouri, 1834; and Kentucky, 1837.[9]

While the states were thus organizing, another important undertaking had been launched nationally. In 1817 the Foreign Missions Convention board had been authorized to expend some of its funds in home missions, particularly in the frontier area, and John M. Peck was one of the first appointees. In a long career as a Baptist emissary to the hinterlands, Peck became known as "the Apostle of the West," and a word or two about him is in order. He was born in Litchfield, Conn., in 1789, and after his conversion in 1807 joined the Congregational Church. In 1811 he moved to Green County, N. Y., and that year became a Baptist. He was rebaptized and two years later was ordained into the Baptist ministry. Feeling that his education had been slighted, he spent a year in Philadelphia under the tutelage of William Staughton, a learned Baptist who was to become president of Columbian College, and the year's study was the only near-formal advanced schooling Peck ever had. After his appointment as a missionary to the West in 1817 he moved to St. Louis, where he set up a small school. Later he shifted his base of operations to Rock Spring, Ill. A tireless worker, Peck was constantly moving about in the Baptist cause. In one seven-month period he preached 78 times, made 38 other public addresses, attended 45 churches, four associational meetings, a college commencement, five state conventions and six ministerial meetings. In that time he traveled 3,310 miles by horseback — reading and writing as he rode.[10] A lesser man than Peck probably would have been discouraged by some of the problems he encountered. The chief one was the lack of continuing support by the Foreign Mission Board, which was far more interested in the fields abroad than in those at home. But Peck put together little pieces of support, notably from the Massachusetts Baptist Missionary Society, and found other ways to raise money. He even published a newspaper, *The Pioneer of the Valley of the Mississippi,* and one of his books, *Guide for Emigrants* (1831), received wide circulation back East and was responsible for bringing in new settlers. Concerned about the quality of the Baptist frontier ministry, Peck established a school at Alton, Ill., for pastoral training. It later became Shurtleff College.[11]

In 1826 Peck spent a night in the home of the Rev. Jonathan Going in Worcester, Mass., and it was an evening which was to give new impetus to Peck's work and to change the life of Going, a college trained Vermonter described as "a vast, walking, magnetic machine, at every step giving off sparks through every pore of his skin, through every hair of his head, through every muscle of his face."[12] Going and Peck threafter corresponded for five years, and in the summer of 1831 Dr. Going went to the Mississippi Valley and traveled with Peck for hundreds of miles through Missouri, Kentucky, Illinois and Indiana. Going waxed so enthusiastic about Peck's work that he became convinced the Baptists should grow more active in the home mission field; with Peck he concluded that properly the denomination should set up a separate agency to supervise that endeavor. Peck's experience had demonstrated that it could not be adequately maintained as a stepchild of foreign missions. Back in Massachusetts, Going was able to bring other influential ministers and laymen to see the logic of a new agency.

Accordingly, on April 27, 1832, the American Baptist Home Mission Society was created, with Going resigning his pastorate of sixteen years to accept a post as secretary.[13] With unusual sensitivity, the Society decided when possible to rely on representatives native to, or at least familiar with, the areas to which they were to be assigned. "Such men," the Society said in its first report, "will be, in several respects, more useful than strangers; they know the people, are acquainted with their wants, their habits, and their prejudices, and can readily accommodate themselves to these; they are also known to the public, and confidence is reposed in them."[14] In the first year of its operation the Home Mission Board employed 50 missionaries, posting them in twelve states and lower Canada. By 1836 the missionary total had grown to 96, and receipts from the churches amounted annually to about $17,000.[15]

At about the time the Home Mission Board swung into action, trouble was developing on another front, requiring for its solution the acceptance by the denomination of another united responsibility. Since its founding in 1816, the Baptists had freely supported the interdenominational American Bible Society, whose purpose was to print and distribute the Scriptures in English and other languages. In 1836 the society refused to publish a Bengali edition, prepared by Baptist missionaries, which used words meaning "immerse" and "immersion" in place of "baptize" and "baptism." This denial was striking at the Baptists on a very sensitive point, and the day after the interdenominational publishing society gave its decision, which was on May 12, a group of prominent Baptists met in New York and founded the American and Foreign Bible Society.[16] Because of internal friction this agency ultimately was replaced, but since 1836 Baptists have not been out of the publishing business, and the large book houses at Nashville, Tenn., and Valley Forge, Pa., are among the denomination's chief prides.

It should not be supposed that the marshalling of Baptists for work in the home and foreign mission fields proceeded without opposition. In 1814 there were more Baptists who opposed mission work than favored it, but for awhile the dissidents were unorganized. In his early travels, even on the frontier, Luther Rice encountered very little serious reservation, and in Kentucky and Tennessee, which were to become storm centers of the anti-missionary reaction, he got larger contributions than in any other state.[17] When Peck arrived in Missouri five years later, he was received cordially. But these conditions were not to last; opposition began to mount in the early 1820s, and it brought on the fiercest kind of internecine wrangling. Churches split, associations fell apart, lawsuits were initiated, state conventions were harassed and their work impeded. A Georgia minister announced to his congregation that "if an angel was to come down from heaven and declare the missionary course was of God," he still would not believe it.[18] In Tennessee, anti-mission sentiment became so rampant that noone dared to oppose it. In Ohio, where $547.09 had been contributed to missions in 1820, nothing was given between 1821 and 1828 and only $10 in 1829. Attempts to form state conventions brought out the anti-mission forces in droves, and they denounced not only missions but education in general, Sunday schools, Bible and tract societies and anything that could be categorized as a "human institution." The conventions, as a result, were generally organized by a minority, and many of the churches which joined found themselves "disfellowshipped" by the anti-mission churches. Churches invoked censure on individual members favoring missions, and pastors denounced missionaries as "howling, destructive wolves" and "ravenous dogs" with "numerous whelps."[19]

It is significant that anti-mission feeling was strongest in areas where education was restricted, and it is equally significant that it did not reach its greatest fury until home missionaries started appearing in areas regarded by the backwoods preachers as their private domain. That there was some jealousy there can be no doubt; illiterate preachers simply feared a loss of their own influence. There was also some suspicion: uneducated Baptists had a profound, inbred distrust of higher learning. Missionaries were paid, and on the frontier the farmer-preacher was still serving in large part without salary. There was a legitimate Baptist objection to the centralization of authority which seemed to be imminent in the formation of boards and conventions. And the anti-missionary forces searched the Bible and found scriptural authority for their objections; but these were probably drummed up to support their other reservations.[20] Riding through the tumult, especially that raging along the frontier, were three men: John Taylor, Daniel Parker and Alexander Campbell.

Taylor, a highly respected and devoted pioneer preacher in Kentucky, set his ideas forth in a pamphlet, *Thoughts on Missions,* in 1819. He held that missionaries and mission societies were primarily interested in grabbing money, and he argued that the whole missionary scheme was contrary to the Baptist idea of congregational responsibility. He carried a lot of weight.

Parker, an even more deleterious influence, also argued in broadsides. A hyper-Calvinist (as the entire anti-missionist movement was), he said that God needed no help in bringing the elect to repentance; and as for the non-elect, they might as well be allowed to go to hell without attempts to head them off, because hell was their destination. John M. Peck, who often encountered Parker, said the frontier preacher was in the grip of "zeal and enthusiasm bordering on insanity." He also wrote of Parker: "Raised on the frontiers of Georgia, without education, uncouth in manners, slovenly in dress, diminutive in person, unprepossessing in appearance, with shriveled features and a small, piercing eye, few men, for a series of years, have exerted wider influence on the lower and less educated class of frontier people."[21] Parker was often lucid in his arguments, but he sometimes seemed to be completely befogged. It was he who originated the Two-Seed-in-the-Spirit doctrine, which put simply, is this: When God created Adam and Eve, he included in their beings an emanation of Himself, which is the good seed; after the two were driven from the Garden of Eden there was implanted in Eve and her daughters the "seed of the serpent." Those born of the divine seed are God's elect, and those springing from the evil seed belong to the devil. To preach the gospel to these latter is an act of gross folly.[22] This is a highly imaginative paraphrase of Calvinism.

Campbell, who was a Baptist minister from 1813 to 1830, attacked the denominational mission program because he thought it had no basis in the Bible. He accused mission societies of greed, dishonesty, embezzlement and downright theft. In 1849, after he had founded the Disciples Church, he became president of the

Missionary Society of the Disciples.

The total effort of these three men and the ministers and parishioners who followed them was to impede the progress of the Baptist denomination at a time when growth could have been more rapid. Churches and ministers were brought into low repute, and in many areas the bad feeling persisted for decades, breeding intolerance and bigotry. Newman, commenting on this era, wrote that "the anti-missionary movement constitutes the saddest and most discreditable feature of modern Baptist history, as the highly successful missionary movement constitutes one of the chief glories of the denomination."[23] The missionary program did survive and did thrive. By 1845 the Board of Foreign Missions was supporting 17 missions in Asia, Europe and West Africa. Representing it were 109 missionaries and 123 native pastors. For the year ending in April, 1845, contributions for foreign missions were $82,302.95. In domestic missions 99 representatives were employed in 18 states, with annual receipts up to $18,675.68. In the United States Baptist membership had risen to more than 720,000 (of whom around 70,000 were in anti-missionary congregations), with 9,385 churches and 6,364 ministers.[24]

It had been a long, hard struggle, but Baptists had achieved a high degree of national unity. And now they were to throw it away.

Chapter Nine: A Parting of the Ways

The issue was slavery, and the controversy it produced among churchmen was not unique to the Baptists. The Presbyterians and Methodists also were to feel its corrosive influence, and all three denominations, partaking more deeply of regional passion than of Christian counsel, were to founder on the shoals of human bondage — foretokening the travail the nation they all cherished was later to face. With the churches the break came earlier, and in it a canny statesman might have found some timely instruction. Moral issues contested so strongly that they rend churches are bound to pose a threat to civil order.

To early American Baptist leaders, the question of slavery contained no dilemma at all. As early as 1637 Roger Williams, acknowledged by Baptists of both North and South as the founder, protested the enslavement of the Pequot Indians.[1] In Virginia, where blacks were first imported to the colonies in 1619, several leading Baptists freed their slaves shortly after the Revolutionary War. Among them were Robert Carter, of Nomini, who was said to have owned more than 600 slaves, and David Barrow, a Mill Swamp minister.[2] Barrow subsequently moved to Kentucky, a center of abolitionist agitation, and became a leader of the emancipation forces there. In the Ketokton Baptist Association the question brought a finding in 1787 that slavery was contrary to the laws of God, but a committee appointed to bring in a plan for the gradual freeing of the enslaved had to suspend its work when controversy developed within the association.[3] Two years later, however, at the instance of the Yankee-born but highly respected John Leland, the state-wide General Committee of Virginia Baptists adopted a resolution declaring slavery "a violent deprivation of the rights of nature" which was "inconsistent with a republican government" and urging its members "to make use of every legal means to extirpate this horrid evil from the land."[4] Half a century later the call of Southern Baptist secession was to issue from the same source.

The shift in attitude reflects the changed role of slave labor in the national economy. In the early years of the Nineteenth Century it had been recognized in the Northern states that slavery was an unprofitable system, and the institution had largely disappeared there. The plantation-farming system of the South rested upon cheap labor, and it had not been demonstrated that workers could be hired as economically as slaves could be supported. Into the ranks of the Baptists had moved more and more landed Southerners who had grown up with slavery and accepted it as part and parcel of the Southern way of life. They were good Baptists, and they brought up their human chattels as good Baptists. Negroes were admitted to membership in Baptist churches, and although the slaves sat as a body, in a segregated section of the sanctuary, it was not uncommon for Negro women to be sprinkled through the congregation, generally as nurses for the children of white members. Black membership was not full membership. The slaves were not allowed a vote in church business, and they were not accorded the right of discussion of church affairs, except as occasionally the business of the church, especially in matters of discipline, might involve a black member. From the ranks of the slaves were chosen special deacons, generally the most pious and Lord-loving, as liaison between the black and white membership, but their authority was not church-wide. Whenever a particularly eloquent and articulate black rose up in slave ranks, he could be ordained as a minister to the slaves, and he held forth at prayer meetings and on holidays, occasionally even being allowed the rostrum of the main sanctuary, all under the supervision of his white pastor. Obviously, it was a discriminatory arrangement, but slave-holding Baptists were honestly concerned for the souls of their Negroes, and the slaves enjoyed the association. Their rich voices were a harmonious addition to congregational singing, and they loved the old Baptist hymns and the simple, human order of worship. In 1835 the First Baptist Church of Richmond, Va., had 2,000 blacks on its membership rolls, five times the number of whites. An estimate based on the national census and church statistics for 1837 placed the number of Baptist-held slaves that year at 115,000. Only the Methodists, with 220,000, held more.[5] And that denomination, too, was by then about ready to explode from internal pressures generated by the institution of slavery. By that time, of course, the abolitionist movement was in full swing, and the Southern churchmen had grown almost hysterically defensive of this most prominent feature of their "way of life." In searching the Scriptures they found authority for slave-holding in the Old Testament, which recognized it, and no prohibition against slavery in the New Testament. The fact that the New Testament advised slaves to be content and their masters to be compassionate was regarded as an affirmation of the necessity and humanity of slavery,[6] and Bible scholars from both sides showed an eager willingness to lock horns.

As early as 1789, before national feeling was polarized, the old Philadelphia Association gave its indorsement to abolitionist societies and recommended that its member churches form local affiliates. Thirty years later, when the sensitive nature of the problem was more apparent, that body was more cautious. Asked by the Vincent Baptist Church at Chester Springs, Pa., in 1820 to consider the advisability of convening a national conference to plan for the freeing of slaves held by Baptists, the Association decided it was "inexpedient to enter on such business at this time."[7] A year later the Association declined to consider the question of fellowship with slave-holding Baptists. In South Carolina, where about one-third of Baptist laymen and two-fifths of their ministers were slave owners, there had never been a strong expression against slavery. In 1799 the Bethel Association there suppressed an inquiry into the right of Christians to own slaves.[8] In a message to the Governor of South Carolina in 1822 the widely revered Richard Furman, himself a slaveholder, said that slavery "was clearly established in the Holy Scriptures both by precept and example."[9] In that year and again in 1835 the Charleston Association defended slavery before the State Legislature.[10] North Carolina Baptists were slightly more moderate, the Sandy Creek Association in 1835 adopting a resolution against traffic in slaves but not against slave-holding.[11] In Virginia in that same year the ministers of Richmond adopted a resolution saying that "the example of our Lord Jesus Christ and His Apostles in not interfering with the question of slavery, recognizing the relation of master and slave, giving affectionate instruction to both, is worthy of imitation by all ministers of the Gospel."[12]

On the frontier the movement against slavery started early. In 1807 the four Baptist churches of Illinois had formed the Illinois Union Association. Two years later there was a rift over a corresponding relationship with Kentucky associations in which slavery was tolerated, and those opposed to continuing fellowship withdrew and, with Kentucky sympathizers, formed an organization famous in the abolitionist battle as the Friends to Humanity.[13] The Friends not only campaigned actively and widely for an end to slavery but also helped man the "underground railway" that spirited runaway slaves from the South to freedom.

In the 1830's abolitionists gained outright control of a number of New England Baptist churches, with a particularly vocal concentration in Maine. The Baptists of New Hampshire and Vermont were also strongly on the side of emancipation. When a State anti-slavery society was formed in Maine in 1834, Baptist laymen and ministers were among its organizers and Baptist churches were used for its meetings. For three years running the Maine Baptist State Convention passed anti-slavery resolutions, and in 1836 the Hancock Association adopted a report declaring that "of all the systems of iniquity that ever cursed the world, the slave system is the most abominable." By 1840, when a National Baptist Anti-Slavery Convention was formed, about 180 of Maine's 214 Baptist ministers were on record as abolitionists.[14] Sentiment was almost as strong in New Hampshire. A Baptist anti-slavery society was formed there in 1837, and all but three or four of the State's 50 Baptist ministers were outspoken against slavery.[15] So enthusiastic against slavery was a Freewill Baptist periodical, *The Morning Star*, that it was twice denied incorporation at Dover.[16] In Vermont Alvan Sabin, for 40 years pastor of the Baptist Church at Georgia and for 26 years a member of the Vermont Legislature, was one of the first agents of the American Anti-Slavery Society. After three years of strong resolutions condemning slavery, the Shaftesbury Association there voted to bar slaveholders from both pulpits and communion in Vermont Baptist churches.[17]

One of the few Northern denominational groups which showed any toleration of the Southern view was New York's influential Hudson River Baptist Association. Directed by men like Jonathan Going, Spencer H. Cone, Rufus Babcock, Jr., and Francis Wayland, that association concluded that the national unity of the Baptists in missions and benevolent work was too important to endanger by backbiting over a controversy which they regarded as social or political.[18] The most rational spokesman for the moderates was Wayland, who opposed both slavery and the tenor of agitation against it. A native of New York City, Wayland had entered the Baptist ministry in 1807 and had held successive pastorates at Poughkeepsie, Albany, Troy and Saratoga Springs. In 1827 he was named the fourth president of Brown University, and he began a 28-year administration which was to be revolutionary in improvements to school and curriculum. His whole life was marked by "abhorrence of meanness and wrong, belief in the divine purpose of life, stern sense of duty, moral courage, passion for truth."[19] In 1831, Wayland wrote a letter to William Lloyd Garrison explaining why he did not wish to receive Garrison's abolitionist newspaper, *The Liberator*. He said he believed slavery was wicked and destructive of the best interests of both master and slave, but he thought immediate emancipation was neither wise nor just. Even if it were, he said, it should not be attained by inciting slaves to rebellion, and he believed Garrison's paper encouraged that kind of violence. Later, in a famous series of letters which appeared in the *Christian Reflector* in 1844, Wayland discounted the alleged Biblical basis for slavery in a debate with

South Carolina's Harvard-trained Richard Fuller. (Fuller later went to Baltimore and was pastor of the Seventh Baptist Church from 1871 — 1876.)

By the late 1830's the slavery controversy had infected the mission boards operated by the Baptists, and although churchmen of the North and South continued to cooperate in home and foreign missions, a showdown was inevitable. Abolitionists tried to inject the slavery issue into the proceedings of the boards; slaveholders argued that it was a subject apart, not within the authority of the boards. Southerners were particularly resentful when they heard that Baron Stowe, recording secretary of the Board of Managers of the Triennial Convention, had addressed a letter to the London Union, under date of January 11, 1839, in which he expressed his personal sympathy with abolitionism and asserted that "it would not be difficult to show that the influence of the American church is, at present, the main pillar of American slavery."[20] He was probably right; without the active support of the churches of the South, slavery could not have survived. But he touched off a general uproar, and it did not subside even with the passage later in the year of a Foreign Missions Board resolution declaring its neutrality on the slavery issue. The formal resolution could not still the talk in the convention corridors, and Baptists of strong anti-slavery conviction could not help but offend Southern messengers, all highly sensitive to Northern criticism.[21]

In April of 1840 the smoldering ashes were fanned by the organization at the McDougall Street Baptist Church in New York City of the National Baptist Anti-Slavery Convention, with Elon Galusha, of New York, as president and O. S. Murray, a Vermonter who was on the board of the Triennial Convention, as secretary. In its three-day session the Baptist abolition society drew up two denominational addresses, one aimed at Northern churchmen and the other at those living in the South. The Northerners were told that they had a Christian and denominational obligation to stamp out slavery, and if the Southern churches "cling to the evil, and defend it as Scriptural right, it will become your duty, in the fear of God, and in a manner the most solemn and deliberate, to withdraw yourselves from this fellowship." The Southerners were told bluntly that slavery was wrong, and therefore unchristian, and that their defense of it brought the whole denomination and all who bore the name Baptist into disrepute in the eyes of God and the world.[22]

Southern Baptists were not in a mood to accept the reprimand gracefully. They suspected that men like Murray, committed to abolition in the Anti-Slavery Convention, could not maintain neutrality on the Foreign Mission Board, and a restatement of the board's middle course in 1843 failed to mollify them. When the Convention held its triennial session in Philadelphia in 1844, the air was highly charged. A total of 460 delegates had gathered, representing the country's 700,000 Baptists,[23] and sensing the explosive mood of the convention its leaders attempted to chart a course which would offend no one. Richard Fuller, still based in South Carolina, tried his hand at it first. He offered a resolution saying that "whereas, some misapprehension exists in certain parts of the country as to the design or character of this Convention, and it is most desirable that such misapprehension be removed; therefore, Resolved, that this Convention is a corporation with limited powers, for a specific purpose defined in its constitution; and therefore, that its members are delegated to meet solely for the transaction of business prescribed by said constitution, and that cooperation in this body does not involve or imply any concert or sympathy as to any matters foreign from the object designated as aforesaid."[24] Missions, said Fuller's resolution in effect, were the business of the Convention, and slavery was not.

Northerners dominated the Convention; only 80 delegates were from below the Mason-Dixon line. And to the majority Fuller's wording left too much unsaid. Slavery was not even mentioned by name. So the South Carolina resolution was withdrawn in favor of a substitute, which was passed unanimously. It said: "Whereas, there exists in various sections of our country an impression that our present organization involves the fellowship of the institution of domestic slavery, or of certain associations which are designed to oppose this institution; resolved, that cooperating together as members of this Convention in the work of foreign missions, we disclaim all sanction, either express or implied, whether of slavery or anti-slavery, but as individuals we are perfectly free both to express and promote our views on these subjects in a Christian

117

manner and spirit."[25]

Shortly after the adjournment of the Philadelphia Convention, some news got around that was particularly distressing to Baptists of the South. It was said that the Foreign Missions Board, through Dr. R.E. Pattison, one of its secretaries, had attempted to force the resignation of John Bushyhead, a Cherokee Indian chief justice who was working under the board's direction as a missionary to his tribe.[26] Bushyhead was a slaveholder, and although he died on July 17, 1844, before the issue could be brought to resolution, the conviction was widespread in the South that thenceforth no owner of slaves could expect appointment as a missionary, agent or officer of the Foreign Missions Board.

In test of this supposition, the Alabama Baptist Convention, acting at the inspiration of Basil Manly, president of Alabama State University, forwarded to the Foreign Missions Board a resolution designed to test the inclination of that agency. Famous in Baptist history as the "Alabama Resolutions," the document said:

"Whereas, the holding of property in African Negro slaves has for some years excited discussion, as a question of morals between different portions of the Baptist denomination united in benevolent enterprise; and by a large portion of our brethren is now imputed to the slaveholders in these Southern and Southwestern States, as a sin at once grievous, palpable and disqualifying,

"1. Resolved, That when one party to a voluntary compact among Christian brethren is not willing to acknowledge the entire social equality with the other as to all privileges and benefits of the union, nor even to refrain from impeachment and annoyance, united efforts between such parties, even in the sacred cause of Christian benevolence, cease to be agreeable, useful or proper.

"2. Resolved, That our duty at this crisis requires us to demand from the proper authorities in all those bodies to whose funds we have contributed, or with whom we have in any way been connected, the distinct, explicit avowal that slaveholders are eligible, and entitled, equally with nonslaveholders, to all the privileges and immunities of their several unions; and especially to receive any agency, mission, or other appointment which may run within (the scope) of their operations or duties."[27]

The Foreign Missions Board, thus put on the spot, replied with dignity and candor. "In the 30 years in which the board has existed," it said, "no slaveholder, to our knowledge, has applied to be a missionary. And, as we send out no domestics or servants, such an event as a missionary taking slaves with him, were it morally right, could not, in accordance with all our past arrangements and present plans, possibly occur. If, however, anyone should offer himself as a missionary, having slaves, we could not appoint him. One thing is certain, we can never be a party to any arrangement which would imply approbation of slavery."[28]

This forthright reply from the central headquarters of the Baptists excited consternation throughout the South. The Alabama Convention's board reacted immediately. In a statement it said that "with much reluctance and grief we are compelled to consider the communication from the Acting Board of the Baptist General Convention to be a full and candid avowal that they are not willing to acknowledge our entire social equality as to all the privileges and benefits of the union and therefore, in the opinion of both parties, our united efforts cease to be agreeable, useful or proper."[29] Southern response was not wholly negative, however. In a letter to the *Religious Herald* of April 17, 1845, Daniel J. Garnett, president of the Shiloh Baptist Domestic Missionary Society in Culpeper County, Va., wrote that "the Foreign Mission Board were pressed to a decision by the Alabama Baptist State Convention. They were put to the test. And in the eyes of the world and the presence of God they had to decide. I am inclined to think they could not have decided differently without doing violence to the authority of conscience."[30]

Meanwhile, the Georgia Baptist Convention had put in motion another test, this time with the Home Mission Society. In April, 1844, its executive committee requested the appointment of James E. Reeves, who owned slaves, as a missionary to that state's Tallapoosa Association, saying, "We wish his appointment so much the more as it will stop the mouths of gainsayers. There are good brethren among us, who not withstanding the transactions of your society at Philadelphia, are hard to believe that you will appoint a slaveholder a missionary, even when the funds are supplied by those who desire the appointment."[31] As news of the Georgia application got around, Northern Baptists rose to the bait. In New Hampshire, Maine, Vermont and Michigan, Baptist associations demanded that their missions contributions be withheld from any appointee who embraced slavery.[32] In October the Board of the Home Mission Society met for fifteen hours on the Reeves application, on five separate occasions. The members ultimately voted, 7 to 5, that the petition had to be denied. In a communication to the Georgia Baptists the board said, "The application of Mr. Reeves, of Georgia, a slaveholder, to be appointed a missionary of the society has been rejected, not on the ground of his being in fact a slaveholder, but because that fact was urged as a reason for his appointment."[33]

Under the guidance of Francis Wayland, a national convention of Baptists in Providence in the spring of 1845 attempted to repair the growing breach with a statement that all Baptists of good standing, whether of the North or the South, were eligible for all denominational appointments. But it was to no avail; the damage, in Southern eyes, had been done, and at the suggestion of the board of the Foreign Missions Society of Virginia, Southern Baptists were invited to hold a rump convention in Augusta, Ga., in May, 1845, for the purpose of launching mission enterprises with a distinctively Southern flavor. James B. Taylor, president of the Virginia missionary board, issued a statement saying the secession from the north was proposed "not because we reside at the South but because they have adopted an unconstitutional and unscriptural principle to govern their future course. The principle is this: that holding slaves is under all circumstances incompatible with the office of the Christian ministry. On this point we take issue with them; and verily believe that when the mists of prejudice shall have been scattered, we shall stand justified in the eyes of the world."[34] Taylor, an honorable man who was not himself a slaveholder, read the future but poorly.

There were those in the North who were not without understanding and compassion for their embattled brethren to the South. In a letter to Virginia's Jeremiah B. Jeter, Francis Wayland said sadly, "You will separate, of course, I could not ask otherwise. Your rights have been infringed. I will take the liberty

120

of offering one or two suggestions. We have shown how Christians ought not to act, and it remains for you to show how they ought to act. Put away all violence, act with dignity and firmness, and the world will approve your course."[35]

They separated, all right. And from the unhappy division, born of human rather than holy considerations, two separate strains of Baptists grew, mirror twins almost to this day. It is a temptation for skeptics to say that Baptists were the bulwarks of slavery, forgetting that there were as many Baptists who opposed that institution, and said so, as there were who defended it. Since the day of that historic division, Baptists have been involved in almost every social and political question which has faced this country — on both sides. And one of the strengths of the denomination is that there is room under the Baptist umbrella for men of varying persuasion, as long as they share a common faith in God.

Chapter Ten: Baptists At War

By train, stagecoach, boat and horseback the Baptists of the South converged on Augusta for the organization of the Southern Baptist Convention on May 8, 1845. While there was a spirit of adventure about their new undertaking, the messengers were not without fears and misgiving. The 30-member delegation from Virginia had covered one leg of their long trip by ship from Wilmington, N. C., to Charleston, S. C., and Jeremiah Jeter recalled later that they encountered a severe storm at sea which raised the specter of shipwreck. "When the peril had passed," he wrote, "this thought forced itself on our minds: If we had perished our fate would have been deemed decisive proof that slavery was wrong, and that God visited its defenders with a just and signal judgment. A thousand pulpits would have proclaimed the instructive lessons of the fearful providence."[1]

The 327 messengers, from the District of Columbia and the states of Alabama, Georgia, Kentucky, Louisiana, Maryland, North Carolina, South Carolina and Virginia,[2] represented 350,000 churchmen in the slave-holding states, of whom 130,000 were black.[3] Looking on from the North, above the Mason-Dixon Line, were 318,000 more Baptists, separated from their dissident brethren — as the nation was soon to separate — over an issue which was not even central to their original union. Doctrinally they were still one people. But at no time since have they been one church.

By common inclination, 4,126 churches in the Southern states pledged their support to such organization as might be formed. And with very little hesitation, the Southerners moved to put their new house in order. Dr. William Bullein Johnson, a South Carolinian who as a boy had shaken the hand of George Washington and who had served for many years as head of the Triennial Convention, was elected first president; Wilson Lumpkin, of Georgia, and Dr. J. B. Taylor, of Virginia, were chosen vice presidents; and Jesse Hartwell, of Alabama, and James C. Crane, of Virginia, were chosen secretaries.[4] A committee of two messengers from each state presented a resolution, unanimously adopted, which stated the purpose of the organization. It said: "That for peace and harmony, and in order to accomplish the greatest amount of good, and for the maintainance (sic) of those Scriptural principles on which the General Missionary Convention of the Baptist Denomination of the United States was originally formed, it is proper that this Convention at once proceed to organize for the propagation of the gospel."[5]

The structure of the Southern order, worked out in large part by Dr. Johnson, was different from the previous national arrangement. The old foreign and home mission boards, which were to continue operating in the north, were in large part autonomous bodies, subject only to the authority of the board members. The scheme proposed by Johnson, and accepted by the delegates, created the Convention as the superstructure to which all church boards would be responsible. In that way the churches, through their messengers, would have final authority over the activities of the Convention's various agencies. At the same time, it was understood — and remains a part of the Southern Baptist tradition — that the resolutions and decisions would in no way be binding upon individual churches. This is at once the great strength and great weakness of the Baptist denomination: no central power can dictate to any church; at the same time, no Convention undertaking can be assured of the total support of the churches. It is literally true that no one can presume to speak for the Baptists: he may speak for himself; he may even be empowered to speak for his church — if not for every member. But because of the autonomy of the local church, it is impossible to speak with denomination-wide assurance on anything except the very few basic Baptist principles. And even those have not gone totally unassailed.

Following Johnson's organizational plan, two boards of managers were formed, one for a foreign missions agency, with headquarters in Richmond and with Dr. Jeter as president, and a second for home missions, to be located at Marion, Ala., with Basil Manly as president.[6] The Southerners were moving quickly into the work from which they felt they had been excluded by Northern pique.

In an attempt to explain themselves to the nation, the Southern Baptists sent out an address "to the brethren in the United States; to the congregations connected with the respective churches; and to all candid men." It said that "a painful division has taken place in the missionary operations of the American Baptists. We would explain the origin, the principles, and the objects of that division, or the peculiar circumstances in which the organization of the Southern Baptist Convention became necessary. Let not the extent of this disunion be exaggerated. At the present time it involves only the foreign and domestic missions of the denomination. Northern and Southern Baptists are still brethren. They differ in no article of faith. They are guided by the same principles of gospel order. . . We do not regard the rupture as extending to foundation principles. . . In parting with beloved brethren and old coadjutors in this cause, we could weep, and have wept, for ourselves and for them; but the season, as well of weeping as of vain jangling, is, we are constrained to believe, just now past. . . "[7]

As the Southern Baptist Convention swung into action, there were some initial difficulties stemming from the old cooperative arrangement with the North. The Boston Foreign Missions Board refused an application from the Southern board for the assignment of some of the work abroad which previously had been conducted jointly. But the South quickly got organized, with beginnings in

China and Africa, and in the first thirteen years of separate operations Baptist churches of the Southern states contributed $266,656 to home missions and $384,399 to work abroad, in a volume of annual giving seven times greater than the Southern churches had produced in the 33 years of alliance with the North.[8] This was despite a slowly evaporating anti-missionary feeling still present in some parts of the South and a rather notorious reluctance on the part of Southern churchmen to overcultivate the "grace of giving." By 1861 the SBC home mission agency, by then called the Domestic and Indian Mission Board, had sent out 750 home missionaries, added 15,000 members to the churches, had been responsible for the construction of 200 new churches, and had spent $300,000.[9]

In the period following the Baptist division, of course, the slavery controversy did not abate. Attitudes adopted by Baptists of the opposing regions reflected popular sentiment, and in the 22 years leading up to the Civil War extremism abounded on both sides. Southern Baptist ministers, regarded as either defenders of or apologists for slavery, were unwelcome in Northern pulpits, and Baptist churches in the South went to great lengths to suppress abolitionist ideas. One of the most lamentable developments in the last years before fighting began was the loss of credit suffered in the South by Charles H. Spurgeon, at that time the most famous Baptist minister in the world. From his London pulpit he preached every week to audiences numbering as many as 10,000, and his reprinted sermons were borrowed for use in many American churches of both North and South. But when Spurgeon started denouncing slavery, Baptists of the South felt that he had "stopped preaching and gone to meddling." And his denunciations were biting. "I believe slavery to be a crime of crimes, a soul-destroying sin, and an inquiry which cries aloud for vengeance," he said. And on another occasion he told his congregation, "Better far should it come to this issue, that North and South should be rent asunder, and the States of the Union shivered into a thousand fragments, than that slavery should be suffered to continue."[10] All over the South Baptist ministers took their volumes of Spurgeon's sermons out and burned them.

When war came, it found the nation's Baptists as ardent in their support of the two opposing causes as they had been united in loyalty to American resistance during the Revolution. Northern Baptists bent their strength to the Union, convinced that not just the eradication of slavery but the nation's existence was at stake. In some areas, Baptists felt that the war, much as they regretted it, was ordered in heaven, and Indiana Baptists in particular believed that here was "a special manifestation of Divine Providence."[11] In Maine, the Baptist State Convention pledged its full cooperation and sympathy to the Washington government. Throughout the North, Baptists enlisted in the Army and churches were involved in relief work. But there was not yet in the North an organization through which the Baptists could speak with a united voice.

That was not true in the South, where many churches had to suspend operations and where Baptist buildings were taken over for use as hospitals, if they were usable at all. Battle left many of them in ruins, and the churches were brought to the same destitution and devastation as other Southern institutions. Baptist schools closed for want of students; Baptist ministers took menial jobs to support their families. But for Baptists scattered, wounded or dead, the Southern Baptist Convention still made cause. In a "Resolution on the State of the Country" at its 1861 meeting in Savannah, Ga., the Convention said: "The Government at Washington. . . now insists upon devastating our land with fire and sword, upon letting loose hordes of armed soldiers to pillage the entire South, for the purpose of forcing the seceded States back into unnatural Union, or of subjugating them and holding them as conquered provinces. . . With astonishment and grief, we find churches and pastors of the North breathing out slaughter, and clamoring for sanguinary hostilities with a fierceness which we would have supposed impossible among the disciples of the Prince of Peace." Accordingly, it "resolved, that we most cordially approve of the formation of the Government of the Confederate States of America, and admire and applaud the noble course of that Government up to this present time."[12]

In May two years later, when the Convention met at Augusta, Ga., during the thickest of Civil War fighting, the mood of the Baptists had not changed. Shiloh, both Bull Runs and Chancellorsville, in which Southern forces had consistently come off well, were behind them, and the Baptists had not lost their dedication to the Confederacy or their belief in final vindication through arms. The State of the Country resolution adopted that year said "that the events of the past two years have only confirmed the conviction expressed by this Convention at its last session, that the war which has been forced upon us is, on our part, just and necessary, and have only strengthened our opposition to a reunion with the United States on any terms whatever; and while deploring the dreadful evils of war, and earnestly desiring peace, we have no thought of ever yielding, but will render a hearty support to the Confederate government against the power and rage of our enemies, and in the signal victories with which He has crowned our arms; and encouraged by the experience of the past, and by the present condition of affairs, and humbly relying on the Divine blessing, we confidently anticipate ultimate success.

"That while we justify ourselves in this conflict with our enemies, we acknowledge that our sins have deserved the terrible calamities that God has sent upon us, and view them as a solemn and imperative call to penitence, humiliation and a hearty turning to God."[13]

The resolution also expressed concern over the "religious destitution of our armies" and spoke of "unutterable grief" over the "death of that noble Christian warrior," Stonewall Jackson. For the moment the Baptists were willing to overlook the fact that Jackson, mortally wounded by fire from his own men at Chancellorsville, was a Presbyterian deacon[14] who was regarded by his men as a religious fanatic.

In the same year the Domestic and Indian Mission Board reported that it had assigned 26 missionaries to Confederate units in Florida, Tennessee, Alabama, Mississippi, Georgia, South Carolina, North Carolina and Virginia. "Sometimes," its report said, "the missionary is accompanying the regiment or brigade upon their long marches, and preaches as he finds it convenient. Sometimes he moves from camp to camp, conversing with the men, distributing tracts, testaments, religious newspapers, and holding meetings for prayer, and exhortation; and sometimes he is found for a time within the massive walls of the strong and defiant fort, where he has access to its defenders, always anxious to wait upon his ministry."[15] In "very imperfect" records, the 26 missionaries to the troops reported that in a year they had preached 482 sermons, made 231 addresses, led 313 prayer meetings, paid religious visits to 1,762 individuals, officiated at 75 baptisms, reclaimed 19 "backsliders," converted 107 unbelievers, attended 24 funerals, traveled 2,383 miles and handed out hundreds of thousands of tracts, Testaments, religious newspapers and hymnbooks.[16]

After the Union blockade of Confederate ports, the Southern Baptist Convention had extreme difficulty in getting funds to its missionaries abroad, by that time based in Shanghai, Shantung, Tung-Chow, Liberia and Yoruba. The Foreign Mission Board, desperate to provide enough support at least to keep its representatives alive, joined in the scheme which was providing a trickle of commerce for the Confederacy. The Board bought $1,500 worth of cotton, through the assistance of a friendly speculator loaded it on a blockade runner, and smuggled it out to Bermuda. From there it was transshipped to England, where the consignment brought $5,000 on the London cotton exchange.[17] London banks conveyed the funds thus realized to Baptist missions in Africa and the Orient, and after the war the Foreign Missions Board was able to report that smuggled cotton had kept the work of the Lord alive.

As Union forces closed in on the South, the situation of the church became more and more desperate. In particular, Baptist ministers in areas of Union occupation were forbidden to preach unless they took an oath of allegiance to the United States. Fragmentary records show that at least ten Southern Baptist ministers were imprisoned for various infractions, and some died from the after-effects of incarceration. One of the ten was executed, not on account of his religion but for the company he kept. Albert C. Willis, a young minister licensed by the Crooked Run Baptist Church in Culpeper County, Va., was a member of John S. Mosby's Confederate raiders when he was captured by Union troops under the command of Gen. William H. Powell. On October 14, 1864, Willis was ordered hanged in Rappahannock in retaliation for the shooting of a Union spy by Mosby's men.[18]

The other ministers arrested were not actively engaged in

military operations, but Mosby was indirectly responsible for the detention of one of them. To forestall attack by the raiders, Union forces compelled Charles C. Bitting, pastor of a church near Washington, to ride all day on the cowcatcher of a locomotive shuttling freight cars between Alexandria and Orange Court House, Va. Bitting then was imprisoned for two months because he refused to take an oath of allegiance.[19]

R.B.C. Howell, a Tennessee minister who had been president of the Southern Baptist Convention from 1851 to 1857, was held in Nashville Penitentiary for two months in 1862 for declining to take the oath. Garnett Ryland, in *The Baptists of Virginia, 1699-1926,* tells of a number of other ministers who ran afoul of wartime regulations. They included:

William F. Broadus, pastor in Fredericksburg, Va., who was picked up on July 29, 1862, with six other residents of that city and taken to the Old Capitol Prison in Washington in retaliation for the jailing of four Federal agents held by Confederate authorities as traitors. Broadus was released two months later in ill health.

Charles W. Dobbs, pastor of the Court Street Church, who was imprisoned in Eastern Virginia on May 9, 1864, by order of Benjamin F. Butler, the Union occupation commander.

George W. Harris, who, according to the records of the Long Branch Church in Fauquier County, was "a prisoner" in October, 1864.

Jeremiah Hendren, pastor at Tanner's Creek, one of a number of Norfolk citizens arrested during Federal occupation there. He is said to have come to an early end as the result of the anxiety and suffering of his incarceration.

Richard Nutt Herndon, Luray pastor, who was removed from a sick bed when he refused to take the oath and confined in a "cold, damp prison" at Culpeper Court House. He contracted rheumatic fever and died the year after he was paroled.

John M. Lamb, of Mt. Pleasant Church in Charles City County. Union troops destroyed his home and he was held in a Northern prison for a year.

Meriwether Winston, who resigned the pastorate of a Philadelphia church at the beginning of the Civil War and returned to Virginia, his native state. In 1864 he was seized at his home in Hanover and forced to walk through sleet and rain to Fortress Monroe, where he was held for three months in company with convicted felons from the Union Army. He contracted pulmonary disease from exposure and died in 1866.[20]

One other Nashville pastor, Reuben Ford, a native of Goochland County, Va., is known to have been imprisoned. His Second Baptist Church was used as a hospital during the war, and he, like Howell, was put in jail for refusing to take a loyalty oath. Soon after his release, on March 12, 1864, he died of the effects of his imprisonment.[21]

A phenomenon which developed toward the end of the war served to widen the breach between Northern and Southern Baptists and is one factor in their decision not to reunite when hostilities ceased. In late 1863, the American (Northern) Baptist Home Mission Society petitioned the War Department for permission to take over and operate abandoned Baptist churches in the areas of the Confederacy under Federal control. Its motives appear to have been completely honorable, and the petition was filed without any thought of permanent seizure.

On January 14, 1864, the War Department, sensing political advantage in the move, instructed Army commanders "to place at the disposal of the American Baptist Home Missions Society all houses of worship belonging to the Baptist Churches South, in which a loyal minister of said church does not now officiate. It is a matter of great importance to the Government, in its efforts to restore tranquility to the community and peace to the nation, that Christian ministers should, by example and precept, support and foster the loyal sentiment of the people. The American Baptist Home Missions Society enjoys the entire confidence of this Department. . . "[22]

By that order, the Northern Baptists could have taken over practically every church in the South, because few Baptist ministers in Dixie could have qualified as "loyal" ministers. To Southerners, the War Department order was regarded as a move to make the church an instrument of the government. The whole thing smacked of one more form of occupation.

But the Missions Board disclaimed any such grand design,

carefully explaining its objectives. "In almost every city, town and village taken by our Army," it said, "there had been found a deserted Baptist meeting house. In many places these houses have been stripped of all that was movable, or converted into hospitals, stables, storehouses, or perhaps, occupied by others than Baptists, who have denied us the privilege of using them as places of worship. Instances are not wanting where colored brethren have been shut out of, or disturbed in the use of, their own houses wherein they had worshipped for years, under plea that the houses formerly belonged to their masters, and now to the Government, and not to them."

The Society added that "in all this the Board have to do only with meeting-houses, or Baptist church property that has been deserted by its former occupants, which property the War Department allows them to hold and use until civil authority can be restored. And their whole object will be accomplished if, by occupying the property, they can save it from being destroyed, or passing into other than Baptist hands, and preserve it as an inheritance for future Baptists who may live to own and occupy it."[2][3]

Dr. J. W. Parker, of Boston, was appointed by the Northern Baptists to follow through on the military order. Agents designated by him were to take possession of the churches in question and to secure pastoral services. In the first four months of the arrangement about 30 buildings were taken over from Virginia to Florida.[2][4] An example of how it worked out is shown by the case of a New Orleans church involved in the operation. According to the Northern board, a missionary sent early in the year to New Orleans "has been able to perpetuate the Coliseum Place Baptist Church, with modern improvements, and now has 30 members, 15 of whom he has baptized, a good congregation, a Sabbath school of three or four hundred children, and, in the basement of the house, a flourishing day and evening school."[2][5]

The Southern Baptist view was a little different, and the Convention later got this report: "In the summer of 1863 a Rev. J. W. Horton, a representative of the American Baptist Home Missions Society of New York, visited New Orleans, as he said, 'to look after Baptist interest.' Finding the church neither desirous of his services, nor willing to surrender the house to him, he obtained a military order from General Bowen, Provost Martial *(sic)* General, and thus forcibly obtained possession. At the time of this military seizure, there were about 65 members of the church in the city; of whom only five, one male (German) and four females, continued to worship in the house under the new administration."[26] In December of 1865 the Domestic and Indian Mission Board filed a military suit to regain possession of the church, and after a long checklist of qualifying papers was produced the church was restored to the Southerners on March 8, 1866.

From that year onward the Southern Baptists, disheartened over the loss of the war, held their conventions annually. In the post-war world they seemed reluctant to engage in civil controversy, but at the 1866 convention in Russelville, Ky., they did set on record a few afterthoughts about the war in a short resolution on "religious freedom." In it they said: "Many of our Christian brethren, of different denominations, and in various portions of the United States, having been restrained and annoyed in their appropriate work of preaching the gospel of Christ, sometimes by civil, and sometimes by military authority, contrary to the fundamental principles of religious liberty, and the paramount claims of Jesus Christ, we, members of the Southern Baptist Convention, deem it proper occasion for reasserting and proclaiming the principles of 'Soul Liberty' which our fathers were the first to publish, for the maintenance of which they suffered persecution, in which they have for ages gloried, and which we should be the last to abandon.

"We solemnly resolve, in the face of the world, and in the fear of god... that all interference with these functions on the part of civil rulers transcends their legitimate authority, and is a usurpation of the rights of conscience, and that when the claims of civil rulers come in conflict with those of Christ, it is our duty to 'obey God rather than men,' and endure the consequences.

"That we express our sincere sympathy and high regard for those ministers, who, in following the dictates of their consciences, and maintaining the authority of the Supreme Lawgiver, have cheerfully submitted to fines, imprisonments and other 'pains and penalties.'..."[27]

"That in adopting these resolutions, the Convention expressly disavow any disposition to interfere with political affairs, and have regard solely to the question of religious liberty."

There was a smattering of talk, both in the North and the South, about a Baptist reunion, but the Southerners resisted it on several grounds: A national convention of Baptists would be too cumbersome; few cities in the nation could accommodate such a crowd of delegates; Southerners would have to travel too far to convention cities (in 1970, they all traveled to Denver); with a regional organization, rank-and-file members could become better acquainted with denominational leaders;[28] and there were remaining, after all, the old scars and bitterness of the war. In 1868 the Southern Baptist Convention proclaimed itself a permanent organization, and although subsequently it offered by both word and deed to cooperate with Baptists of the North, there has since been no serious effort to achieve reunification. The obvious permanence of the breach was in part responsible, in 1907, for the organization, along Southern lines, of the Northern Baptist Convention, as overseer of the multitude of agencies and activities which had grown up since 1814. "American" was substituted for "Northern" in 1950. If there is a difference now in the two major organizations, it is a matter of nuance. As a body, American Baptists are more liberal in Christian practice and belief than the still largely conservative Southern Baptists.[29] American Baptists, for example, are members of the National and World Council of Churches, while the Southerners have resisted such affiliation as a dilution of the purity of their faith. Other than in matters of interpretation, however, Baptists are the same, wherever they are found. Strip away the trappings and you will find, all Baptists believe, the nearest modern equivalent of the New Testament church.

Chapter Eleven: God, Man, and the Lower Orders

For more than fifty years after the Civil War, the Baptists of America expended their energies in a sometimes acrimonious, often bitter, quest for doctrinal purity. Across the nation, invisibly, had swept a new tide. Science was in the ascendancy; old beliefs were being examined and questioned; new ideas were no longer rejected without study. The growth of communications, the emergence of well-edited newspapers and magazines, a rapidly rising level of literacy all tended to compete with the pulpit for the attention of church-goers. And smoldering under all this challenge to orthodoxy was a time bomb which had been planted by an almost unheard-of English naturalist, Charles Darwin, with the 1859 publication of an obscure book, *Origin of Species.*

That the first assault on the bedrock belief of the Baptists of Dixie should emanate from the Southern Baptist Theological Seminary was wholly predictable. It had been established in Greenville, S. C., in the same year that Darwin's book appeared in England, as an adjunct to the Convention, and its most enthusiastic supporters were a minority of educated ministers and laymen. Baptists generally, and it was especially true in the South, did not favor theological schooling for the clergy. The lingering suspicion from the Colonial days, when the trained ministers of the established Episcopal Church were the symbol of Baptist oppression, endured in the hinterlands, and among Baptists there was still strong belief in the old saw: "God never called a man to a job he wasn't prepared to perform." If a man got the "call," he would be endowed by heaven with all the understanding he needed.

But the divinity school was founded, and even though it operated under a cloud of mistrust, nothing startling occurred there to justify the reservations of its opponents until after its removal to Louisville, Ky., in 1877. At that time there was on the faculty, as professor of Old Testament interpretation, a young scholar of towering ability, Crawford H. Toy.[1] About two years after the move to Kentucky it began to be noised about Baptist backwaters that a smart aleck in Louisville was defiling the mind of fledgling parsons with the suggestion that perhaps not all of the books of the Old Testament were divinely inspired. This was heresy of the most painful order; it was basic to Baptist faith that all of the Bible was from God, and this raising of doubts was a motion of the devil.

And Toy's background, in the Southern view, was impeccable only to a point. Born to a prominent Norfolk, Va., family in 1836, he had done his preparatory work at Norfolk Academy and then gone on to the University of Virginia. So far so good. After three years of teaching at a Charlottesville girls' school, he went to the seminary at Greenville for a year with the hope of becoming a missionary to Japan. Entirely honorable. With the outbreak of the Civil War he scrapped his missions plan and entered the Confederate army, serving first as an artillery private and later as infantry chaplain. In July, 1863, he was captured at Gettysburg, but upon his exchange in December he returned to the army. As much as the most fervent patriot could ask. But after the war, Crawford H. Toy spent two years studying Semitic languages and theology in Berlin. Later it became clear to the orthodox Baptist that in his visit abroad young Toy had been "tampered with." Appointed to the Southern Baptist Theological Seminary faculty in 1869, he won a large following among students.[2] But he was also teaching heresy, and across the South, in pulpits, associational meetings and denominational papers, a clamor arose for his head. Officials of the seminary drew back in alarm, fearful that denominational support might be withdrawn, and Toy was asked to submit to his superiors a written statement of his views, accompanied by a letter of resignation. After inspection of both, the Board of Trustees told Toy his services would no longer be required in the precincts of Louisville. The rascal was thrown out — and catapulted to a position of much greater eminence. For almost immediately he was hired by Harvard University as Hancock Professor of Hebrew Languages, and in thirty years there he became one of the giants of the campus.[3]

Twenty years later an even more highly placed official of the seminary was ousted because of his offensive ideas, President William H. Whitsitt. Although Whitsitt was five years younger than Toy, the similarity between their careers is remarkable — both of good Southern stock, both respectably schooled, both possessors of records of honorable service to the Confederacy, both going abroad for their later education, both returning to the seminary to come to grief. Whitsitt was born near Nashville in 1841 into a family with an old Baptist tradition. Fifty years earlier, his grandfather, James Whitsitt, had left the ministry of a church in Virginia to introduce and spread Baptist principles in Tennessee. William Whitsitt graduated from Union University in Jackson, Tenn., in 1861, and enlisted in the Confederate Army as a scout under Gen. Nathan B. Forrest. After a year in the service he was ordained as a Baptist minister, and for the rest of the war he was a chaplain. In 1866 he studied briefly at the University of Virginia, and then, until 1868, he was a student at the seminary in Greenville. To round out his work there he spent two years at the universities of Leipzig and Berlin. Upon his return to the United States he was for a short time pastor of a church in Albany, Ga., but in 1872 he was appointed professor of ecclesiastical history at the seminary. He was so well regarded there that he was named president in 1895, and it was as the seminary's chief administrator that he got into trouble.[4]

As a contributor to the New York *Independent,* Whitsitt had at first anonymously published his view that the idea of the immersion of adult believers had been lost by the English Baptists and that they had "invented" the practice about 1641. He said Roger Williams probably had been sprinkled.[5] When Whitsitt later admitted the authorship of these assertions, a storm began to rage about his head. What was at stake here was the Baptist claim, then widely asserted and popularly enjoyed, that through an unbroken chain of heretics the church could honestly trace its lineage back to Jerusalem and that immersion was at all times part of that line. To accept Whitsitt was to discount the claim of antiquity, and right up to the convention level the controversy raged for several years. The principle of academic freedom had not then been introduced into Baptist practice — nor is it on unshakable footing yet — and Whitsitt's resignation was all that prevented a church split. The trustees accepted Whitsitt's withdrawal in 1899, and he became a professor of philosophy in Richmond, Va.[6]

While this purging of the seat of denominational learning had been going on, the Baptists, over a period of many years, had been involved, at first only tentatively, in the prohibition movement. In principle, although not in practice, the Baptist church has been dry for a hundred years. But it was not always dry, and its movement, as a denomination, into the anti-liquor camp was very gradual.

For a fact, and in common with most early American churchmen, the Baptists of the Eighteenth and early Nineteenth Century drank and didn't try to hide it. The congregation drank, the preacher drank, and many of the members made and sold their own liquor and consumed it in copious quantities. This is not to say that the Baptists were bigger boozers than other denominations. It says only that in this regard they were not unlike other religious people. The colonists, including the Puritans, referred in their laws to liquor as "the good creature of God," and practically no one went very long without a pull at the rum tap. Whisky was food, drink, medicine, an illness preventer and a health restorer, a comfort to the aged and an opiate for the very young. The rare teetotaller was regarded as queer.[7] All ceremonial occasions, including marriages, funerals, ordinations, barn-raisings, corn-huskings or elections, were celebrated with enormous consumption of whisky, and ministers as a matter of face and propriety were required to drink with the best —and worst — of them. Even if he had wished, the minister probably could not have abstained: to offer a guest a drink was a matter of hospitality; to accept it was a mark of politeness; and no one visited more than the preacher. But he was expected to be able to hold his liquor, and he was suspected of theological unsoundness if he couldn't.[8]

Outright and repeated drunkenness was, of course, a matter for church discipline, especially in the pastor. The Middletown, N.J., Baptist Church held in 1792 that its minister, Samuel Morgan, "does at times drink spirritous liquer to access — which report is rather an injury to his publick character and a great embarrassment to his usefulness in the ministry of the everlasting gospel." Morgan did not deny it but was offended that it should be called to his attention and requested that he be allowed to serve another church. He was subsequently ejected from the pulpits of two other churches.[9]

On the Western frontier the prowess of Baptist ministers in handling the bottle was legendary. A Methodist circuit rider, the Rev. Peter Cartwright, who moved around among the new settlements a great deal at the turn of the Nineteenth Century, said in his autobiography that "it was almost universally the custom for preachers, in common with all others, to take drams. I recollect at an early age, at a court time in Springfield, Tenn., to have seen and heard a very popular Baptist preacher, who was evidently intoxicated, drinking the health of the company in what he called the health the Devil drank to a dead hog."[10]

There was, however, no embarrassment and no stigma in the purchase and use of the rather large quantities of alcohol which were then held to be moderation. Dr. Jonathan Going, cited in an earlier reference as a pioneer in Baptist home missions, was asked in 1815 to give a Massachusetts church some advice on how it might improve its financial situation. Dr. Going, no tippler himself, investigated and concluded that the members might be in a better position to support the church if they spent less on booze. When he asked one of the churchmen if some saving might not be accomplished there, he was told, "I think not, sir; I buy mine now by the barrel, at the lowest wholesale rates."[11]

Although Baptists as a group were slow to join the anti-liquor crusade — which nationally was spearheaded by Methodists — there were pockets of pioneering, often against strong opposition, in this cause, too. Without knowing of the organization of the American Temperance Society in Boston in February, 1826, a Virginia Baptist pastor, Abner W. Clopton, was instrumental in the founding, in October, 1826, of a Virginia Society for the Promotion of Temperance. In its initial meeting at Clopton's Ash Camp Baptist Meeting House in Charlotte County, the society offered membership to "any sober person, whether a member of a church or not, who will consent to abstain from the habitual use of spirituous liquor, and use it as medicine only, and, provided he be the head of a family, shall enforce the same rule upon his children and domestics." Only nine persons joined at the founding session, eight of them preachers. A year later 23 Baptist ministers were among the 84 members.[12]

Although the temperance movement was a primarily lay undertaking at its beginnings, many Baptist laymen were suspicious of it. On March 17, 1832, the members of the Salem, N.J., First Baptist Church refused to accept this resolution offered by the pastor: "That the men of this church believe that the use of ardent spirits of any kind are to persons in health, not only unnecessary but hurtful. . . Therefore (we) promise that we will abstain from the use of distilled spirits except as medicine, that we will not make use of them in our families, nor provide them for the entertainment of our friends."[13] Three years later, however, the New Jersey Baptist Association declared that "it is morally wrong in all, and especially in a professor of religion, to manufacture, vend, or use such liquors (alcoholic, whether distilled or fermented) as a common article of luxury living."[14]

By mid-century the idea was taking hold in many Baptist circles that drinking was a mortal sin, and more and more the church, although not all members, moved into the camp of the prohibitionists. It did not sweep up all Baptists in a great wave of righteous indignation, though: as late as 1854 Primitive Baptist congregations in Kentucky were expelling members who joined temperance societies,[15] and in some Virginia churches which adopted a rule of total abstinence, minorities of dissenting members pulled out and formed "wet" congregations.[16] Through the church as a whole, though, the idea began to permeate that despite the repeated references to the use of wine in the Bible, drinking was a sin. Its opponents dreamed up all sorts of explanations for the Scriptural indorsements of alcohol, and some (e.g., the contention that the wine into which Jesus converted the water at Cana, as his first miracle, was not alcoholic) persist to this day. Prohibition became a denominational cause, and in both 1876 and 1896 Baptists supplied the Prohibition Party candidate for the presidency. Neither got very many Baptist votes. A Baptist minister, Gen. Green Clay Smith, who earlier had barely escaped becoming President (at the Republican Convention of 1864 he lacked one vote of being chosen Abraham Lincoln's running mate; Andrew Johnson, who got the spot, assumed the Presidency upon Lincoln's assassination), was the 1876 Prohibition Party candidate. He got 9,737 votes.[17] At his death in 1895, Smith was pastor of the Metropolitan Baptist Church of Washington. A layman, Joshua Levering, later (1908-1910) to become president of the Southern Baptist Convention, was the Prohibition candidate in 1896.[18] He polled 130,753 votes.

In the interim the American Baptist Home Mission Society had resolved in 1890 that "we declare ourselves among its (the liquor traffic) most pronounced and relentless foes, believing that it has no defensible right to exist, and that it can never be reformed: and that it stands condemned by its unrighteous fruits as a thing unchristian, un-American and perilous utterly to every interest of life. That we stand pledged by every legitimate means to work and pray and vote for the absolute abolition and overthrow of the iniquitous traffic in State and Nation."[19] Ten years later the Southern Baptists, in convention, threw their weight into the fight to outlaw booze. Their resolution said that "in brief we favor prohibition for the nation and the state and total abstinence for the individual, and we do believe that no Christian citizen should ever cast a ballot for any man, measure or platform that is not opposed to the annihilation of the liquor traffic."[20] In that year there were about 4 million Baptists, and the Prohibition Party candidate got 209,469 votes. It was in this period that the Baptist devotion to the dogma of abstinence became firmly rooted, and the memory of the time when Baptists drank openly, instead of secretly, was totally obliterated.

Baptists might have been more devoted to the temperance cause in the first quarter of this century had not a campaign of far greater significance engulfed them. This was a fight not in the conquest of man but in the defense of God. And at the bottom of it was that old devil Darwin. It was he who spawned the hellish theory of evolution, which to the orthodox, conservative Baptist challenged the Biblical account of creation. Sure, on the question of drinking the Bible might just have been a little hard to read; but on the question of the origin of man it was unequivocal. The Seventeenth Century Archbishop of Armagh in Ireland, James Usher, had figured the date of Creation as 4004 B. C. and had got it printed in the King James Version of the Bible,[21] by which association the date itself had assumed a mantle of inspiration. To suggest that the earth was untold millions of years old, and that man over a period of millions of years had evolved from lower orders, was regarded by religious conservatives as direct contradiction of Holy Writ.

In 1895 a number of divines troubled by the increasing challenges of science to true faith had converged in the Niagara Bible Conference and reduced Christian faith to five basic points: (1) the absolute infallibility of the divinely inspired Bible, (2) the divinity of Jesus Christ, (3) His virgin birth, (4) His penal substitutionary atonement, and (5) His physical resurrection and imminent second coming.[22] Under the sponsorship of Lyman and Milton Stewart, brother millionaires who founded the Los Angeles Bible Institute, a committee of ministers and laymen illuminated the Five Points in a series of twelve pamphlets called *The Fundamentals: A Testimony of the Truth,* widely circulated after their appearance in 1910.[23] With the financial support of the Stewarts, packets of *The Fundamentals,* which condemned Darwinism and modernist criticism of the Bible, were sent to "every pastor, evangelist, missionary, theological student, Sunday School superintendent, YMCA and YWCA secretary in the English speaking world, so far as these addresses can be obtained."[24] One of the general editors of the booklets was Amzi C. Dixon, a Northern Baptist evangelist, and among the contributors was Edgar Young Mullins, later to become president of both the Southern Baptist Theological Seminary and the Southern Baptist Convention.

Mullins' ideas were not completely ossified, however, and he was to be a target of conservative censure.

From *The Fundamentals* derived the term "fundamentalist," signifying those who accepted the Five Points without reservation, and anyone straying from the five-fold path was attacked as a "modernist." Although it cannot be said absolutely, fundamentalist zeal thrived upon ignorance. Only a few of its arch loyalists had impressive educational credentials, and for the most part it drew its supporters from the ranks of the poorly schooled in rural communities or the South. Absence of higher instruction, in fact, became a matter of pride with the fundamentalists: it signified a heart and soul uncontaminated by the doubtful conclusions of human scholars. By 1918, it was estimated, fundamentalist ministers may have controlled as many as 75 percent of American churches, with a total following of 20 million.[25] Since bedrock fundamentalism was — and is — primarily a rural and Southern phenomenon, it follows that the Baptists, serving those areas as well as others, were the most ardent of conservative champions. To classify all Baptists as dinosaur fundamentalists, however, would be unfair, for among the Baptist ranks were enlightened scholars and ministers who braved the wildest and most vitriolic assaults from their brethren in teaching and preaching the truth as they saw it. Since their "truth" was sometimes at variance — or so it seemed — with the "truth" proclaimed by the fundamentalists, there ensued a period of public brawling during which errant professors were ejected from the classroom and ministers tumbled from the pulpit by the legions of orthodoxy. The fight pervaded not only religious circles but rippled out into education and politics, and much of the splashing was done by Baptists.

To conservative diagnosticians, the clearest symptom of the deadly virus of modernism was evolution; Darwinism so certainly represented the drift from orthodoxy that wherever it appeared, fundamentalists rose up with the cry that here was an assault on the pillars of the Christian church. They warned that it would turn the whole country into a wilderness of paganism. Most often quoted by the conservatives was William Jennings Bryan, whose oratory was characterized by more rhyme than reason. He was fond of saying, "If we have come to the stage at which we must decide between geology and Christianity, I think it is better that we know 'the Rock of Ages' than that we know the age of rocks."[26] On close examination, that doesn't mean very much, but it has a nice ring. And to the simple and emotional it made a precious distinction.

Among the Baptist champions of fundamentalism were William Bell Riley, the voluble, hard-working pastor of the First Baptist Church of Minneapolis; John Roach Straton, who attacked liquor, dancing and evolution from the pulpit of the Calvary Baptist Church in New York City; T. T. Martin, a Blue Mountain, Miss., evangelist; J. W. Porter, of Kentucky, one of the stalwarts of the Anti-Evolution League; J. Frank Norris, Alabama-born pastor of the First Baptist Church of Fort Worth, Texas, and "Cyclone Mac" McLendon, a former Bennettsville, S. C., barber who switched from the Methodist to the Baptist faith when he hit the sawdust circuit.

As in all controversies involving Baptists, there were equally high-principled men on the other side, in this case opposing the fundamentalists either in tactics or belief. Among them were Harry Emerson Fosdick, who, though remaining Baptist, served a New York Presbyterian Church before mounting the pulpit of Park Avenue Baptist; William Louis Poteat, Berlin-trained biologist who was president of tiny Wake Forest College in North Carolina; Douglas Southall Freeman, Baptist editor of the Richmond, Va., *News-Leader*, and Dr. William Faunce, president of Brown University.

Obviously, the first job of Baptist fundamentalists was to put their own house in order. In the Southern Baptist Convention they made short work of it, because there was no contest. As a denomination, Southern Baptists were naturally fundamentalists, and if a statement condemning evolution and modernism were required it could be had for the asking. Anything condemning sin could get a hearing, because the Baptists, experienced at fighting sin in the prohibition controversy, were now flailing away at all its forms. In Chattanooga, Tenn., during the Convention of 1921, the messengers endorsed a Social Service Commission report which condemned motion pictures because they "appeal to and create depraved tastes." It went on to darker doings: "Another gross and growing evil must be mentioned. It is the modern dance. One of the most serious and menacing byproducts of the World War is the great increase in the dance evil, and the extravagant extremes to which it has gone. Accompanied, as it is, by immodest dress, by close physical contact of the sexes, by its lack of restraint, it is undoubtedly doing much to undermine the morals of our young people. It is beyond question that in many cases it leads to moral wreck and ruin. . . The time has come when our churches must take a positive position against this corrupt and corrupting evil."[27]

With the controversy over Darwinism growing, it was inevitable that the Convention should shortly stake out its ground, and it did so repeatedly, beginning in 1922. At Jacksonville, Fla., that year the delegates concluded that the theory of evolution and the Bible were in direct conflict and that the former must then necessarily be wrong.[28] At the same time the authorities of denominational schools were cautioned to weed out any textbooks which attempted to present Darwinism in an objective manner.[29] The following year, in Kansas City, the Convention endorsed a statement by President Mullins of the Louisville Seminary saying that scientists, if they wished their work to be authoritative, must begin their investigations by accepting the infallibility of the Bible, the atonement, the Virgin Birth, the physical resurrection of Christ and His second coming.[30] This was but a restatement of the Five Points, but the messengers felt an obligation to demonstrate their devotion to principles they judged to be eternal. The 1925 Convention, in Memphis, had to choose between two doctrinal resolutions: "Man was created by the special act of God, as recorded in Genesis," and "we believe that man came into this world by direct creation of God and not evolution." The two seem to be saying the same thing, but since the first contained no specific disavowal of evolution, the fundamentalists demanded the second. They were defeated by a vote of 2,013 to 950.[31] A year later, in Houston, after an uproar about modernist teaching in Baptist schools, the delegates supported a statement that "this Convention accepts Genesis as teaching that man was a special creation of God, and rejects every theory, evolutionary or other, which teaches that man originated or came by way of lower animal ancestry." The faculty and administration of all Baptist schools

144

and colleges were asked to affirm the declaration, and many of them did. But some ignored it and others opposed it outright. Dr. S. P. Brooks, president of Baylor University and a frequent target of the Texas Tornado, J. Frank Norris, said later, "I would die and rot in my grave before I would sign the Houston resolution."[32]

Although the evolution fight continued to blossom at the local and state level in the South, this was about its height in the Convention. One reason is that Norris, who in large part had masterminded the strategy in the Baptist body, had fallen into personal disrepute.[33] Remembered as "the most violent and pugnacious American preacher of his day,"[34] Norris was always a controversial and colorful figure who made so many enemies he habitually carried a gun. During a Fort Worth church quarrel in 1912 over the hiring of a professional quartet for the choir (which Norris opposed), the church burned to the ground. Pastor Norris was indicted on charges of arson and perjury, tried and acquitted. Although a lot of Baptists despised him thereafter, he became pastor of Fort Worth's First Baptist Church, which under his pastorate attained a membership of 8,000 — making it the largest Baptist church in the world. He soon got a wide radio following and added to his own personal prestige with a pastoral newspaper called "The Searchlight," whose front page showed him brandishing the Bible toward a cowering Satan. He denounced loudly against all of Satan's works, and loudest of all against evolution, which he called "hell-born, Bible-destroying, deity-of-Christ-denying, German rationalism." His particular target for several years was the group of teachers who taught evolution, and he claimed to have been responsible for the dislodgement of six professors from their posts. His probing searchlight ranged as far away as North Carolina, where he joined in the hue and cry for the scalp of Dr. Billy Poteat. In 1926 Norris turned his attention to the Catholic Church, which he also hoped to demolish. In the course of his campaign he got into an altercation with an unarmed official of the Knights of Columbus and shot him three times, killing him. Although he was acquitted of a charge of murder, his power waned, and for the next 25 years he preached in a succession of small Baptist churches, one of which burned — along with the parsonage.[35]

In the Northern Baptist Convention the fundamentalists were never able to take over, as they had done in the South, but the denomination was kept in considerable turmoil because of the violent agitations of the minority. In 1919 Minnesota's William Bell Riley, descrying in evolution a shoal which would sink the Christian ship, founded the World's Christian Fundamentals Association, which he described as "an event of more historical moment than the nailing up, at Wittenberg, of Martin Luther's ninety-five theses."[36] He also joined with John Roach Straton, Curtis Lee Laws, editor of the anti-evolution *Watchman-Examiner*, Jasper C. Massee, of Brooklyn, Amzi C. Dixon and Cortland Myers in the founding of the National Federation of Fundamentalists of the Northern Baptists. This group engineered a drive for doctrinal purity in Baptist educational institutions of the North and was responsible for much of the dissension on the Convention floor in succeeding years. It also tried for three years to induce the Convention to accept a fundamentalist creedal statement.[37]

Hostility was thick at the Des Moines Convention of 1921 when a fundamentalist investigating committee reported that because certain teachers were guilty of unsound theology, "it is the duty of Baptist communities... to displace from the schools men who impugn the authority of the Scriptures as the word of God and who deny the deity of our Lord."[38] Sensing the necessity to organize for their own defense, the liberal ministers of the North, under the leadership of New York's Cornelius Woelfkin, formed an "Evangelical Movement" to combat the fundamentalists and others seeking to disturb the harmony of the denomination. At the Indianapolis Convention of 1922 Woelfkin's group foiled a fundamentalist drive for a creedal adoption by offering a resolution that "the New Testament is the all-sufficient ground of our faith and practice, and we need no other statement." This was approved, 1,264 to 637 — a vote which pretty well showed the relative strength of the two colliding groups.[39]

In the interval before the next Convention President William H. P. Faunce, of Brown University, wrote an article for *World's Work* in which he stirred the fundamentalists to new passion. In it he said, "The doctrine of evolution, rightly understood and interpreted, is today one of the most powerful aids to religious

146

faith. It has delivered thousands from perplexity amounting to despair. . . . The doctrine of development has cleared away most of the difficulties in Old Testament ethics, and enables us to reconcile teachings which, given in different centuries, are yet united in one book. It has furnished the church with a powerful apologetic, which many of our leaders are now using." In the same article Faunce tried to counsel compassion for his opposing brethren. "Wise men," he wrote, "will not seek to exclude any fundamentalist from church fellowship. He is mistaken; he is undermining the faith of thousands; but he is sincerely wrong, and hence on the way to become right. He needs not violent objurgation, nor condescending pity, but simply continuous education."[40] The fundamentalists did not accord Faunce the same kind of tolerance. At the Atlantic City convention a few months later John Roach Straton climbed on a chair and demanded that Faunce not be allowed the floor because he had "in recent times aggressively expressed views subversive to our faith."[41]

Faunce was not the chief Northern heretic, though. That spot was held indisputably by Harry Emerson Fosdick, whose name alone was sufficient provocation to keep a passionate fundamentalist in pulpit fodder for a month. Fosdick, a Buffalo, N. Y., native, was a product of Colgate University and Union Theological Seminary. Ordained to the Baptist ministry in 1903, he accepted a call to the First Baptist Church of Montclair, N. J., and almost immediately established a reputation as a religious liberal. After the Jersey ministry, Fosdick became professor of practical theology at Union and concurrently accepted the associate pastorate of the First Presbyterian Church in New York City — which allowed him to retain his Baptist affiliation.

For a while he stayed away from theological squabbles, but after a trip to China, where fundamentalist missionaries were proclaiming the Five Points and condemning their more liberal brethren, Fosdick took off after the fundamentalists from his Presbyterian pulpit. He condemned the diehard conservatives for their rule-or-ruin divisiveness and left no doubt that as minister and teacher he rejected several of the fundamentalists' basic tenets.[42] He also made it plain that he felt God's creation of man by a

147

process of evolution through lower animal orders was no less wondrous than an on-the-spot transformation of a handful of dust. This bold challenge brought the fundamentalists out in droves, and Fosdick was denounced as a "renegade Baptist" peddling "bootleg theology."[43]

Largely at the insistence of fundamentalists the Presbyterian General Assembly in Indianapolis in 1923 ordered the New York Presbytery to get rid of Fosdick, and in 1924 he submitted his resignation to the First Church. An assembly in which 700 people stood in the aisles and adjoining rooms came to hear his farewell address, and he did not back away from his convictions. "We have stood here for an inclusive church," he said. "And this other thing we have stood for: the right of people to think the abiding verities of Christianity through in modern terms. . . There is no use in trying to turn the clock back. Ideas like scientific law and evolution are here to stay. . . The day is past when you can ask thoughtful men to hold religion in one compartment of their minds and their modern world view in another." He said he didn't mind being called a heretic. "I am proud of it. I wouldn't live in a generation like this and be anything but a heretic." For a Baptist, he also expressed some startling views on the rite most honored by his denomination. "If I had my way, baptism would be altogether an individual affair," he said. "Anyone who wanted to be immersed I would gladly immerse. Anyone who wanted to be sprinkled I would gladly sprinkle. If anybody was a Quaker and had conscientious scruples against any ritual, I would gladly without baptism welcome him on confession of his faith."[44]

When subsequently Fosdick was called to the pastorate of the Park Avenue Baptist Church, he accepted the position on condition that he be allowed to baptize in accordance with the wishes of the candidate, and the church agreed. Northern Baptist fundamentalists raved about that, too, and they sought to get Fosdick ejected from the denomination. At the Seattle convention of 1925, Fosdick's foes pictured him as a symbol of the devilish theology that was creeping into the church through the pulpit, but the best they could get out of the delegates was a bland resolution expressing sorrow over the policies of Fosdick's church. It was neither directive nor binding on the Park Avenue Church: being Baptist, it was autonomous and was required to take orders from nobody. In 1930 Fosdick became founding pastor of Riverside Church, erected by John D. Rockefeller, Jr., on condition that it be interdenominational and inter-racial. He was thus beyond reach of the fundamentalists; they continued to blacken his name, but to little avail — until his death in 1969 Fosdick remained one of the most powerful influences in American religion.

To the South, Fosdick's co-defender as prime whipping-boy of the fundamentalists was not a minister but the president of a North Carolina Baptist college, Wake Forest's William Louis Poteat. Like Toy and Whitsitt before him, "Dr. Billy" was an authentic son of the South who went abroad for educational refinement — and was suspect in some minds because of it. Born in Caswell County, N. C., in 1856, Poteat graduated from Wake Forest in 1877 and studied at the zoological institute at the University of Berlin the following year. Later he spent some time at the marine biological laboratory at Woods Hole, Mass. From 1878 onward, when he joined the Wake Forest faculty as a teacher of natural science, Poteat was associated with his alma mater, including a long term as president extending from 1905 to 1927.[45]

Unlike Fosdick, Poteat was not in all respects a theological liberal. His views for the most part were so orthodox that Southern Baptists had not hesitated to elect him to positions of honor and trust. He served as president of the North Carolina Baptist Convention and the State Anti-Saloon League, and in 1921 signed the Southern Baptist Social Service Commission report condemning motion pictures and "the modern dance." But Poteat's great sin, in fundamentalist eyes, erased all the good that he might otherwise have accomplished. For from the beginning of his career in the college classroom he taught evolution. He was, in fact, the first Southern educator to do so, and he was the first in the South to use the laboratory method in his biology classes.

Gerald W. Johnson, the historian and biographer who was a student of Poteat's, recalls that "Dr. Billy" had a quality of personal charm "far too elusive to be portrayed in words, yet it had power to disarm many an opponent who was impervious to logical argument and to make ardent defenders of some who never fully accepted Poteat's philosophy."[46] Undoubtedly under the influence of Johnson (they worked together on the *Baltimore Evening Sun*), H. L. Mencken, normally wasting no kind word on anyone professing Christian belief, paid tribute to Poteat as the "liaison officer between Baptist revelation and human progress" who through his personal influence had made North Carolina "the most intelligent of the Southern states."[47]

Not everyone was so fond of the country college president, and in 1920 Poteat became the center of a fundamentalist controversy which raged for five or six years. He had, in fact, rarely been spared. As early as 1907 a prominent North Carolina Baptist layman, D. F. King, had questioned Poteat's fitness to teach in a Baptist college, and although he was repulsed at every turn in North Carolina, King finally won strong outside support for his campaign. In 1920 the Mississippi evangelist Thomas Theodore Martin, acting on information supplied by King, wrote an article in the *Western Recorder* blasting the "fatal teachings" of the German-trained biologist as "Bible-warping" and soul-destroying." In subsequent broadsides he attacked Poteat as a "rank infidel" deluded by doctrines which had caused World War I and which were injurious and insulting to the belief of every true Christian. "Every honest man knows," Martin said, "that accepting evolution means giving up the inspiration of Genesis; and if the inspiration of Genesis is given up, the testimony of Jesus to the inspiration of the scriptures goes with it; and if his testimony to the scriptures is given up, his deity goes with it, and with that goes his being a real Redeemer and we are left without a Savior and in the darkness and in our sins."[48] With King and Martin blazing the trail, other leading fundamentalists, including Amzi C. Dixon and J. Frank Norris, joined in the hue and cry. North Carolina Baptists, under pressure from the outside, divided into pro-Poteat and anti-Poteat camps, but the college president, under personal provocation of the lowest order, never recanted and never lost his good humor. He insisted that there was no conflict between Christian faith and scientific investigation, and with that charm which Johnson described he won over all but the bitterest of his enemies. In the state Baptist magazine, the *Biblical Recorder* he wrote in April, 1922: "I have been ... teaching biological sciences forty years. I have discredited neither the Genesis account of the origin of man

150

nor the Gospel account of the origin of Jesus Christ. And there has been no concealment of my attitude. I have published two books on the relation of science and religion. Whenever I have referred to the creation account in Genesis I have taken pains to say two things — that the Bible is not a textbook in science and the affirmation there is of the divine agency in the process without a word about the method of creation. I frankly believe that God created all things and animals, man included, by the method of evolution. I find myself unable to resist the considerations in support of that method. There I stand, and I cannot help it."[49]

While Poteat had the support of the college board of trustees, the student body, most of the alumni and a majority of the educated Baptists across the state, the fundamentalists were determined to make a test case in education, and they thought North Carolina was the place to do it. Baptists were the largest denomination in the state; they had their fingers in the government, the schools, the courts — every public institution. And Poteat's scalp was a trophy the fundamentalists needed. The high point in the campaign to destroy him came at the annual meeting of the State Baptist Convention, which controls Wake Forest, on December 13, 1922, at Winston-Salem. Invited to speak on the subject of Christian education, Poteat sensed that he was facing a command performance, before a potentially hostile audience, and that he was fighting not only for his own professional life but also for the integrity of his Wake Forest classrooms.

His Baptist training served him well. Rather than make a frontal assault on cast-iron intellects he knew he could not dent, he decided instead to give what amounted to his personal testimony to the saving grace of Jesus Christ. As he mounted the rostrum of the Salem Baptist Church he held up the New Testament. "Permit me to read to you a little passage out of a little book," he began, "I love the little book and accept all it says. It has been the light and joy of my life. I commend it to you. It is our final authority for faith and practice. If you hear of anybody who flouts its authority and threatens to destroy it and to dislodge it from the minds and hearts of men, blow your trumpet, turn the bell of it Wake Forest way, and our little company, little but loyal, will be at your side on the dot." He did speak of the relationship of

151

Christianity to education: "If I am asked for a definition of Christian education, I reply, Christian education is Christianity operating in the field of enlightenment." But the most telling portion of his short address came when he spoke of his own conversion as a young man. "The cross," he said, "is the central fact toward which all previous history converges, from which all subsequent history diverges with a crimson tinge forever. Redemption is there, or it is nowhere, individual redemption and social redemption. Christ crucified works in the individual life a revolution so universal and so radical that there is no describing it save in His own immortal figure, the new birth. When the name of our dear brother, F. M. Jordan, was called this morning, you cannot guess what I thought about at once. I recalled a revival meeting which he held in Wake Forest College away back in the seventies, and but for the renovation of the building I could point you out the pew on the back of which I wept my heart out as I said to my Lord that the experience which I had at the age of twelve might have been genuine or not, one thing was certain now, that He was mine and I was His forever. I do not know what occurred in the deeps of my nature then. I have no psychology of conversion. I do not have to understand it in order to be assured of its reality. And you do not know what occurred in the deeps of your nature when you had the same happy experience and you do not have to understand it. I only know that when I yielded my heart to Him my surrender was my victory; this slavery of love these intervening years has been my emancipation."[50]

In a man of lesser principle Poteat's tactic of fighting fire with fire might have been dismissed as a histrionic trick. But most of the messengers to the Convention *knew* beforehand, and those who did not were quickly persuaded, that Poteat *believed* everything he said. When he concluded his address, on a rousingly inspiring note, the audience descended upon him en masse. Friends and former foes alike shook his hand in admiring congratulation, and a High Point couple who had cancelled a $2,500 pledge to Wake Forest because of the suspicion of Poteat's radicalism paid the full amount.[51] In the North Carolina press, generally elated over Poteat's convention victory, only one dissenting voice was raised. The Elizabeth City *Independent* accused Poteat of "chloroforming"

Poteat was subjected to about four more years of sniping, from both within the state and without, but by the time of his retirement as Wake Forest president in 1927, for reasons of age, he had shown the fundamentalists that a large segment of the Baptist church, even in the South, could not be stampeded. The National Cyclopaedia of American Biography remembers this dauntless little man as "a lifelong student, a gifted teacher and an accomplished college administrator, lecturer, author and civic and religious leader. He was witty, urbane and courteous and universally esteemed for his decision of character, his erudition, his intellectual integrity, his courage in the face of criticism and opposition, the breadth of his interests and his distinguished contributions to culture, social progress and public morality in the South."[53] Poteat died March 12, 1938. His alma mater over the years has produced senators, representatives, governors, editors and many other men of high principle and deep conviction. None ever fought more bravely, or with more telling effect, than "Dr. Billy."

While the fundamentalists gave a great deal of attention to "heretics" like Fosdick and Poteat, they were also active on a much broader front. They determined that if they could not kill the evolution heresy by pressure in the churches and colleges, they could attempt to have it banned from the public schools through legislation. They had found a weak spot, too, because politicians, living off the ballot box, are more sensitive to public outcry than are preachers and college presidents. Between 1921 and 1929, thirty-seven anti-evolution bills were introduced in twenty State legislatures, mostly in the South.[54] Inspiring most of these legislative proposals were fundamental Baptists, and where they did not inspire they aided and abetted. But that tells only half of the story. Time and again, sometimes singly and sometimes collectively, Baptists rose up in unexpected places to frustrate the anti-evolution goals of their denominational brethren.

Typical of this Baptist vs. Baptist showdown was the case in Kentucky, where in 1922 a bill to prohibit the teaching of the evolution theory in the public schools was introduced in the State Legislature largely through the prodding of J. W. Porter, a Baptist minister later closely identified with the Anti-Evolution League.

When the measure came to a decision in the House, it was defeated by one vote, 42-41. The deciding ballot was cast by Bryce Cundiff, a Hard-Shell Baptist who regarded the proposal as "an infringement of personal liberty."[55] Piqued by the loss, the state's General Association of Baptists, in which were represented 279,000 churchmen, vowed to wage political war against the opposing legislators. The fight extended over a period of eight years, but the fundamentalists never came close again.[56] Virginia was the only Southern state in which anti-evolution legislation never got as far as the floor of the Legislature. The fundamentalists were pressing there, not only for a Darwinism ban but also for a measure making Bible reading in the public schools compulsory. Under the leadership of Douglas Southall Freeman, the Richmond editor, and Dr. Robert H. Pitt, editor of the *Religious Herald,* Virginia Baptists drenched the fires of the fundamentalist anti-evolution crusade and condemned the proposed Bible-reading measure as "an unholy alliance of state and church."[57] In Minnesota William Bell Riley, the Northern Baptist firebrand, worked for six years to get anti-evolution legislation to a vote only to see it defeated,[58] but in Arkansas and Mississippi his sympathizers were more successful. The 1926 success in Mississippi was in large part the work of the Bible Crusaders,[59] a fundamentalist organization heavily populated by Baptists; in Arkansas the bulk of the credit goes to one man, the Rev. Ben Bogard, a Baptist of the J. Frank Norris school. Anti-evolution legislation there had been successfully thwarted until Bogard organized the American Anti-Evolution Association, in which he offered membership to everyone except "Negroes and persons of African descent, atheists, infidels, agnostics, such persons as hold to the theory of evolution, habitual drunkards, gamblers, profane swearers, despoilers of the domestic life of others, desecrators of the Lord's Day and those who would depreciate feminine virtue by vulgarly discussing sex relationship."[60] Through the collection of signatures on petitions, Bogard brought the evolution question to referendum, and in the election of November, 1928, Arkansas voters approved a monkey law by a vote of 108,991 to 63,406.[61]

Actually, the Arkansas and Mississippi statutes were anticlimactic, because the greatest success of the fundamentalists —

and the greatest exposure of the decrepitude of their ideas — had come in Tennessee in 1925. The Tennessee Legislature, not one of the most enlightened in the land, already had proven itself willing to consider seriously almost any extremist idea put forward under the auspices of a Christian religious sect. Prior to its writing an evolution ban into the law, the Legislature, at the request of the Holiness Baptists, had actually toyed with the idea of a law declaring the earth flat.[62] The measure failed of passage, but it was not long before the much more mischievous Monkey Law sailed through both chambers of the assembly.

The act itself was proposed by John Washington Butler, a Macon County legislator who was clerk of the Round Lick Association of Primitive Baptists. The only piece of legislation for which history has remembered him read:

"An act prohibiting the teaching of the Evolution Theory in all the Universities, Normals and all other public schools of Tennessee, which are supported in whole or in part by the public school funds of the State and to provide penalties for the violations thereof.

Section 1. Be it enacted by the General Assembly of the State of Tennessee, that it shall be unlawful for any teacher in any of the Universities, Normals, and all other public schools of the State which are supported in whole or in part by the public school fund of the State, to teach any theory that denies the story of the Divine Creation of man as taught in the Bible, and to teach instead that man has descended from a lower order of animals.

"Section 2. Be it further enacted, that any teacher found guilty of the violation of this Act, shall be guilty of a misdemeanor and upon conviction, shall be fined not less than One Hundred ($100.00) Dollars nor more than Five Hundred ($500.00) Dollars for each offense.

"Section 3. Be it further enacted, that this Act take effect from and after its passage, the public welfare requiring it."[63]

Asked why he had proposed the bill, Butler said, "In the first place, the Bible is the foundation upon which our American Government is built... The evolutionist who denies the Biblical story of Creation, as well as other Biblical accounts, cannot be a Christian... It goes hand in hand with modernism, makes Jesus Christ a fakir, robs the Christian of his hope and undermines the foundation of our Government."[64] Among those who rushed to his immediate support was Dr. W. F. Powell, influential pastor of the First Baptist Church of Nashville and thus representative of the largest denomination in the State. Baptists and other fundamentalist groups pelted the Legislature with demands that the Butler Act be passed, and on January 28, 1925, the House of Representatives accommodated them with an approving vote of 71 to 5. By mid-March the Senate had concurred, 24-6, and on March 21, Baptist Governor Austin Peay signed the bill into law. Peay had not at first favored the Butler Act, but he changed his mind after a visit from a Baptist delegation headed by Dr. Powell. In yielding the Governor said the anti-evolution bill was "a distinct protest against an irreligious tendency to exalt so-called science, and deny the Bible in some schools and quarters — a tendency fundamentally wrong and fatally mischievous in its effects on our children, our institutions and our country."[65]

The resulting trial of the young substitute biology teacher, John T. Scopes, for defying the law was initiated as a publicity stunt for the little town of Dayton, Tenn., and Baptists had nothing to do with originating it. But once the battle lines were drawn, with William Jennings Bryan and Clarence Darrow arrayed against each other, Baptists were all over the place. As far away as Brooklyn, N. Y., Charles F. McCoy, pastor of the Greene Avenue Baptist Church, dismissed evolution as "a lie of hell" and characterized Scopes, an admitted infidel, as "an ambassador of the devil."[66] On the twelve-man jury sat six active Baptists and a seventh man who, though a non-member, had been reared in a Baptist home.[67] They were unmoved by Darrow's opening plea: "My friend the attorney general says that John Scopes knows what he is here for. Yes, I know what he is here for — because the fundamentalists are after everybody who thinks. I know why he is here. I know he is here because ignorance and bigotry are rampant, and it is a mighty strong combination."[68] The jury was equally unimpressed by Darrow's dismantling of the fundamentalists' general, Bryan. In one of the most celebrated trials of the century they found Scopes guilty.

A few years later Arthur Garfield Hays, one of the defense attorneys, recalled his foray into the Deep South stronghold of the Baptists: "I should have been startled and somewhat doubtful had anyone told me that at this late date there were great numbers of people in the United States who held the religious views of the Middle Ages, who, in spite of railroads, steamboats, the World War, the telephone, the airplane, the radio, all the great mechanistic discoveries and all the advancement in science and philosophy, in spite of education in the public schools in geography, biology and kindred subjects, still thought that the earth was flat; that doctors were a menace; that lawyers were predestined to damnation, and that failure to observe literally every word of the Bible would send one to eternal hell, a material region where the flames leap high and where the doors are sealed for eternity. Had anyone suggested that there were millions of people who believed it possible to build up a theocracy in the United States under the leadership of Bryan, I should have thought the statement that of a madman — that is, before I went to Dayton."[69]

Although the fundamentalists scored a few more successes, the Monkey Trial really was the turning point in their crusade, for at Dayton they were shown to be largely neanderthal types. Looking back upon the carnage in 1928, Walter Lippmann, well aware that the carnage was in large part expressive of Baptist zeal and energy, wrote: "These assaults upon the freedom of teaching have been supported by the ignorant part of our population, the spokesmen of these new inquisitions have often been mountebanks, and invariably they have been ignoramuses."[70] Not everyone believed him, least of all those about whom he wrote. As late as 1931, Editor Curtis Lee Laws, who was neither mountebank nor ingoramus but an honest, God-fearing conservative, wrote wistfully in his Baptist *Watchman-Examiner:* "The spectacular days are over, but so long as old-fashioned Baptists exist there will be protests against false doctrines and against methods that are contrary to God's Word."[71]

And Laws was right. Old-fashioned Baptists do still exist, in large numbers, scattered through the rural areas of the South and Southwest, and not only in the backwoods but also in the hamlets, the towns and the cities. And to paraphrase Mencken, you may go there, anywhere, and find yourself a Baptist church. From that spot, cast a stone in any direction. And where it falls, within five minutes, you can get an argument on evolution, the whale that swallowed Jonah, the fires of hell, or whether Moses, author of the Pentateuch, actually was inspired by God to report his own death.

Chapter Twelve: The Black Baptists

While the Northern and Southern Baptist colossi had been developing, spreading, merging, disuniting, regrouping and fighting out their internal conflicts with almost self-obsessed zeal, a companion body of Baptist believers had survived both persecution and neglect in becoming the most powerful and representative organization of blacks in the world. In America today nearly half of the Negro population is Baptist,[1] and that statistic is not an accident. In the days of slavery, beginning about 1740,[2] the Baptist church had deliberately set out to convert the blacks, and although black members of the white churches were never regarded as full-fledged affiliates the influence of the church on those untutored Africans was profound.

The slave hungered for religious expression, and the formal ritual of the high churches to which many of the slave-owners adhered was unappealing. In the soulful hymns, earnest prayer, simple service and fervent preaching of the early Baptist ministers the black found a freedom of spirit he could not elsewhere experience. For a few moments each week, in the back pews or the slave gallery of the Baptist church, he could lift his rich voice

159

in worshipful song; he could hear an appeal to some mysterious force in his own breast; he could approach the throne of grace in what the Baptists liked to call "soul liberty". Some of those who felt these stirrings yearned to preach themselves, and out of this response to white Baptist tutelage the first exclusively Negro Baptist congregation was born.

The early history of the black Baptists is at best vague and imprecise. Few of the early Negro ministers could read or write, and only the scantiest written records were left for posterity. It has been established fairly definitively, however, that the first Negro Baptist church in America was founded between 1773 and 1775 on the estate of a generous planter named John Galphin at Silver Bluff, S. C., twelve miles from Augusta, Ga.[3] The congregation was formed, with Galphin's blessing, after a number of visits to the plantation by an itinerant black minister remembered only as "Brother Palmer."[4] The first preacher to appear at the church on a regular basis was George Lisle, and Galphin later permitted the ordination of one of his own slaves, David George, to succeed Lisle.

Lisle, born in Virginia about 1750, was the property of a moderate slave-holder named Henry Sharpe. When Sharpe moved to Burke County, Ga., during Lisle's youth the young slave naturally was taken along, and he often accompanied his master to meetings of the local Baptist church, where the Rev. Matthew Moore was pastor. Sharpe became a deacon, and he noticed that the young Negro, who had a natural oratorical gift, was deeply interested in religion. Accordingly, he and Moore agreed that Lisle should be baptized and ordained as a preacher to the blacks. Under the sponsorship of Moore's church, and with the written encouragement of Sharpe, Lisle ranged in his evangelical duties all the way from Augusta to Savannah, preaching to the slaves gathered on plantations or at Sunday meetings of the workers of several settlements. For his methods Lisle is criticized by today's black historians,[5] because he shrewdly realized that he could operate only within the framework of the white establishment. Accordingly, he always cleared his messages with the authorities, and he refused to give religious instruction to slaves who did not have the permission of their owners. It is probably true that emancipation did not figure in Lisle's thinking; but without the precautions he took, he could not have preached at all. Soon Lisle's work became so manifestly important that Sharpe gave him his freedom in order that he might operate as he wished.

That began a new phase of Lisle's career. Although he continued to travel the back roads, he concentrated his activities more in the region of Savannah and was living there when the American Revolution broke out. Sharpe, his old master, was killed in the early days of fighting and Sharpe's heirs, who had never approved of the master's freeing the black minister, tried to have Lisle re-enslaved. He was thrown in jail in Savannah pending a hearing and was languishing there when the British occupied the city in 1778. A Colonel Kirkland of the British forces heard of Lisle's plight, had the claim against him dismissed and employed the Negro minister as a servant. During the British tenure a number of slaves, promised freedom by the occupying forces, had run away from their masters and settled in Savannah, and from these and permanent black residents of the city Lisle, in 1779, formed the first Negro Baptist church there — the second established *by* Negroes in America (but the third *for* Negroes; in 1776 the white Baptists of Williamsburg, Va., had set up a church for blacks[6]). Lisle continued as its pastor until 1782, when the British evacuated the city.

With the withdrawal of his benefactors Lisle faced an uncertain future. He feared that if he stayed in South Carolina, or anywhere within American jurisdiction, he would be persecuted and perhaps even re-enslaved as a British sympathizer. To avoid that fate, he indentured himself to Kirkland in exchange for passage for himself and his family to Jamaica, where Kirkland was settling. His last act on American shores was to baptize Andrew Bryan, Bryan's wife Hannah, Kate Hogg and Hagar Simpson, a gesture which would pay handsome Baptist dividends. Lisle, working off his indentureship and gaining his complete freedom in two years, subsequently became the spiritual father of the Baptist church in Jamaica, and his memory is honored there to this day.[7]

David George, who had succeeded Lisle as pastor of the Silver Bluff church, brought many of its members to Savannah during the British occupation, and he, too, thought it the better part of

161

wisdom to quit the country when the British withdrew. For a time George, who could both read and write, although born a slave in 1742, lived in Halifax, N. S., where he gained considerable fame as a pulpiteer. In 1792, to repair his failing health, he moved to Sierra Leone, where he established a Baptist church.[8]

After the war the Silver Bluff church was reorganized by one of its original members, the Rev. Jesse Peters, and it has been continously in existence since that time.

In many ways, however, the history of the early Negro Baptist church in America is the story of the Rev. Andrew Bryan, the same Andrew who was baptized by Lisle as his last act of grace in Savannah. Bryan, born a slave in Goose Creek, S. C., about sixteen miles from Savannah, in 1737, was brought to Savannah as a young man and soon came under the influence of George Lisle. So intense was Andrew's religious fervor that he felt compelled to preach, and he was soon delivering sermons to black and white congregations in the city. Upon the departure of Lisle from Savannah, Andrew Bryan became the spiritual leader of the church Lisle had founded, and it was his dearest wish to obtain a permanent building for use by the church. Edward Davis, a rich white landowner, allowed the black congregation to erect a rough wooden building on a plot of land he owned at Yamacraw, on the outskirts of Savannah, but conservative slave-holders, fearful of rebellion by their human chattels, so vigorously objected that the black Baptists abandoned the building and met in secret — which was against the law. With a brother, Sampson, Andrew held the congregation together, often persecuted, sometimes taking refuge in the South Carolina swampland. Once, under arrest, Andrew and Sampson were " 'inhumanly cut and their backs were so lacerated that their blood ran down to the earth as they, with uplifted hands, cried unto the Lord; but Bryan, in the midst of his torture, declared that he rejoiced not only to be whipped but would freely suffer death for the cause of Jesus Christ.' "[9]

On that occasion Jonathan Bryan, the white master of Andrew and Sampson, came to the aid of his two slaves, had them freed and allowed them to hold their church meetings in his barn. Even so, white patrols often eavesdropped outside the premises to see if rebellion were being plotted. With the assistance of Jonathan Bryan and the indorsement of a number of other slave-holders, Andrew got a court order permitting him to conduct worship services in the Bryan barn without hindrance anytime on Sunday between sunrise and sunset. One of the indorsers, John Millen, gave this reason for backing Andrew's request: "I signe the above petition finding that my Negros that atend publicly worshap ar to be Trusted."[10]

With these beginnings of white support, Andrew Bryan once again began a campaign to obtain a church building. He started a fund-raising drive, soliciting white contributions, and in 1794, he and his congregation put up the first permanent church in America built by Negroes for Negroes. It stood at what is now Mill Street and Indian Street Lane in Savannah, and it was not a thing of beauty. One historian says that the rectangular church, 42 feet by 49 feet, "was slow in building, as facilities for getting materials were difficult, but the framing timber was good and solid, hewed out in the forest by its members, and the weatherboarding was all neatly planed smooth. The building was very plain, without any attempt at architectural beauty, almost square and boxlike, high-pitched roof, with small windows; one wide door in the west center of the building and two smaller doors near each end on the south side... the pulpit (was) in the east center, built very plain, shaped like an acorn, with a raise from the floor of about three feet, plain board front, a neat cushioned pad for the Bible, and a board' seat which would accommodate three. No part of the building inside was ceiled, rafters and studs in their rough state, straight-back pews without doors; and the only pretense to neatness was in the smoothing of the backs and seats and rounding and beading the edges and tops. No part of the building was painted or white-washed, but plain and pure as from the carpenter's hands."[11]

In 1795, Jonathan Bryan, Andrew's master, died, and the Negro minister, who seems to have been remarkably frugal, was allowed to purchase his freedom. Thereafter he devoted his full time to his church, and he so assiduously converted the blacks of Savannah that by 1800 his First African Baptist Church had 700 members — more than his rude sanctuary, now blackened by weather, could accommodate. By 1802 the overflow was so great that the Second

African Baptist Church of Savannah was established, with Henry Francis, a slave owned by a Col. Leroy Hamilton, as pastor.[12]

Andrew Bryan remained a vigorous minister, patriarch of all the Negro Baptists of upper Georgia, until his death, at the age of 75, in 1812. He left a modest estate, and he was held in such esteem in the community that the white Savannah Baptist Association passed this resolution: "The Association is sensibly affected by the death of the Rev. Andrew Bryan, a man of color, and pastor of the First Colored Church in Savannah. This son of Africa, after suffering inexpressible persecution in the cause of his divine master, was at length permitted to discharge the duties of the ministry among his colored friends in peace and quiet, hundreds of whom, through his instrumentality, were brought to a knowledge of the truth as 'it is in Jesus.' He closed his extensively useful and amazingly luminous course in the lively exercise of faith and in the joyful hope of a happy immortality."[13]

While the Baptist faith was being firmly implanted among the Negroes of the coastal South, black congregations were springing up independently elsewhere, sometimes on their own initiative, sometimes as wards of a white congregation. Before 1780 the Harrison Street Baptist Church of Petersburg, Va., had been founded under the example of the black church at Williamsburg. In Kentucky, the First Baptist Church of Lexington came into being in 1790, and in Augusta, Ga., the Springfield Baptist Church was established in 1795.[14] All have survived into modern times.

In many places where there was no black Baptist church there were black Baptist ministers, and some of these men, without formal education whatsoever, were recognized as such powerful and compelling preachers that they were popular with both whites and blacks. A particular favorite in Virginia, widely known as "Uncle Jack," was so highly regarded by the whites that they formally licensed him to preach and raised a fund with which to purchase his freedom. They bought him a small farm, and for 40 years "Uncle Jack" was an itinerant minister, moving from one plantation to another in his rounds and bringing about the conversion of a large number of blacks and whites.[15] In Portsmouth, Va., in 1795 a Baptist church with a mixed congregation actually called a black man as pastor. The church, organized in 1789 as a member of the Isle of Wight Baptist Association, had had a run of bad luck with white ministers, and upon hearing a guest sermon by Josiah Bishop, a Northampton County Negro slave, the congregation not only offered him the pulpit but bought his freedom and that of his wife and eldest son. White resentment in Portsmouth, however, soon made it clear that a black man would not be tolerated as pastor to whites even if it was the will of his congregation, and Bishop, a powerful, gifted preacher, moved on to important black congregations in Baltimore and New York.[16] Some years later in Alabama there rose up a powerful Negro preacher named Caesar McLemore. The Alabama Baptist Association was so impressed with his godliness and diligence that it purchased his freedom for $625. At that time Alabama law did not provide for freedmen, so Rev. McLemore's owner of record became the Baptist Association, and a committee of three whites was appointed to supervise his work as a plantation missionary.[17] In most states of the South prior to the Civil War it was not legal for slaves to hold property in their own names. When property was acquired by the early churches it had to be vested in white trustees for the benefit of the blacks. Generally Negro ministers, even when ordained, did not acquire those civil rights denied to slaves; thus, when they performed marriages, as they often did, the contract established in the eyes of God was not sanctioned by law.[18]

No account of black religious figures of this period would be complete without reference to Lott Carey, even though the work for which he seems to have been destined was not carried on in America. Born a slave about 1780 in Charles City County, Va., Carey was exposed from his earliest years to Baptist training. His father was widely known for his piety. In 1804 Lott was taken to Richmond, about 30 miles away, where he was sent to work in a tobacco warehouse. By his own account he became debauched for a while in the big city, but after two or three years he remembered his earlier training, repented, was baptized in 1807 and joined the First Baptist Church (white) of Richmond. One Sunday he heard the pastor, John Courtney, preach a sermon on the Third Chapter of St. John, which contains an account of a conversation between Jesus and Nicodemus and which also has, at the sixteenth verse, lines dear to the heart of all Baptists: "For God so loved the world that he gave his only begotten Son, that whosoever believeth in him should not perish, but have everlasting life."

Carey was so taken with the passage that he resolved to learn to read it himself. He got a New Testament, and, badgering the literate whites at the warehouse, quickly learned to read not only that chapter but the whole book. And soon after he learned to write. Feeling an urge to preach, Carey switched his membership to the First African Church, was licensed as a minister and began to hold services in and around Richmond. Still popular at the warehouse, and often the recipient of small gifts of money, Carey by 1813 had saved enough money to buy his own freedom and that of his two children — a total bill of $850. After that he went on salary at the warehouse and bought a small farm.

About 1815 he became obsessed with the idea of the African mission field. He helped found the Richmond African Missionary Society to raise money for the work there, and then he decided to send himself. There was more to his resolve than religion: also involved was his own self respect. On one occasion he said, "I am an African, and in this country, however meritorious my conduct and respectable my character, I cannot receive the credit due either. I wish to go to a country where I shall be estimated by my merits, not my complexion; and I feel bound to labor for my suffering race."

Accepted by the American Colonization Society as an emigrant, he won appointment from the Board of the (white) Baptist General Convention as a missionary to Africa and sailed for Sierra Leone on January 23, 1821. Upon his arrival there he worked first as a mechanic, but with the establishment of Liberia he moved to Monrovia and, over a period of several years, founded a church and a school and became familiar enough with African diseases and their cure to serve as colony physician. Appointed acting governor of Liberia, Lott Carey died in 1828 when a powder keg exploded during an attack by unfriendly natives.[19]

Although no black Baptist church was established in the North during the Eighteenth Century, a considerable number of blacks were members of the white churches, and in the first decade of the Nineteenth Century they began to regroup in Negro congregations.

In Boston the Joy Street Baptist Church was founded in 1804 on the initiative of the Rev. Thomas Paul, a New Hampshire-born black minister who served the Boston congregation for 25 years. Five years later, when some Negro members of New York's First Baptist Church on Gold Street wished to launch out on their own, Paul supervised their withdrawal, prevailed upon the Gold Street whites to provide financial assistance, and helped the fledgling congregation acquire a recently vacated white church on Anthony Street for its house of worship. It was in that manner, with nineteen charter members, that the Abyssinian Baptist Church, to become the most famous and influential black church in America, was founded on July 5, 1809.[20] Bishop, who had been ousted fifteen years earlier by prejudiced Virginia whites, arrived to become the minister. He was part of a long line which was to include Adam Clayton Powell, Sr., and his controversial son. In 1809 a similar separatist movement in Philadelphia, involving thirteen black members of a white church, resulted in the organization of the African Baptist Church there.[21] By 1846 there were three Negro Baptist churches in Philadelphia, New York's Abyssinian church had a membership of more than 500, and churches had been established in Baltimore and Washington.[22]

With black churches in the North beginning to prosper, the Negro Baptists of the South entered a period of severe repression, inflicted in part as a result of the Southampton (Va.) Insurrection led by Nat Turner in 1831. Turner believed himself to be divinely appointed to lead the slaves to freedom, and Southerners, reacting to the specter of 54 white dead, were quick to suspect all slaves who claimed spiritual enlightenment of any kind. Hastily enacted laws in Virginia, dated 1832, made it impossible for Negro ministers to preach except in the presence of white men. Alabama followed with laws requiring black ministers not only to have a supervised audience but also to obtain the sponsorship of a neighboring white church; Georgia set up rigid certification requirements, almost impossible to fulfill, and provided that without the new license a Negro might preach to an assembly of no more than seven. All the Southern states, in fact, tightened up their laws, to the extent even of forbidding the teaching of reading and writing to Negroes. Although some masters refused to acknowledge the new measures and allowed their slaves to worship as before, the laws were generally effective and served to inhibit the spread of religion among the blacks. Even so the slaves occasionally managed, at great risk, to circumvent the law — as in the case of the invention of "before-day prayer meetings," an illegal assembly called after the night patrols of the plantation watch had gone to bed.[23]

The slaves were, of course, still permitted to attend white churches; South Carolina, in fact, had rarely permitted the blacks to separate. The result was that Negroes so outnumbered whites in many Baptist congregations that the assemblies were effectively all-black. Of the 1,643 members of Charleston's First Baptist Church in 1846 only 261 were white; in that city's Second Baptist Church there were 312 blacks and 200 whites; Georgetown Baptist had 298 Negroes and only 33 whites; and so it went in town after town. Another way to stay within the law, and to provide in the eyes of the authorities a superior kind of religious institution, was to supply white ministers for black congregations, and this practice was widespread.

The concurrent movement of freedmen and fugitive slaves toward the west in this period served to implant Baptist principles among the black populations of the frontier, and well before the Civil War Negro Baptist churches came into being in Pittsburgh, Cleveland, Columbus, Cincinnati, Buffalo, Detroit and Chicago. In a short time there were more black Baptist churches west of the Alleghanies than there were in either the North or South. The first inter-church agency, in fact, came out of the new territory when in 1836 a number of congregations in Ohio joined in the Providence Baptist Association. Two years later a number of churches in Illinois formed the Wood River Baptist Association, and in 1853 these two associations along with other outlying churches united in the Western Colored Baptist Convention.[24] The only other considerable organization of Negro Baptists at that time was a Missionary Convention formed in 1840 by the churches of New England and the Middle Atlantic states. It distinguished itself during the Civil War by petitioning the Union government for permission to send black ministers into the South with the Union Armies to preach to newly freed slaves — an arrangement which

President Lincoln approved on August 31, 1863.[25]

The war itself worked considerable hardships on Negro Baptists, particularly those in the South. It is true that they did not have fine churches to be destroyed, but the loss in war of such crude buildings as they owned represented severe privation. The churches were disrupted even more, however, by the removal of slaves from one place to another. As the Union forces advanced, slaves often were hidden in the fields and swamps for their own "protection." Many of these were Baptists, and their churches ceased to function. It has been estimated that on the effective date of the Emancipation Proclamation — January 1, 1863 — there were 400,000 Negro Baptists in the United States, most of them in the South.[26]

Emancipation, of course, meant nothing to those slaves in territory dominated by the Confederacy, and it was not until the war's end that the bulk of the slaves faced the question of their religious future. In some areas of the South ugly situations developed when the freed blacks were callously advised to seize the white churches of which they had been majority members. One recorded instance of such a confrontation occurred in Selma, Ala., and accounts in part for the intensity of residual race prejudice there. Told that the blacks were planning to take over his church, the pastor, J. B. Hawthorne, and some of his white friends armed themselves and threatened to shoot anyone who attempted to capture the building. A mob which had gathered dispersed without bloodshed, and B. F. Riley, who tells of the incident, says it would not have happened but for "white instigators."[27]

The white Southern Baptist Convention, itself severely unsettled by the loss of the war, manfully attempted to extend at least a gesture of friendship toward the liberated blacks. At its 1866 convention in Russelville, Ky., the whites appointed a "Committee on the Religious Instruction of the Colored People" which returned the following resolution:

"Resolved, that in our changed relations to the colored people, we recognize, as heretofore, our solemn obligations to give religious instruction to them, by all those means which God has ordained for the salvation of men.

"Resolved, that we earnestly commend to our brethren to

169

increase the work of Sabbath School instruction among them, and that when practicable, a Sunday School be established for them in every church.

"Resolved, that we suggest to the pastors of our churches the duty of giving theological and other instruction to such colored brethren as are now engaged in preaching, and to such as, in the judgement of the churches, may be called to this work.

"Resolved, that we recommend to our people to encourage the Negroes to establish day schools for the instruction of their children, and also encourage our young men and women to engage in the work of teaching them.

"Resolved, that while we are not opposed to any right-minded man aiding in this important work, it is our decided conviction, from our knowledge of these people, and of the feelings of our citizens, that this work must be done mainly by ourselves."[28]

Several ideas were imbedded in that resolution. For one thing, the Southern Baptists assumed that many of the blacks would choose to continue as members of white churches. And many did. It also assumed that whites were in the best position to serve as religious instructors to the blacks, and there was a renewal of the old practice of sending white ministers to the pastorate of black churches. In 1866, for example, Dr. Robert Ryland, who since 1832 had been president of Richmond College, became pastor of the First Colored Church in the Virginia Capital. He remained for 25 years, baptizing 3,800 new members in that time, and be it said to his credit that he was well-loved by his Negro constituents.[29] Also part of the 1866 resolution was a conviction among Southern whites that they, and not Yankee infiltrators, were best equipped to serve the needs of the Negroes. That idea was expressed a year later at the 1867 convention when the delegates, noting that the American Baptist Home Mission Society wanted to help, said, in effect, "Fine; send money."[30] By 1868 the Domestic and Indian Mission Board of the Southern Convention was able to report that in a year of work among the Negroes 30 new congregations had been constituted, 24 meeting houses had been commenced, with 11 finished, and 611 blacks had been baptized.[31] The following year those in charge of that work noted that "the colored race are exceedingly disposed to religious excitement, and are alarmingly exposed to the artifices of fanatics and demagogues." They said the blacks were being preyed upon by fake preachers interested not in Christ but in "filthy lucre."[32]

Whatever the circumstances, and despite all hardships, the postwar period was one of phenomenal growth for the black Baptists — despite the fact that white Baptists of the South had most ardently advocated the Confederacy and among all churchmen had most vigorously defended the hated institution of slavery. The most tangible sign of growth, from this distance, is in the organization of black state conventions. In the South the first was established in North Carolina in 1866, and Alabama and Virginia followed in 1867. By 1880 Negro Baptist conventions had been formed in every Southern state.[33] A companion tendency was to affiliate with large, regional organizations, and between 1865 and 1895 a number of these sprang up, some to endure, others to lead relatively short lives. One of the most important was the Foreign Mission Convention of the United States of America, which was organized in Montgomery, Ala., on Nov. 24, 1880, largely on the initiative of the Rev. W. W. Colley, who for two years had represented the Southern Baptist Convention as a missionary in Africa. One hundred fifty-one delegates from churches in eleven states attended the founding session.[34]

Another of these larger bodies was the American National Baptist Convention, constituted in St. Louis on August 25, 1886. Its moving spirit was the Rev. William J. Simmons, one of the nation's foremost black educators. Born a slave in Charleston in 1849, Simmons was smuggled aboard a ship in Charleston with his mother and two sisters when he was 10 and taken to Philadelphia. He was first a shoemaker and then an apprentice to a dentist. In 1864 he ran away from his apprenticeship to join the 41st Division of U. S. Colored Troops, in which he served for a year before being honorably discharged. Back in civilian life he became the first Negro member of the Baptist Church at Bordentown, Pa., and when he declared an interest in the ministry the church sponsored his education. Ordained in 1878, he was pastor of a church in Lexington, Ky., when the trustees of the Normal and Theological Institute of Louisville offered him the presidency. In the direction of that school (which later became Simmons University) he became

171

interested in unity as a means of making the black Baptist churches more effective and laid the groundwork for the St. Louis convention. The 600 delegates elected him president, and he held that post until his death in 1890.[35]

The first truly nation-wide organization of black Baptists, however, was established in 1895 through the merging of Colley's Foreign Mission Convention (by then known as the Tripartite Union), Simmons's American National Baptist Convention and a new organization known as the Baptist National Educational Convention. One of the chief incentives for the formation of a strong national body was the refusal of the American Baptist Publication Society, whose quarterlies and other materials were used in the black churches, to include in its output the writings of Negro authors. The blacks decided they needed their own publishing house, and one way to get it was through an organization which could guarantee large circulation. And so it was that the National Baptist Convention of the U. S. A. was established in Atlanta on September 28, 1895.[36] Its first president, to serve for 28 years, was the Rev. C. E. Morris, born a Georgia slave in 1855. Like Simmons he, too, was for a short time a shoemaker, and also like Simmons he went into the ministry, serving in Arkansas. In addition he was an editor and educator, and his influence on the nation's Negro Baptists was profound.[37] Another of the large figures of the convention was Lewis G. Jordan, who was to become the principal historian of the black church. He, also, had been a slave, born about 1860 in Lauerdale County, Mississippi. He ultimately became pastor of the Union Baptist Church in Philadelphia and at one time ran unsuccessfully for Pennsylvania Congressman-at-large on the Prohibition Party ticket. Jordan was chosen to direct the work of the new convention's Foreign Mission Board, a role he played for 25 years.[38] By the turn of the century there were in the United States more than 1.8 million black Baptists. Most of them, in 10,000 churches, were represented by the National Baptist Convention, but there were still 300,000 in white churches and churches associated with white conventions.[39]

A word must be said about the role of the black churches in American life between the end of the Civil War and the dawning of the Twentieth Century. They were poor, it is true, and very often their theology left a lot to be desired. The ministry was in large part uneducated, the congregations even less trained. But the judgement of Pelt and Smith is unassailable: "The church played a central role in the great movement 'up from slavery.' It was the door to full citizenship responsibility, a door that was open when others were still closed. Here a man could rise as far as his abilities could carry him, and here he entered a moral universe where his status and dignity as a human being were absolutely affirmed."[40] The transition from slavery to freedom was very difficult for the blacks, and through much of the period of adjustment the church undoubtedly acted as a rock and a beacon on the shore of some very troubled seas. That the blacks did not turn on their erstwhile tormentors, even when urged to do so by vengeful advisers, was in great part the result of the stabilizing influence of the church.

As time passed, however, a "generation gap" could be discerned in the black church. Up until the end of the Nineteenth Century, most of the ministers and leaders had known slavery and it had left its mark upon them. While many slave-born blacks could and did assert their independence as free men, equal under the law, there were just as many who retained the old second-class attitude, fearful for themselves, fearful of offending the power structure of the whites. For the black community this was agonizing; younger men were springing up who did not wish to give offense to their revered elders but who were determined to stamp out the last vestiges of the mark of the shackle; they have not, of course, done it yet.

In the National Baptist Convention the blacks did, indeed, get their publishing house — but in a way that was later to spell division. At the convention's second annual meeting a publishing board was established, supposedly to operate under the wing of the Home Mission Board. The corresponding secretary of that board, the Rev. R. H. Boyd, set up the publishing house — but in such a way that it became a highly personal venture. Boyd incorporated the publishing house in Tennessee and used part of the fast accumulating proceeds to build a fine plant on property of which he was part owner. The annual volume of business was in the millions of dollars. So possessive was Boyd of the enterprise, however, that when in 1915 the parent National Baptist Convention of the U. S. A. asked for an accounting and tried to institute stricter reporting procedures, Boyd withdrew, taking many of the Negro churches with him, and founded the National Baptist Convention of America.[41] It was one of the few splits in Baptist history that did not involve a doctrinal or theological disagreement of some kind. Today the two conventions exist side by side; the older, with more than 5.5 million members, 27,500 ministers and 26,000 churches, is the largest Negro denomination in the world and the third largest Protestant denomination in America.[42] (It underwent another division in 1961 when delegates from 14 states, protesting the failure of the old convention to limit the tenure of officers, organized the Progressive Baptist Convention of America.[43]) Publisher Boyd's National Baptist Convention of America claims more than 2.6 million members. All together there are about 10 million black Baptists in America, organized in around 40,000 churches. They represent four of every ten Baptists in North America and account for 44 per cent of the blacks on the continent.[44]

It is difficult to gauge the effectiveness of the Baptist church in the Negro community in modern times. Almost by default, some of its functions have been taken over by the National Association for the Advancement of Colored People, the Congress on Racial Equality and the Student Nonviolent Coordinating Committee. Belatedly, black Baptist organizations have begun to sponsor such undertakings as voter registration drives and voter instruction, but they have been largely preempted in this field.

Nevertheless, the churches have provided the community centers from which secular organizations have operated, and the Baptists produced the two most effective Negro leaders of modern times. Both were Negro ministers, and the sons of Negro ministers. Otherwise there was no similarity in their styles. Chronologically, the earlier of the two was Adam Clayton Powell, Jr., born in Harlem, where his father was pastor of the Abyssinian Baptist Church, in 1908. He was trained at Colgate, and he was fighting, as he often boasted, for equal opportunity for the Negro long before most of today's black activists were out of diapers. In the Depression years of the Thirties Powell raged through Harlem, operating soup kitchens and demanding equal job opportunities for the deprived blacks. He had help, but it was largely his crusade, and it was barely beginning when in 1937 he succeeded his father as pastor of the Abyssinian Church. In 1941 he won a seat on the New York City Council, and in 1945 Harlem's Eighteenth Congressional District, 300,000 strong and 89 per cent black, sent him to Congress, where he was to become a powerful committee chairman. In his heyday, Powell had become what every black man dreamed of — a charismatic figure who could beat whitey at his own game.[45] Powell knew that he was a new breed, and he gloried in it. "My father," he once said, "was a radical and a prophet — I am a radical and a fighter."[46] And fight he did, tooth and nail, breaking down doors in Washington that had always been closed to all black men. But Powell changed. He was a perfect example of the corrupting influence of power, and as he turned more and more to women and Scotch whiskey he seemed to be only a cynical, windy shadow of the dynamic force he had once been. To some Negroes, he was a white man in a black man's skin. "It is widely believed," writes Murray S. Stedman, Jr., rather mildly, in *Religion and Politics in America,* "that Rep. Adam Clayton Powell cannot at the same time fulfill the duties assigned to the Rev. Adam Clayton Powell. To many Americans, there is more than a touch of the medieval in the Harlem clergyman's blending of church and state in his person."[47] At his death in 1972 he was no longer either minister or lawmaker, having been turned out of office by his constituents and having resigned the pastorate of the church his father made great. Somewhere in his make-up were the seeds of his own destruction.

Quite a different figure was Martin Luther King, Jr., a black American Baptist minister from the South who forged a powerful force in the nation without ever forsaking his principles or his church. King, one of three children of a Baptist minister as highly regarded in the South as the elder Powell was in the North, was born in 1929 in Atlanta, where his father was pastor of the Ebenezer Baptist Church. After public schooling young King attended Morehouse College in Atlanta and won a theological degree from Crozer and a doctorate from Boston University. It was during his pastorate of the Dexter Avenue Baptist Church in

Montgomery, Ala., that King suddenly emerged as the most effective civil rights leader in the country. He was only 27 at the beginning of the 382-day bus boycott there in 1955, and it fell to him to organize the resistance. He did so, doggedly but calmly, rallying the blacks of the city despite arrest and the bombing of his house. He led sit-ins, protests and other demonstrations, clinging always to the principle of non-violence, exhorting his crowds as a passionate minister of the South preaches to a revival congregation. When the boycott ended, with a total victory for the blacks, King was clearly the figure to watch on the national civil rights scene.[48] He organized the Southern Christian Leadership Conference, headed it, and as a black man, a Baptist, a Christian and a human being, he showed up at rights protests in almost every part of the country. His "I Have a Dream" testimony (". . . I have a dream that one day this nation will rise up and live out the true meaning of its creed: 'We hold these truths to be self evident; that all men are created equal'. . . "[49]) before a crowd of 200,000 gathered at the Lincoln Memorial in Washington August 28, 1963, will long live in the annals of American oratory. To liberal Baptists one of the ironies of King's career was the degree to which he was disliked by white Southern Baptists. On the Sunday in March, 1965, when King led his faithful out of Selma, Ala., in the march toward Montgomery, a group of reporters heard the minister of the leading Baptist church in Montgomery pray, in a broadcast sermon, that God would deliver Alabama of the "pestilence" of the marchers; a short while later, from the steps of the Brown Memorial Church in Selma, King prayed to the same God for His blessings on the protest undertaking.[50] By then, of course, King had already won the Nobel Peace Prize (1964), which says something of the regard in which he was held in the world community, and only a few years later, on April 4, 1968, he would be assassinated on a Memphis motel balcony — which says something else entirely.

In *Black Religion,* Joseph R. Washington tried to explain the secret of King's enormous appeal. Writing before the assassination, he said, ". . . King is an outstanding example of the Baptist preacher. He has that Baptist hum which makes what is said only as important as how it is said. The key to being a successful

Baptist preacher is being able to speak at once as a philosopher and a man of religion, without distinguishing between the two. This is accomplished by using a tone of voice which so absorbs one's audience in emotion that anything which is said is cushioned."[51] Without doubt, King had all the equipment necessary to do the job he set out to do. And he had much more — things reminiscent of Gandhi and Tom Paine and the prophets of the Old Testament. Without doubt, he is one of the finest products to date of the black Baptists of America, and his like will not soon be seen again.

Chapter Thirteen: Baptist Schizophrenia

The organization of the black Baptists into churches, associations and conventions of their own was in truth a relief to the white Baptists of America, because otherwise the whites would not have known what to do with their black brothers. In the South a segregated society had evolved, and the separation occurring in public transport, restaurants, domicile, schools, at water fountains and restrooms, at public beaches and places of amusement was complete. Few Southerners after the Civil War could have accepted the idea that a separation occurring six days of the week should not be extended to the seventh. When the blacks withdrew from their secondary role in the white churches to form their own, they were encouraged and in some degree aided. In the North black Baptists formed into congregations of their own not out of necessity but out of desire, and for a time Baptists across the nation were able to submerge their long-time preoccupation with the Negro in denominational matters that seemed more pressing — as in the drives for orthodoxy in the pulpits and classrooms, the wars against demon rum and the fierce assaults on modernism, Darwinism and assorted evils ranging from card-playing, gambling and motion pictures to the wearing of lipstick, rouge and fingernail polish.

As the great fundamentalist controversy began to wane in the Twenties, however, it suddenly dawned upon the American conscience that the black citizen, though emancipated in body, was still a slave to prejudice, economic exploitation and inequality before the law. Baptists tended to view these things in the light of their regional heritage: the Southern Baptist had withdrawn his fellowship from the Northern churches over the institution of slavery; he had shed his blood in its defense, and he had been forced to submit to vengeful reconstruction when he could not perpetuate his view by force of arms. The Northern Baptist, on the other hand, had leaned toward abolition, had just as joyfully rushed to battle to extinguish the Southern evil, and had opened his territory — if not his heart — to the freedmen. By tradition that has not yet been widely expunged, the Southern church looked upon the Negro as an inferior, admissible to the white sanctuary only on terms which clearly preserved the master-menial relationship. To this day the average Southern Baptist, honestly upright and God-fearing, is able to read his Bible, attend his church and say his prayers without relenting in his advocacy of segregation. To suggest to him that as a Christian he is a walking paradox is to give serious offense. The Northern churches, although content with the ghettoization of the black, liked to think of themselves as the friend and possibly the savior of the chattel. Thus rooted in slavery a schizoid attitude toward the black endured in the Baptist church.

From the black point of view, the trouble was not in the Baptist church alone but in the whole white Christian community. The black historian Carter G. Woodson, writing in 1921 in *The History of the Negro Church,* said that "the white people of this country are not interested in the real mission of Christ. In the North the church has surrendered to the capitalistic system and developed into an agency seeking to assuage the pains of those suffering from the very economic evils which the institution has not the courage to attack. In the southern portion of the United States, the white churches have degenerated into perfunctory machines engaged in the service of deceiving the multitude with

179

the doctrine that the Anglo-Saxon, being superior to other races by divine ordination, may justly oppress them to maintain its supremacy and that the principles of Jesus are exemplified in the lives of these newly-chosen people of God when they permit their so-called inferiors to eat the crumbs let fall by those whom their idol god has carefully selected as the honor guests at the feast. If the humble Nazarene appeared there disturbing the present caste system, he would be speedily lynched as he was in Palestine."[1]

Twenty-five years later, in 1946, the president of Atlanta's Morehouse College, Dr. Benjamin E. Mays, saw little change. "I would tremble for the Christian cause," he said, "if 50 Negroes were to enter an average local church in this country on a Sunday morning and ask to become members. Fundamentally we are afraid. . . to practice the Christian religion."[2]

But although it might not have been apparent in the part of the country familiar to Dr. Mays, there had been change in the church, in the Baptist church, too, and it began with the kind of violence envisioned by Woodson for the Nazarene. In 1922 a Northern Baptist resolution condemned the subjection of the black to physical atrocity. "All good citizens, North and South," the convention said, "deplore lawlessness in the form of lynching and mob violence in the treatment of Negroes and all unchristian acts as well as illegal discrimination of race against race."[3] On into the Thirties and Forties the Baptists of the North wrestled repeatedly with the degradation of the black, urging equal rights and equal protection for all citizens, opposing forced segregation and discriminatory laws, anti-racial organizations and unfair labor tactics, and, by 1944, dedicating themselves to a policy of expansion without discrimination.[4] When in 1952 the convention went on record as favoring unsegregated churches, there were already 232 black churches with a membership of 45,000 affiliated with the organization, and Negroes were attending white Baptist churches of the North in 22 states. What the convention set forth as policy the local churches to a large degree accepted, and in the last decade, as the American Baptist Convention, the churches of the North have crusaded actively for individual and governmental action in the areas of housing, employment, education, and the eradication of all nuances of discrimination.

Typical of the resolutions approved by the convention in the last ten years are these, given in condensed form:[5]

Acceptance of "the basic affirmation that in Christ God has broken down the wall between all men and the barriers between races, cultures, nations and classes have been removed."

Recognition of "the irony that the divisions of the world are often mirrored in the divisions of the churches."

Reaffirmation that "the church has a responsibility to be open to all in the community without regard to class."

Support for the agents of change which may bring about an inclusive world community.

A call on members to support "open occupancy" in housing through personal practice and a recommendation that they "refuse to participate in panic selling" when persons of another race become neighbors.

Recognition that "any form of segregation based on race is contrary to the gospel of Jesus Christ and is incompatible with the doctrine of man and with the nature of the church of Christ. Whenever and wherever Christians, individually or collectively, practice segregation by action or inaction, we betray Christ and the fellowship which bears His name."

A "confession" that "un-Christian racial attitudes and conformity to the unjust mores of secular society have produced segregated churches which have failed to challenge unjust practices in the world."

A resolve to "continue to strengthen citizens in Southern states who are working quietly and prayerfully for the peaceful acceptance of civil rights in their communities."

An assertion that "the racial crisis we face as a nation often requires the support of Christians by dramatic acts of non-violent demonstration to arouse the nation to end injustices."

A determination to oppose segregation in country clubs, sororities, fraternities, service clubs, organizations of property owners, cemeteries and all inclusive groups.

A call to all American Baptist city, state and national organizations "to make sure that all offices (including the ministry), staff positions and lay leadership are open to all qualified persons without regard to race."

181

An affirmation of the defensibility of "black power," which read: "At this moment in our nation's history the cry of 'black power,' with its varied and conflicting meanings has served to call attention to the hidden as well as open, the subtle as well as violent ways by which 'white power' has been used to keep Negroes powerless in our nation's major political, economic, social and religious structures, with the resultant indignities to one-tenth of our population. Our faith impells us to reject the double standard which makes it a virtue for white men to use power, but makes it a vice for Negroes or other American minority groups to advocate the use of that same power."

These forthright positions taken by the Northern Baptists on the race issue have encouraged black churches to affiliate with the convention and black churchmen to attend the white churches of the North. The largest single addition of blacks to the convention came in May, 1971, when 131 Southern congregations, 110 of them predominantly Negro and 11 mostly white, were voted into membership at the annual meeting in Minneapolis. Those admitted came from 14 Southern states, and Dr. J. B. Henderson, pastor of a black church in Norfolk, Va., said the churches had declined to join the Southern Baptist Convention because it offered "only tokenism."[6] The new bloc, which corresponds for the South with regional groupings of American Baptists in the Northern, Central and Western states, Henderson called the "first thoroughly integrated Baptist organization to encompass the South."

The integration of the Northern convention has created a few problems, some of which reflect the new mood of black militancy. Before the annual convention in Boston in May, 1968, a group styling itself the Black Churchmen of the American Baptist Convention presented a list of demands which had all the earmarks of an ultimatum. The demands included: (a) the right of veto over all appointments to committees, boards and commissions operated by the convention; (b) the employment of additional blacks on the convention administrative staff; (c) the creation of the position, Associate General Secretary for Urban Ministries, to be filled by a black; (d) the employment of Negroes as executives of state conventions and city agencies and the calling of pastors without regard to color; (e) a program to double the enrollment of blacks in the 27 Convention-supported colleges and universities, with guarantees of financial aid to such students; (f) reorganization of the denomination's news media with the employment of blacks at policy-making levels; (g) the contribution to the Southern Christian Leadership Conference of all funds collected as a memorial to the late Dr. Martin Luther King, who had been an American Baptist minister; (h) placing under black direction all convention personnel working in black communities; (i) withdrawal of all convention funds on deposit with financial institutions practicing racial discrimination; (j) the pledging of 10 per cent of the convention's investment portfolio as a credit guarantee for new black businesses, and (k) the election of a black as president of the convention.[7] The General Council of the convention, meeting in advance of the formal sessions, reacted sympathetically to the black demands, in particular those having to do with education and the support of the SCLC, now headed by Dr. Ralph Abernathy, another American Baptist minister. It also said there would be no objection to the election of a black president if a candidate could rally sufficient support. On the assembly floor one minister announced that he was pulling his church out of the convention, and a minority of messengers banded together as the Group Concerned for Democratic Process deplored the attempt by the blacks to secure a favored status. Direct collision was avoided, however, and the convention adjourned on a note of harmony without surrender to the black ultimatum but also without seriously offending the Negro members.

While it would be inexact to say that every American Baptist church everywhere adheres scrupulously to convention policy or faithfully avoids all overtones of racial discrimination, the denomination by and large has compiled an excellent record in civil rights and has the respect of the moderate element of the black community. The story of the Southern Baptists, still mired in the morass of the past, is totally different — at least at the practicing local level, which is the true test. The involvement of the Southern church in the civil rights struggle began gingerly in 1929 with convention passage of an anti-lynch resolution affirming unalterable opposition to mob violence and expressing faith in orderly court processes and the impartial administration of justice.

183

Various versions of this same sentiment were put through the convention in 1930, 1931, 1933, 1934, 1935, 1936, and 1937, and in a slightly more affirmative mood the convention in 1939 pledged its support of efforts to correct racial inequities in the distribution of school funds, the administration of justice and the wages paid Negro workmen. In the early Forties the convention promised to attempt to cultivate interracial goodwill so as to eliminate frictions, bitterness and injustice, and on one occasion the convention seemed to descry an abatement of racial misunderstanding.[9]

Not until 1947 did the resolutions of the Southern church take on a specific ring. In a statement that year which for Southerners was rather bold the convention pledged "to think of the Negro as a person and treat him accordingly" and to "strive as individuals to conquer all prejudice and eliminate from our speech terms of contempt and from our conduct actions of ill-will." The messengers also promised to "teach our children that prejudice is un-Christian and that good will and helpful deeds are the duty of every Christian toward all men of all races."[10] The resolution stopped far short of advocating open church membership, however, and indeed it was impossible in many Southern associations to get that idea considered.

In 1946, for example, the North Carolina Baptist State Convention, meeting in Asheville, carelessly approved a Social Service Commission report saying that the "segregation of believers holding to the same tenets of faith because of color or social status into racial or class churches is a denial of the New Testament affirmation of the equality of all believers at the foot of the Cross and alien to the spirit of Christ, the Head of the Church." That it was passed carelessly is demonstrated by the fact that it went through unanimously, and when news of the action moved out over the press wires into the dark corners of the state a rain of protesting telegrams poured in on the messengers. The following day the convention recanted; the whole clause relating to the equality of believers quoted above was deleted, and for a section advocating voting rights for blacks a weak job opportunity plea was substituted.[11] Only occasionally was a stronger stand permitted, but there were exceptions. In 1946 the Georgia Baptist

Convention, prodded by a minister who had been a Navy chaplain, indorsed a resolution urging "all Christian people of Georgia, particularly Baptists, (to) speak forth with every ounce of energy by word, deed and thought against the so-called patriotic groups which... claim race superiority, which is neither American nor Christian." The resolution also urged that "no man shall be discriminated against because of race, creed or color."[12] The moving spirit behind the action was the Rev. Joseph A. Rabun, after his military service pastor of the McRae Baptist Church. His leading member was Eugene Talmadge — who for many years was the symbol of white racist demagoguery in the South.

In the Fifties the high-water mark of the Southerners at the Convention level occurred in 1954, three weeks after the Supreme Court had outlawed segregation in the public schools. Meeting in St. Louis, the Baptists approved a statement, in a vote of 9,000 to 100, which said; "We recognize the fact that this Supreme Court decision is in harmony with the constitutional guarantee of equal freedom to all citizens, and with the Christian principles of equal justice and love for all men." The convention called on "Christian statesmen and leaders in our churches to use their leadership in positive thought and planning to the end that this crisis in our national history shall not be made the occasion for new and bitter prejudices."[13] In keeping with that resolution, the convention's president, Dr. J. W. Storer, pastor of the First Baptist Church of Tulsa, Okla., told the messengers that "as Christians we are to love all men regardless of color, even as God does... Since the Supreme Court has made its ruling it is the duty of all Christians to respect that ruling and pray that God shall guide its implementing within the framework of mutual understanding and consideration."[14] Dr. A. C. Miller, head of the Christian Life Commission, which was to become the cutting edge for progress in the Southern convention, told the assembly that the court decision, repugnant to much of Dixie, was "the inevitable result of social progress based on the Christian teaching that all men are included in the love of God and have dignity and worth in the sight of God."[15]

It was the Christian Life Commission which in the following year won convention approval of a report which said: "We do not feel that an easy solution (to the race problem) can be found. But

185

we cannot wave aside this issue on the pretext that it is exclusively a political question. Nor can we accept the claim of some that any action by our churches or conventions on this question does violence to the scriptural principle of separation of church and state. The spiritual and moral responsibilities involved in this question far outweigh the political aspects of it. In this great day of world awakening the mighty arm of God must not be hindered by political expediency nor by the racial exclusiveness of those who follow Him."[16.]

Even though the convention had come a long way from white exclusiveness, there were still widespread signs of Christian timidity. One of these came to national attention in 1963, shortly after the bombing of a Negro Baptist church in Birmingham, Ala., which took the lives of four young girls. An administrative subcommittee of the convention's executive board, urged to take some notice of the outrage in the name of Southern Baptists, floundered and failed. It had had the opportunity to make a significant expression, because Charles A. Trentham, of Knoxville, Tenn., had offered a resolution which read: "To the pastor and members of the Sixteenth Street Baptist Church of Birmingham, Ala. We, your fellow Baptists and members of the executive committee of the Southern Baptist Convention in session Sept. 18, 1963, join you in mourning your dead and lamenting the tragedy which lies heavily upon every Christian conscience in the bombing of your church. We would pledge our prayers and our energetic efforts in healing the rift between the races. Furthermore, we would encourage our people to contribute money toward the restoration of your building." The committee rejected that resolution in favor of a pious declaration generalizing about racial strife and not mentioning the Birmingham bombing at all. A dozen Baptist editors present for the meeting were forbidden to report the details of the deliberations, and for the most part they meekly complied. Not so the independent magazine *Christian Century*, which accused the Baptists of "adroitly ducking the issue" and asked, "Is the leadership of the Southern Baptist Convention afraid to face up to the racial crisis in the South? Evidently so . . . "[17]

The following year, 1964, the Southern Baptist Convention celebrated the Baptist Jubilee at Atlantic City, N.J., by holding its annual session concurrently with the American, Seventh Day, North American and Negro Baptists, and while the Northern churches in one part of the city passed resolutions advocating the withholding of church loans from segregated congregations and the insertion of fair-employment clauses in all construction contracts, the Southerners resisted even the mildest recommendations asking an open door policy in the churches.[18]

But the Southern church, as a body, could not forever ignore the march of progress or defend its reluctance to accept the brotherhood of man. Under the urging of liberal leaders like Foy Valentine, the Texas minister who is executive secretary of the Christian Life Commission, the 8,000 messengers to the 1965 convention acknowledged that "our Southern Baptist witness for Jesus Christ continues to be challenged more seriously and more fundamentally by the racial crisis than by any other ideological movement or moral problem in our time." They agreed that "the ultimate solution of the racial problems lies on distinctively spiritual grounds" and that "what the New Testament says is far more demanding than what the Civil Rights law says." And then the Southern Baptists, in a great outpouring of Christian humility, made their most penetrating declaration of modern times: "We. . . confess before God and the world," they said, "that we have been guilty of the sin of conformity to the world, that we have often followed the vain traditions of men instead of the mind of Christ, and that our silence and fear have all too frequently made us stumbling blocks instead of stepping stones in the area of human relations. In a spirit of true repentance, we prayerfully rededicate ourselves to the Christian ministry of reconciliation between Negroes and whites and between segregationists and integrationists. We recognize anew that the churches of which we are members are not *our* churches but *Christ's* churches and we acknowledge His complete lordship over them as well as over us, so that we shall undertake to bear witness to the truth that the doors of salvation, fellowship and ministry are open to all men and closed to none. We earnestly hope that we will begin to see more and more Southern Baptists involved actively and redemptively in seeking specific cures for such specific racial ailments as personal prejudice, unfair housing practice, discriminatory employment, unequal justice under the law, and denial of voting rights. We hereby affirm our purpose to do whatever we can, with God's help, beginning now, to undergird our Christian witness in missions and evangelism at home and abroad with an uncompromised and uncompromising testimony at the point of race."[19]

Conservative forces tried to throw out the declaration but succeeded only in adding a final paragraph noting that "this convention of Baptists recognizes the authority and competence of every local church affiliated with the Southern Baptist Convention in dealing with any question, social or otherwise." And that, of course, is the crux of the Baptist racial problem, because in practice it is the local church that demonstrates the depth of Baptist commitment to any principle.

The conservatives, since Dallas, also have been trying to dismantle the Christian Life Commission, which dreams up this language they find offensive, but thus far the convention has supported the commission. Valentine, its executive, said after the Dallas convention that he was not "suggesting that we lightly cast aside our cherished traditions. I am suggesting that we throw them aside with great vigor wherever they violate the spirit of the Bible." Valentine is not essentially a social reformer; he is a deeply dedicated Baptist minister whose objections to racism are based on what he finds in his Bible. "We need to abolish racial discrimination in our country and our churches not because of a clause in the Constitution or because of the Communist challenge," he said, "nor yet because we need the votes of the watching world. We need to conquer race prejudice because it is a sin against almighty God and a rejection of the precious blood of Jesus Christ." Southern Baptists, he added, "are abandoning the culture which has had us very much captive, and we are abandoning it in favor of Christ."[20]

The action of the Convention has had some trickle-down impact. In November, 1965, Virginia Baptists convening in Richmond, the capital of the Confederacy, were as forthright as the national convention had been. "We acknowledge before God," they said, "our partnership of guilt in the long, dark night of injustice and discrimination. Under the cloak of moderation, we have maintained a conspiracy of silence, while extremists at both

188

ends of this issue have set the tone of debate and action."[21] They were brave words for the Old Dominion.

The year 1965 was a turning point in convention policy at the national level, because since that time the assembly has regularly stated its concern over segregationist practices. At Houston in 1968 the messengers, admitting that the church had "come far short of our privilege in Christian brotherhood," voted to "personally accept every Christian as a brother beloved in the Lord and welcome to the fellowship of faith and worship every person irrespective of race or class."[22] In Denver in 1970 the convention applauded warmly when told by Dr. Billy Graham, the Baptist crown jewel in the field of interdenominational evangelism, that they should join hands with the blacks. "They need us, but we need them more," Graham said, and the convention did not deny it.[23] A few hours earlier the convention had voted ten minutes to an unheralded group of black students from Metropolitan State College in Denver to present their views. Jeff Thomas, black spokesman for the group, confronted the messengers with a clenched fist and a prayer describing the Southern Baptists as "bigoted," but he failed to get a rise out of the convention.[24]

Racial accommodation at the convention level, slowly as it has moved, has not been reflected in the local churches, however, and today no more than 10 per cent of the 34,000 congregations affiliated with the convention are integrated; the ones which have admitted Negroes or are willing to do so are for the most part not located in the South. The vast majority of Southern Baptist churches pitched on Southern soil have not only resisted but have actively opposed open membership, to the extent of physically barring entry to would-be black visitors. That ugly manifestation, surely not Christian or Christ-like or even humane, is an open scandal in Christendom.

Six years ago, in the January, 1967, issue of *Atlantic,* Marshall Frady, Atlanta-based newspaper and magazine correspondent who is the son of a Baptist minister, wrote that "any indictment. . . of Christianity's posture in the South during the last ten years of moral crisis is inevitably an indictment of the Southern Baptist church. The fact is that by its very structure. . . the Southern Baptist church has had the effect of reflecting and confirming local prejudices rather than challenging them."[25] The trail-blazing declarations approved by the convention Frady called "sporting resolutions. . . that vaguely resembled conscience-wrestling,"[26] and to show their ineffectiveness he recalled what was happening concurrently at the church doors: "Throughout the anguished course of the Negro revolution in the South, one would frequently open the Monday morning paper to find a picture of a dozen or so funereal-faced deacons standing shoulder-to-shoulder on the steps of some small brick church, all of them bareheaded, squinting a little in the Sunday morning sunshine, mouths clamped tightly shut, arms unanimously folded (usually hiding their hands), their blank gazes fixed just an inch or two over the heads of a small delegation of Negroes clustered on the sidewalk below them. It was one of the most curious spectacles produced by the most profound moral crisis of our time."[27]

Frady's portrait was not overdrawn. The cruel tableau he described was repeated over and over in the South, sometimes erupting into shoving and pushing matches at the church entrance while the white congregation worshipped nervously inside. That more of these painful incidents did not occur is the result of the forbearance of the blacks rather than the Christian brotherhood of the whites, because scores of churches which were not challenged were prepared, almost eager, to bar entrance to the house of God.

Here and there a church with progressive leadership or under deep conviction over the intent of the scriptures did open its doors. Very often the barrier was first lowered in college towns, and then generally at the insistence of the young. Seven of ten Baptist churches are rural (although 61 per cent of the total membership is urban), and in the rural areas integration of the churches has hardly occurred at all. But in most large Southern cities there is at least one forward-looking church, and their example has been that open membership resulted neither in a great inpouring of blacks nor in painful disruption of the church. As early as 1945 the University Baptist Church of Austin, Texas, voted "to abandon separated seating forever." The first black member, admitted in 1950, came under peculiar circumstances. A non-commissioned black officer had approached the Austin pastor, Blake Smith, with a request for baptism when Smith was participating in a preaching mission in San Antonio. No Baptist church in that city would permit the use of its baptistry for such a purpose, and Smith was forced to baptize the soldier at midnight in the YMCA pool. Thereafter he asked his own church in Austin to admit the Negro to membership, a move which was speedily accepted. Since then young blacks from the University of Texas have joined, often taking leading roles in the choir and the Training Unions. In that church "race awareness has so faded that merit is recognized by everyone and the fact of color is scarcely mentioned."[28] Over the period of integration four families have withdrawn in protest.

Another Texas church, the First at Dallas, is pastored by Dr. W. A. Criswell, who was Southern Baptist Convention president in 1969 and 1970. Doctrinally Criswell is about as conservative as Baptists come in the Twentieth Century, and in the South segregation is most often championed by doctrinal mossbacks. Criswell, however, is not in that camp. Several years ago he told his members, "I stand in that pulpit to press an appeal for Jesus, for the gospel of the Son of God on the basis of what He has done to save us from our sin. . . I am done with the emptiness of an appeal to say it and to preach it and to fear that somebody of different pigment might accept it and come forward. . . Not in dramatics, not in fanfare, but in the spirit of Jesus, humbly, simply, the First Baptist Church of Dallas is now and forever a Philadelphian church of the open door. Anybody can come and may God bless him and attend him in the way as he comes. Our gospel shall be to all men everywhere."[29]

Criswell is, of course, in an extremely protected position. His stature among Southern Baptists is such that his tenure as a pastor is assured. But lesser ministers, when they themselves have not been outright segregationists, have failed to prod their brethren on the race issue simply out of fear of losing their jobs or out of concern for dissension. These ministers have followed, rather than led, their congregations, and lay Baptists have tended to shape their own spiritual lives, and that of their churches, after the prevailing attitudes of the community. In many churches of the South at the present moment the first question asked about a prospective new pastor is not "How does he stand on doctrine?"

but "How does he stand on race?" And if he is "right" on race it generally follows that his spiritual beliefs are acceptable. If he forthrightly acknowledges that he believes in integration he will not get the call — although that will not be the reason cited. And so many Southern Baptist ministers whose hearts are pure cannot bring their sentiments on race to articulation. Frady wrote of these men in the *Atlantic,* saying that "for them the past decade has been another kind of anguish — perhaps the loneliest kind. Isolated from civil rights workers in their communities, with a genuine and even passionate private identification with the Negro struggle, they have been men without a country, trying Sunday after Sunday to smuggle into the hearts of their congregations some sort of compassion, some sense of outrage and pity like their own, with an endless series of sermons about brotherhood and God's universal love for mankind, aware all the time that the instant they drop their abstractions they will most certainly lose their pulpit."[30]

The threat of dismissal is a real one. In Macon, Ga., in 1966 a Southern Baptist church within hailing distance of the campus of Baptist-supported Mercer University threw the pastor out when he protested the blockading of the church steps as a bar to Negro students.[31] Elsewhere pastors have been dismissed, and lay whites who favored integration have been hounded out of churches, harassed at home and even boycotted in their businesses. Ridiculous measures have been dredged up to prevent open membership. In Richmond in January, 1965 (the year Virginia Baptists confessed their "partnership of guilt" in "the long, dark night of injustice") the application of two blacks to join the First Baptist Church, one of the state's most influential, precipitated a lawsuit. The blacks, Abe Oshoniyi and Gideon S. Adegbile, were the sons of Baptist ministers in Nigeria — and thus associated with Southern Baptist mission programs abroad. After the church voted 755-540 to admit the two students, dissident deacons of the church provoked a court test on the basis of a forgotten 1827 constitution which reserved voting privileges to male members. The court rejected the minority petition. Pastor of the church at that time, and considerably agonized over the controversy, was Dr. Theodore F. Adams, former president of the Baptist World Alliance and one of the outstanding churchmen of this country.

192

To suppose that the decade of the Seventies has ushered in a new feeling of racial understanding in the Southern churches is erroneous. The battle is continuing, from church to church, and no skirmish is ever easily won. The division of the First Baptist Church of Birmingham, Ala., is illustrative. When the Rev. J. Herbert Gilmore accepted a call to the pastorate of that church in 1968, he did so with the understanding that there would be an active inner-city ministry and that membership would be open to all. In response to the appeal of the urban ministry Mrs. Winifred Bryant, a black, and her 11-year-old daughter, Twila, were converted and applied for membership in the church responsible for their salvation. A fierce battle broke out over their admission, entailing long business meetings lasting far into the night, and at one point the segregationists failed by only four votes in an attempt to fire the church staff. During part of the controversy Gilmore was absent in attendance at the Baptist World Alliance meeting in Japan. During his absence the racist forces tried to discredit him on the grounds that he held unscriptural views and that he had created congregational dissension. When in a standing vote the blacks were rejected as members, Dr. Gilmore resigned, saying, "I will not be pastor of a racist church." Three hundred members walked out in his support, withdrew from the First Church and formed the Baptist Church of the Covenant, with Mrs. Bryant and her daughter as charter members. In a letter to a friend afterward Dr. Gilmore wrote, "The hour is very late for us to set our house in order, both as a nation and as a church. Some of us, when we have the opportunity, have got to drive some nails in the coffin of racism."[32]

Reaction among Southern Baptists to the Birmingham eruption was generally condemnatory; but even in the expressions of regret there was concession that almost the same thing could happen anywhere in the South. Kenneth L. Chafin, of Atlanta, a former seminary professor who is now evangelism director of the Southern Baptist Home Mission Board and therefore quite close to the problem, acknowledged that "many of our churches are controlled by racists. . . When a great church in a great city is confronted by a little woman and a 10-year-old *(sic)* daughter who have been converted as a result of the church's ministry, and they (the church members) sit up until 3 in the morning, and by four votes finally agree not to fire the staff, we are not as far along as I thought."[33]

State Baptist papers were deluged with letters of outrage, some of them conceding that Birmingham goes by many names. In a letter to North Carolina's *Biblical Recorder,* W. D. Kiser, of Shelby, N. C., took note of warnings that Baptists should pray the Birmingham contagion did not reach their churches. "That means," he said, "that we will have to pray that no Negro family will ask for church membership; for I am convinced that in most of our churches the very same controversy would develop. Only the names, places and faces would be different. . . Could it be that since we Baptists became the 'Fat Cats' of the religious establishment in this area, that we have replaced *His* church with *our* church? Certainly in regard to our black neighbor we preach *His* love and practice *our* prejudices. Maybe the 'fullness of time' has come when God is crowding the churches (supposedly representing Him) into a corner and saying, 'Start practicing, or stop preaching'."[34]

Such criticism rarely provides learning or guidance for Southern Baptists. During the summer of 1970, Jim Cooley, a 23-year-old honor graduate of Davidson College and one-time student at Union Theological Seminary in New York, spent a few months working among Carolina blacks under the auspices of the Pilot Mountain Baptist Association. At the conclusion of his employment Cooley told a newspaper interviewer that he had come away from the experience with a realization of how deeply imbedded racism is within the churches. Alarmed by his remarks, his employers chose not to examine their validity but instead voted thereafter to screen applicants for summer jobs more carefully.[35]

To suggest that Southern Baptists are incapable of sustained and effective interracial ministry, however, would be erroneous. One of the most imaginative projects ever to be undertaken in the South in the cause of Christianity began in 1942 when Clarence Jordan and Martin England, both graduates of the Southern Baptist Theological Seminary and both ordained ministers, bought 440 acres of rundown land near Americus, Ga., 100 miles south of Atlanta, and founded Koinonia Farm.

Koinonia, the Greek New Testament's word for fellowship or community, was conceived as an interdenominational, interracial body of Christians banded together after the pattern of the early church as a living witness to the true meaning and spirit of the Jerusalem fellowship of believers. The members of the community would work the soil, produce enough to be self-sufficient, live in an atmosphere of humility and worship, and provide a ministry to the poor, the oppressed and the downtrodden. "Our real interest is more in the soul of Georgia than in the soil," Jordan explained.[36]

Over the years the size of the farm grew to 1,103 acres, and through scientific methods the soil was gradually improved to the extent that the property was valued at more than $150,000. Cash crops included peanuts, corn, cotton, goats, cattle, hogs and poultry, and one of the principal sources of revenue was from eggs sold at a neat roadside produce stand. The operation was conducted as a true cooperative, with all members sharing profits and reverses, all participating in the farm's basic mission of worship and ministry.

At first Negroes were related directly to the enterprise only as workers, but in 1955 those who wished to join were admitted as full members with the privilege of living in the farm compound. By 1956 about 60 people shared the premises, half of them children and 15 of them Negroes. Since the earliest days Koinonia's neighbors had viewed the farm with hostility and suspicion, but the introduction of Negroes to the common living quarters set off a round of terrorism, intimidation and boycott. Four times the roadside market was dynamited; hand-painted signs advertising Koinonia products were repeatedly ripped down; night after night shots were fired into the living quarters by night-riders; merchants refused to handle Koinonia produce and livestock; suppliers cut off their stores; insurance companies cancelled policies on Koinonia buildings, thereby wrecking the farm's credit; a feed dealer ordered by his parent firm to supply the Koinonians was subjected to a dynamiting; a cropdusting firm refused to treat Koinonia cotton, and local mills declined to gin it; the persecutors got an injunction prohibiting the farm from conducting an interracial summer youth camp (one farmer complained that the camp would breed immorality because the children might see live pigs born); and an

Americus Baptist church expelled the Koinonians as members. [37]

At the height of the persecutions in 1957, George Mathews, chairman of the Sumter County Commissioners, expressed to an interviewer the general attitude of the community toward the farm. "We got a good county here," he said, "and God knows we treat our niggers right. We aren't going to have a gang down here stirring up our Americus niggers. . . We got no room for people like them here, and we don't aim to have them around much longer." [38] Although this feeling of deep hatred appears to have been fairly general and the economic boycott complete, a visitor to the farm at about that same time found the spirit of its people unbroken. "Koinonia," he wrote, "seems to have struck its surrounding community with awe and dread, as though one of the schools of the prophets of the ancient Hebrews had appeared in their midst. . . The prophetic judgment which Koinonia exerts by continuing not only to exist but to present to its enemies the face of friendship, of forgiveness, of courageous affirmation of right human relations, is a wonderful and terrible thing at any time. But right at this time in Georgia it thunders as the voice of God thundered through Elisha before the prophets of Baal." [39] He found the farm community not a center of rabble-rousing racial agitation but "a church, and our difficulty in recognizing it as such comes about because we have forgotten what the church of the New Testament was really like. Koinonia is more profoundly moved by the living presence of Jesus Christ than by the spirit of any other person, living or dead. It remembers Him, seeks to persuade others to recall Him and strives to fulfill His ministry among men. It gathers for worship several times a week, and especially seeks the spirit of worship when it makes decisions concerning human relations. Prayer and rigorous discussion of the inner life are an unceasing occurrence. There is here a deep joy in Christian love toward each other and toward all men, especially enemies." [40]

Koinonia survived, and its example is living witness to the kind of imaginative Christian enterprise Baptists are capable of when they approach the challenge of race and injustice in the spirit of the Master. Unfortunately that is not the tactic of the average Southern Baptist, most of whom are far more willing to contribute to the conversion of the black in the jungles of Africa than they are to accept the black from the jungles of America. This attitude has made the Baptist Church of the South the great derelict in human relations, because if the churches of Dixie were truly dedicated to Christian love and understanding, the corrosive influences of bigotry could be eradicated almost immediately. In the two decades just past, race has been the single greatest challenge of the Southern church; ministers have retreated before it, and laymen have allowed their prejudices to drown their Christianity. It is not a record in which Southern Baptists generally can take pride.

Chapter Fourteen: Quo Vadis?

In a paper prepared for Baptist teachers in the spring of 1970, W. C. Fields, an official of the Executive Committee of the Southern Baptist Convention, attempted to see the place of the Baptist church in the decade of the Seventies. "We will be embroiled, inevitably and willy-nilly," he wrote, "in the issues afflicting all sectors of religious life in America today: conservatism vs. liberalism, evangelism vs. social action, tradition vs. innovation, youth vs. age, institutionalism vs. the unstructured, the Establishment vs. the rebels, right wing vs. left wing, authority vs. freedom, unity vs. diversity, doctrine vs. activism, separatism vs. ecumenism, and a host of others."[1] He was optimistic that Baptists will confront these problems squarely, emerging with a deeper and broader spiritual life. "Our confrontation with the overriding issues of the day — war, crime, poverty, injustice, overpopulation, pollution, an unregenerate nature in man, and others — may very well bring us out of a wilderness of isolation and egocentricity into a new day with a new sense of mission and message."[2] He recognized that Baptists often are regarded as "reactionaries, mossbacks, anti-intellectuals and antediluvians" but said new

198

approaches are possible within the church because "a growing throng of people throughout the denomination is concerned with integrity, genuineness, warmth in human relationships, openness, freedom to be onself under God, and readiness to move in new directions."[3] He was aware of Baptist liabilities — "reluctance to change, an orientation to a Southern folk-faith which confuses culture with Christianity, preoccupation with the past, a structure which sometimes makes us slow to respond" — but he saw in the church a number of "truly great" assets: "a large and energetic fellowship of believers, a long-standing commitment to missions and evangelism, a willingness to take courageous stands; a structure that places responsibility on the individual church member and gives him opportunity to exercise his own initiative; a long history of remarkable cohesiveness in spite of a loose-knit organization; skill in cooperative work in the midst of vast divergence . . . These are elements of strength on which we can build."[4]

Fields speaks for Nashville, a propaganda and promotional center unrivalled outside Madison Avenue. He is one of the exhorters, the whippers, the cosmeticians. But he knows his people intimately, seriously shares their concerns, and is fully aware in his optimism that the church speaks with more than one voice. A voice which may seem at variance was raised at the 1971 Southern Baptist Convention in St. Louis, when Dr. Carl E. Bates, pastor of the First Baptist Church of Charlotte, N.C., and incumbent president of the convention, told the 15,000 messengers that "many pastors and churches are sick of each other, and this carnal nausea has turned many of our church-houses into nothing more than irrelevant grandeur." A generation of Baptists has been reared, Bates said, "who are almost totally ignorant of our doctrine."[5] And yet, despite this dour view, Bates, a one-time bellhop converted while reading a Gideon Bible, would be the last to characterize the Baptists as a dying or totally irrelevant sect. At the convention he chaired, for example, the Baptists quite unexpectedly gave their approval to the concept of legalized abortion—specifically in cases of "rape, incest, clear evidence of fetal deformity and carefully ascertained evidence of the likelihood of damage to the emotional, mental and physical health of the mother."[6]

The many voices of the Baptist church sometimes support the view that it is backward in outlook. In November, 1970, the

Baptist State Convention of Tennessee sent a directive to the board of trustees of Carson-Newman College asking the rescission of a new policy allowing dancing on the campus. During the debate, Mrs. James W. Adams, of Memphis, argued that the decision should be left up to the students, who she said have a right to make up their own minds about the propriety of dancing. She was booed roundly, and a Knoxville minister, the Rev. John Buell, reprimanded her with a pastoral assertion that any man who claims he can dance with a woman and keep his mind pure "is either less than a man, or a liar." Despite a warning from M. T. Harris, a Nashville layman, that they would make Tennessee Baptists look "ridiculous in the eyes of the world" the Buell forces carried the day, inflicting upon the Baptist students of a Baptist college the Baptist social standards of 50 years ago.[7]

Baptists are not always as unfeeling for changing times and changing life styles. Almost concurrently with the Carson-Newman uproar, a Baptist church across from a shopping center in Newton, Mass., found its property invaded by hippies. Swarms of young long-hairs, of both sexes, set up camp on the lawn and defied the church to remove them. After a great deal of discussion during which some old-time members withdrew from the congregation, the church decided to call for police help only to correct flagrant violations of the law (as in the use of narcotics). Beyond that the church launched a ministry to the hippies, employing a trained counselor to work and pray with the young people, many of whom were rootless and troubled.[8] The church probably would have been legally justified in having the campers removed on the grounds of trespass. But compassionate members argued successfully that in the unwanted encroachment of these young people the church had been challenged to Christian action. Elsewhere Baptist churches of the North and South, white and black, have been involved in drug programs, poverty relief, ghetto day care, draft counseling, alcoholism prevention, unwed mother referrals and other aspects of contemporary problems.

This is not to say that Baptists, through the unique washing of their linen in public, never look ridiculous. They frequently do, and never more than in the fundamentalist paralysis that is endemic to almost every Southern Baptist assembly. A case in point is the controversy which raged ten years ago over a book, *The Message of Genesis,* written by Prof. Ralph Elliott, then on the faculty of the Midwestern Baptist Theological Seminary in Kansas City. In the book Elliott made what *Newsweek* called "a mild, cautious argument for symbolic interpretation of Old Testament stories like Adam's fall and Noah's flood," and even that tippy-toed questioning of orthodoxy enraged Baptist literalists. They first castigated the 54 members of the Sunday School Board for allowing the book to be published through Broadman Press, the vigorous house which the board controls. The board responded that the publication was "in keeping with the historic Baptist principle of the freedom of the individual to interpret the Bible for himself." That reminder had no impact on the anti-Elliott forces, strong in Texas, Oklahoma, Kansas and Missouri. In a naked bid for control of the seminaries, they ordered the theology schools to check on the "orthodoxy" of faculty members. When Elliott refused to repudiate his book, he was fired by the Midwestern trustees. Elliott called his dismissal a "horrible blow — a setback for theological education," and straightway accepted a call to the pastorate of a Kansas City Baptist church which saw nothing sinister in his beliefs.[9]

Elliott's persecution made the Baptist convention seem to be a seething hotbed of paranoid inquisitors, but the resulting bad press in no way diverted the literalists from sniffing out heresy — particularly as it applied to the first book of the Bible. At issue at this moment is the initial volume of the new *Broadman Bible Commentary,* the most ambitious project ever undertaken by the Baptist publishing house. After ten years of planning and the assembly of a company of consultants, advisers and writers "carefully selected for their reverent Christian faith and their knowledge of Bible truth," Broadman had the first of the twelve-volume series ready for release late in 1969. The whole undertaking had been under the general editorship of Clifton J. Allen, a Baptist of impeccable credentials and wide esteem who had resigned his long-time post as editorial secretary of the Sunday School Board to devote full time to the commentary.

When advance copies of the commentary were circulated, however, the literalists recoiled in horror, and before 13,000 messengers to the 1970 convention in Denver in June, 1970, the commentary was denounced as "a denial of the word of God" and a "pernicious attack" on the infallibility of the scripture. In a rude, rowdy debate Dr. Herschel H. Hobbs, pastor of the First Baptist Church of Oklahoma City, Okla., former convention president and a member of the commentary staff, tried to defend the study on the basis of enlightened scholarship only to be greeted with derisive hoots and cries of "Hogwash!" "You can holler me down," Hobbs roared, "but you cannot holler down the truth I am speaking." The upshot was that the first volume was ordered withdrawn,[10] in a paper ballot which showed 5,394 for suppression and 2,170 against.

The passages so gravely offending the Southern messengers would hardly cause a ripple in most Christian churches. In an introductory essay John I. Durham, associate professor of Old Testament Interpretation at Southeastern Baptist Theological Seminary, had written that study of Biblical sources "has led most contemporary scholars to the view that the Pentateuch known to us, is neither a unity nor, when considered as a whole, a composition of Moses."[11] This, of course, does not set well with the traditionalists, who have always been suspicious of "the higher criticism" of a scholarly community which they hold to be theologically bankrupt. Even more distressing to the conservatives were several passages in the Genesis commentary written by G. Henton Davies, principal of Regent's Park College in Oxford, England. In particular the opposition objected to a discussion of Abraham's near-sacrifice of his son, Isaac, in honor of God. "Did God make, would God in fact have made, such a demand upon Abraham or anybody else, except himself?" Davies asked. "There are those of course who would accept the command literally. Our answer, however, is no. Indeed what Christian or humane conscience could regard such a command as coming from God?"[12]

Some of the messengers also declared objection to the commentary's handling of Adam and Eve and the Flood, but an examination of the text at those points seems to give little ground for conservative complaint. It appears certain that the literalists had some deeper reservations. One was that Davies was not only non-American but also non-Baptist. His selection as writer of the opening commentary, dealing with a book as controversial as Genesis, does seem to have been a lapse in psychology on the part of Allen and his colleagues. Another consideration may be that Allen had been associated with some of the more liberal pronouncements of the Christian Life Commission. Some of the delegates at Denver had tried — and failed — five times to clip that commission's wings. The commentary therefore made a perfect substitute target.

Whatever the case, the action of the 1970 convention was affirmed in 1971, and Broadman was told to get a new writer for Genesis.[13] In the meantime the entire press run of the first volume — except for a few bootlegged copies — has been locked up in a Broadman warehouse, a British edition is being sold widely in the United States, and the whole Broadman project has been sabotaged.

Following the 1970 action the Religious Publishers Group of the American Book Publishers Council protested the Baptist action, saying that "as publishers of religious books, we are committed to the proposition that it is our responsibility to make available the widest diversity of views and expressions including those which are unorthodox or unpopular. To suppress or bowdlerize a book on the ground that it questions traditional thought is to deny the value of thought itself. Those who would resort to such methods threaten our democracy by limiting the freedom of citizens to change society by exercising their right to choose widely from conflicting opinions offered freely to them."[14]

Argument over the state of perfection of the Bible is always perilous in Southern Baptist circles, as Dr. William E. Hull, dean of the School of Theology at Southern Baptist Theological Seminary, discovered shortly after the Denver convention when he wrote an article on that subject for *The Baptist Program*.[15] He said it is not really "wise" to call the Bible infallible because it was set down by fallible men in versions which no longer survive. Furthermore, "grotesque perversions of Scripture are possible if we glibly assume that everything in the Bible is to be taken as absolute truth without asking whether human factors are also present for which allowances must be made." And anyway, he said, "the fate of the Bible does not hang in the balance as we deliberate. The reality of the Scripture is not altered by anything we may say about it. Whatever our confessions, they cannot make the Bible any more or less true than it always has been. What is at stake is not the authenticity of the Bible but the integrity and credibility of our witness to it."

Hull's discussion seemed perfectly reasonable to reasonable men, but reason does not always infect Baptists. George Smith, pastor of Carmel Baptist Church in Meridian, Miss., wrote the editor that "your magazine has never appealed to me very much, and after the article by William E. Hull I don't care for it at all. Therefore would you please take my name off your mailing list. This will save you postage, and me the trouble of disposing of your trash." From Roy Batchelder, pastor of the First Baptist Church in Stilwell, Okla., came the comment: "It was with bitterness of soul, shame, and disgust that I read the article by Dr. Hull. I could expect it from some one of the dead, liberal, modernistic denominations of which we have many, but coming from the dean of the School of Theology of one of our seminaries, it is almost unbelievable . . . Dr. Hull can go on teaching that the Bible is not infallible, that it is full of errors, but I will continue to tell my people that they can depend on the Bible, that it doesn't contain any errors, that it is all the word of God, *every word of it*." And from the same direction Laurence Justice, pastor of the Kentucky Avenue Baptist Church in Oklahoma City, wrote: "I hope that you will repent and pray that the Lord will be able to repair the damage that has been done."[16]

Any departure from orthodoxy can spell trouble for a Baptist or a Baptist agency. F. Eugene Garman, a graduate of Midwestern Baptist Theological Seminary, was ousted from the membership of the First Baptist Church in Zion, Ill., after he argued that the Bible is not infallible. The church vote ostensibly was aimed not at his argument but at the dissension he was thought to have aroused.[17] Almost concurrently, the Christian Life Commission got into hot water for sponsoring a seminar on "authentic morality" in Atlanta in which the speakers included Julian Bond, the black Georgia legislator; Joseph Fletcher, an Episcopal theologian; Anson Mount, public affairs director for *Playboy* magazine; and Dr. David Mace, a Baptist sociologist who is trying to popularize sex as a thoroughly wholesome Christian interest.[18] The commission was denounced, editors of church papers condemned the seminar and some churches withdrew their support of convention programs in protest.

But what must be remembered in all this tempest is that there were Baptists on all sides of these issues, that Ralph Elliott had his defenders, that the *Broadman Commentary* is thoroughly acceptable to a large number of churchmen, that Dean Hull was applauded by as many ministers as condemned him, and that the Christian Life Commission is still in business and not likely to go out.

From all of the foregoing, it must be obvious that it is impossible to make any generalization about where Baptists stand as a body — except on those few basic premises of common doctrine: the authority of the Bible (whether infallible or not) as the sole rule of faith and practice; the responsibility, through his own intercession, of every man to God; the autonomy of the individual church and its body of believers; the ordinances of the Lord's Supper and baptism; and the separation of church and state. On all other issues there are almost as many points of view as there are Baptists.

Where the Baptists are headed is also impossible to state with certainty. That their times will be turbulent goes without saying: if they were not fighting joyfully about something, they would have lost their Baptist gumption. Undoubtedly racial controversy will continue — although it is abating with the advent of the lamentable trend toward black separatism. Renewed emphasis on evangelism may dilute the tentative movement into social action, and more and more the Baptist church probably will recede from its early anti-establishment position. It will be possible for some future historian to catalog all of the problems W. C. Fields envisions. It is too early for that now.

But clearly shaping up at the moment, particularly in the Southern churches, is a bitter struggle over the baptismal rite — whether "alien" baptism will be acceptable as a qualification for church membership. The conservative minister M. O. Owens, Jr., writing in *The Sword and the Trowel*, sees that question as potentially the most destructive among Baptists today, and he leaves no doubt as to where he stands. "For a church to call itself 'Baptist' when it does not require immersion is to fly under false colors," he wrote.[19] Associations already are falling apart over that issue, and churches are splitting. But note that, "splitting." The Baptist church perpetuates itself like the amoeba, by fission. When dissidents withdraw in a body, they form a new Baptist church; when a group of churches secede, they form a new convention. The result is that the entire Baptist movement profits in growth and revitalization.

This is occurring at a time when most other Christian denominations are having to cut back in their operations because of declining membership and dwindling receipts. In 1970, for example, the Episcopal Church had to trim its budget by $1 million; the United Presbyterian Church whacked its expenditures by 7 per cent, and the Christian Church ended 1969 with a 3.5 per cent deficit.[20] Although the American Baptists are feeling a slight pinch, the Southern Baptists are not. They are the fastest growing denomination in the country, at a 1.4 per cent rate nationally and at an 8.6 per cent annual rate in so-called "pioneer" territories,[21] and their giving, largely through the device of the tithe, is increasing at the rate of 5 per cent a year — belying the old saw, "The quickest way to kill a Baptist is to shoot him in the pocketbook."

The question naturally arises, why? There are several answers. Obviously some Southern conservatives and others unwilling to accept social change, particularly in race relations, are moving over to the Baptist church because they do not want their beliefs challenged or because they object to liberal leadership in other denominations. To them the Southern Baptist church is a haven in which they hope to weather the storms of progress. But to say that that is the only reason for the rise in Baptist membership would be both unfair and untrue. Talks with a number of denominational leaders suggest that the Baptist church once more is beginning to attract the young, the generation which has come to the verge of maturity through years of national conflict — physical, emotional and intellectual — and which now seeks a refuge for the spirit. Many of these claim to be "turned on to Jesus," and their number is growing. Furthermore, if one believes a cross-section of ministers, large numbers of the previously unchurched, the bewildered and confused, are joining the Baptists not out of fear or conservatism or social hostility but because they honestly have a yearning, a hunger for nourishment of the human soul. In the Baptist church they find it, in an atmosphere of easy informality but also of reverence and praise. They join a church, but they also join a movement, because the Baptist church, however fragmented, however invisible the lines of discipline, is an institution. It is something big, something sweeping, something vibrant and throbbing. That it may also be an anachronism does not matter, because these people feel that they are also anachronisms — obsolete, expendable, adrift in a world which has moved too fast for them and which they had no hand in making. For now and eternity, they find hope in the red-brick church with the white steeple which somehow manages to withstand the assaults of time, change and unbelief.

When all of us who read these lines are gone, the Baptist church will still be here, a refuge and a forum.

The Baptist forum is one in which a pastor like the Rev. Lewis Rhodes, of the Broadway Baptist Church in Knoxville, Tenn., can stand up and say, as he did at the Christian Citizenship Seminar in Washington in 1968, that the Southern Baptist Convention had in fact a shameful origin and that some aspects of its posture in the modern world are just as shameful. Specifically, he said: "We were born from a womb of cultural reactionism. The organization of the Southern Baptist Convention in 1845 was not for theological or missionary reasons but for the preservation of a slavery centered culture. Doubtless there were flourishes of oratory setting forth the justifications for the convention, but after all the stage scenery is removed, there is the life and death struggle to preserve segregation as a social and cultural value, higher than the claims of Christ. A clear confession, one . . . never heard at a state or Southern Baptist Convention, must include the fact that we were organized to preserve injustice, exploitation, and human slavery. A common loyalty to a social structure has been our cohesiveness, and a prevailing fear of division over the race issue is convincing evidence that our loyalty to Christ is not stronger than our loyalty to our culture. . . Pastors, deacons, Bible teachers of children and adults, and women in missionary unions are prisoners to culture. It is clear now to all of us that the church will be the last to surrender its cultural values and loyalty."[22]

Many voices, many jangling sounds, a maze of contradictions. That is Baptist. And that so many divergent opinions and personalities can be accommodated in a single church, and if not in this church, in another just down the street, is one of the glories of the Baptist faith. Yet knowing all this, all these facts set down over all these hundreds of pages, one could still hardly come up with a definition of a Baptist. "If all data about Baptists were fed into a computer with the question of who we are, the computer would likely answer: Baptists do not exist," Rhodes said.[23] But they do exist, alive and kicking, in Rhodes no more than, but as much as, in Gray Allison, the Ruston, La., evangelist, who during the *Broadman Commentary* fracas said, "When the Bible says so and so happened, we ought to preach it just like that — take it as it is."[24]

It is Baptist to protest the dispatch of an American envoy to the Vatican, as the Southern churches have been doing for decades in state and national conventions, and it is Baptist to turn the convention podium over to Bishop Fulton J. Sheen, the Catholic prelate, as the Northern church did in 1968 — thereby striking horror into Baptist hearts all across the Southland.

To be Baptist is to be a Fosdick or a Billy Poteat, or to be their antagonists. It is to be a Billy Graham or an Isaac Backus, to be willing to suffer the stripes of an Obadiah Holmes or a Swearing Jack Waller or an Andrew Bryan. It is to say with Roger Williams in Boston, "I dare not officiate to an unseparated people;" or it is to say with J. Herbert Gilmore, almost two-and-one-half centuries later in Birmingham, "I will not be pastor of a racist church;" and in each instance it is to be opposed by friends whom you love. It is to be Adam Clayton Powell raging through Depression Harlem toward meaningless retreat on Bimini or Martin Luther King trudging out of Selma on the road to martyrdom. It is Adoniram Judson converting to the Baptist faith on the sea lanes to the mission fields, and Lott Carey seeking his dignity as a man in Africa.

To be Baptist is to read this, and to take pride in it because you know it is said of you: "The greatest achievement ever made in the cause of human progress is the total and final separation of church and state. If we had nothing else to boast of, we could lay claim with justice that first among the nations we of this country made it an article of organic law that the relations between man and his Maker were a private concern, into which other men have no right to intrude. To measure the stride thus far made for the emancipation of the human race, we have only to look back over the centuries that have gone before us, and recall the dreadful persecutions in the name of religion that have filled the world."[25]

Diversity, many voices, many moods. And yet, if all the Baptists who ever lived got together, these "peculiar" people, the song they undoubtedly would sing, fervently, with tears flowing down their cheeks, would be, "Blest Be the Tie that Binds."[23] And for the moment all their differences would be forgotten.

APPENDIX A

A Listing of the Various Baptist Denominations in the United States:[1]

American Baptist Association — This large group of Baptists, strong in the South and Southwest, is the result of a 1905 break from the Southern Baptist Convention which followed a decades-long argument over doctrinal purity. They are sometimes called "Landmarkers," a name derived from an 1854 tract by J. M. Pendleton titled "An Old Landmark Reset." J. R. Graves, a fervent traditionalist, elaborated on Pendleton's ideas in a book, *Old Landmarkism: What Is It?* published in 1880. Graves argued that the Southern Baptists were allowing orthodox Baptist ideas to slip away from them. Orthodoxy, he said, holds that (a) a true church is a local church patterned exactly after the Jerusalem original; (b) that any baptism not authorized by such a local church is unacceptable; (c) that only the properly baptized members of a local church may partake of communion; (d) that only ministers ordained by such local churches are genuine teachers of the gospel, and (e) that the line of these true churches goes back in continuous succession to the original. Today's members of this association hold themselves separate from all other religious groups and are among the most conservative of Baptists. With headquarters in Texarkana, Texas, they have 790,000 members in 3,295 churches attended by 3,312 ordained clergymen.[2]

American Baptist Convention — This is the principal association of white Baptists in the North (although it has affiliates in 38 states and the District of Columbia). Its origins go back to the founding of the first Baptist church in America by Roger Williams in 1639. The Northern churches were among the leaders in the establishment of the first nationwide organization of Baptists, a Triennial Convention formed in 1814 to promote missionary work (see Chapter Eight). It was from this arrangement that the

Southern Baptists withdrew in 1845 over the issue of slavery. The Baptists of the North continued their cooperative work through a group of autonomous boards until 1907, when they formed the Northern Baptist Convention at a meeting of delegates held in Washington. The name American Baptist Convention was adopted in 1950. In general American Baptists are known as the most liberal of Baptists, and although the original Baptist split was over the issue of slavery, there are today other distinctions. The Northern churches believe in interdenominational cooperation (they have joined the National Council of Churches, which the Southern Baptists reject), in open communion and in progressive race relations. The American Baptist Convention also has been the most active in taking positions on social issues, including current affairs, international relations, the population explosion, women's liberation, peace, the generation gap, drugs and other present-day concerns. The American Baptists operate 14 children's homes, 48 homes for the aging, 7 hospitals, 10 theological seminaries, 6 academies, 27 senior colleges and universities, 4 junior colleges and a school of nursing. Headquarters are in Valley Forge, Pa., and there are 1,472,478 members in 6,090 churches, with 6,307 ordained ministers.[3]

Baptist General Conference — This was originally the forum for Swedish Baptists, who organized their first church in America in 1852. The conference dates from 1879. National headquarters are in Evanston, Ill., and in the 677 churches there are 103,955 members and 919 ministers.

Baptist Missionary Association of America — This represents a group of Regular Baptist churches which came together in May, 1950, at Little Rock, Ark., as the North American Baptist Association. The present name was adopted in 1968. These are evangelical, missionary, fundamentaal and premillenial Baptists who have 187,246 members in 1,408 churches with 2,000 ministers.

Bethel Ministerial Association, Inc. — This organization was founded as the Evangelical Ministerial Alliance at Evansville, Ind., in May, 1934. In 1960 it began to call itself the Bethel Baptist Assembly, and upon incorporation that year it became legally the association as now titled. There are 15 churches in this branch, with 2,500 members and 55 clergymen.

Christian Unity Baptist Association — Organized out of the Macedonia Baptist Association in North Carolina in 1934, this group requires of its members belief in the Holy Trinity, the divine inspiration of the Bible, spiritual regeneration, universal (rather than particular) atonement and the perseverance of the saints. It has 5 churches, 9 clergymen and 345 members.

Conservative Baptist Association of America — This group of Baptists, with headquarters in Wheaton, Ill., broke away from the American Baptist Convention in 1947 when the parent body refused to require a creedal test for membership. By the Conservatives both the Old and New Testaments are regarded as the divinely inspired word of God, supremely authoritative and absolutely infallible. They describe themselves as "a back-to-the-Bible fellowship of autonomous churches dedicated to soul-winning, missions, church planting, and the defense of the faith,... opposed to modernism, all forms of theological inclusiveness and ecumenalism."[4] The founders were active in the Fundamentalist movement of the 1920's (see Chapter Eleven). The Association has 300,000 members in 1,127 churches.

Duck River (and Kindred) Associations of Baptists — A group of Baptist churches formed into associations in Tennessee, Alabama, Georgia, Kentucky and Mississippi, they are fairly standard in belief and practice. There are 81 churches, with 8,492 members and 128 ministers.

Free Will Baptists — An evangelical group of churchmen organized in 1727 by Paul Palmer in North Carolina and in 1780 by Benjamin Randall, a former Congregationalist, in New Hampshire. These Baptists rejected the Calvinist view of predestination and taught free grace, free will and free salvation. In the days prior to the Civil War they were unpopular in the South and made little headway because they were opposed to slavery. Although many churches merged with the Northern Baptists in 1911, there remain 2,163 congregations with 186,136 members and 2,300 ministers. The national offices are in Nashville, Tenn.[5]

General Association of General Baptists — An Arminian (see Chapter Three) group of Baptists. They are closely related to the Free Will Baptists through Paul Palmer but claim the Rev. Benoni Stinson, who established a congregation in Evansville, Ind., in

1923, as their American founder. The main strength of the Association lies in the central Mid-west and the border states, with active congregations as well in Ohio, Michigan, Illinois, Iowa, Kansas, Nebraska, Colorado, Arizona and California. Unlike most Baptist groups, the General Baptists have an associational "presbytery" made up of all ordained personnel which has control over the official standing of ministers and deacons and lays down the qualifications for those offices. They also hold that neither baptism nor church membership is a prerequisite to the partaking of communion. Otherwise they are orthodox Baptist in belief. There are 859 General Baptist churches, with a membership of around 70,000.[6]

General Association of Regular Baptist Churches — This, again, is the result of dissension in the American Baptist Convention. The Regular Baptists parted company with the Baptists of the North in May, 1932, as a protest against what they saw as modernist tendencies, the trend toward centralization and other organizational differences. Churches affiliating with the Regulars are required to "withdraw all fellowship and cooperation from any convention or group which permits modernists or modernism" within its ranks. These churches will not participate in union revivals, union holiday services or mixed ministerial associations. There are 1,426 churches with 210,000 members and 1,571 ministers.

General Six-Principle Baptists — The "sixth principle" is the laying-on of hands, practiced as a formal rite in these churches. The movement dates back to 1653 in Rhode Island, and it has never gained wide acceptance. There are only eight Six-Principle churches, with a membership of 486 and 8 ministers.

Independent Baptist Church of America — A small body of Swedish Free Baptists dating back to 1893, for the most part residing in Minnesota.

National Baptist Convention of America — This is the younger of the two large associations of black Baptists (see Chapter Twelve). It withdrew from the parent organization, at the urging of the Rev. R. H. Boyd, in 1915 in a dispute over the operation of a publishing house which Boyd controlled. It claims more than 2.6 million members, 11,400 churches and 7,500 ministers and is orthodox Baptist in belief and practice.

National Baptist Convention of the U.S.A. — Organized in 1895, this is the first truly national association of black Baptists. Through various forerunner organizations, it can trace its ancestry back to the first Negro Baptist church in America, which was established at Silver Bluff, S.C., about 1773 (see Chapter Twelve). As one with the white Baptists, the blacks acknowledge Roger Williams as the founder of the Baptist faith in America and their own spiritual forebear. This convention, which has more than 5.5 million members, 26,000 churches and 27,500 ministers, is the largest Negro denomination in the world.

National Baptist Evangelical Life and Soul-Saving Assembly — This Negro organization, with headquarters in Detroit, was founded in 1921 by A.A. Banks. It has 60,000 members in 260 churches.[7] Mead reports that the assembly operates a correspondence school which offers degrees (in from 60 to 120 days) in "evangelology, deaconology, missionology, pastorology and laymanology."

National Primitive Baptist Convention of the U.S.A. — This is the black counterpart of the white Primitive Baptists. Although this convention does have local associations and state affiliates, the primitives in general oppose elaborate organization. The Negro Primitives, who formed their national convention in 1907, have their headquarters in Tallahassee, Fla. Attached to the national organization are 2,196 churches with 1,523,000 members and 597 ordained clergymen. (Many of the Primitive ministers do not bother with ordination.)

North American Baptist General Conference — This Bible-centered, missions-oriented organization grew out of the immigration of German Baptists a century ago. Largely instrumental in its founding was Konrad Anton Fleischmann, who founded the first German Baptist church in America at Philadelphia in 1843. Attached to the present headquarters at Forest Park, Ill., are 347 churches with 55,000 members and 445 clergymen.[8]

Penetecostal Free—Will Baptist Church, Inc. — A small group of Baptists in southeastern North Carolina who took this name in 1959 after originally organizing as the Cape Fear Conference of Free Will Baptists. They are faith healers, with emphasis on the

Second Coming, sanctification and the pentecostal baptism of the Holy Ghost. There are about 13,500 members.

Primitive Baptists — In some respects these are the modern-day counterparts of the anti-mission movement of the early 1800's (see Chapter Eight). They are grouped largely in the South, are generally from the poorest class of whites, and they oppose centralization. Although they have headquarters in Thornton, Ark., they have never been organized as a denomination and have no administrative bodies whatsoever. Strongly Calvinistic, they continue to protest "money-based" mission efforts. These are the genuine "Hard-Shell" Baptists, and some still practice footwashing. Because there is no central organization, their total number is unknown, but it is believed that there are about 525,000 of them, with an estimated 655 churches. These are not included in the figures above for the National Primitive Baptists.

Progressive National Baptist Convention — This Negro organization, now contemplating merger with the predominantly white American Baptist Convention, is a result of dissension within the National Baptist Convention of the U.S.A. It was formed in 1961 by delegates from 14 states representing churches which were dissatisfied with the failure of the older convention to limit the tenure of officers. It has over half a million members in 411 churches.

Separate Baptists in Christ — This is a very exclusive sect of Baptists found in Indiana, Ohio, Kentucky, Tennessee and Illinois with roots going back to an association formed in North Carolina in 1758. The members practice footwashing and assert that their church is not Protestant. There are more than 80 churches, with a membership of about 7,500.

Seventh Day Baptist General Conference — Originally called Sabbatarian Baptists, these churches derive their name from their practice of observing Saturday as the week's holy day. The first such church was founded in Rhode Island in 1672; the General Conference was organized in 1801, and the conference formally took the name "Seventh Day Baptist" in 1818. They are strong on missions and otherwise orthodox in Baptist belief, except that they are not rigidly opposed to ecumenicity. They are members of the National and World Council of Churches. With headquarters in

Plainfield, N. J., they administer to 66 churches with 5,308 members and 75 clergymen.[9]

Seventh Day Baptists (German) — This body, one of the smallest adhering to Baptist principles, was organized in 1728 by refugees from the German Palatinate. At that time the members were also called Brethren or Dunkers. There are only 3 churches, with perhaps 150 members.

Southern Baptist Convention—This is the largest of Baptist denominations and, with 11.6 million members, the largest Protestant denomination in America. With all the other regular Baptists, it acknowledges common roots in England and common beginnings in New England. Its churches, not then organized in a convention, joined with the Baptists of the North in 1814 to promote foreign missions (see Chapter Eight), a loose union which lasted until 1845, when the Southerners withdrew over the issue of slavery (see Chapter Nine) and formed their own convention (see Chapter Ten). Although the word "Southern" has since been retained in the name of the organization, it is now national in scope, with affiliated churches in every state (holding property valued at almost $4 billion) and 31 state conventions (one of which is in the District of Columbia). Most of the churches lying outside the South have been formed by displaced Southerners, who feel ill at ease in other Baptist congregations. The conservative theology of the Convention thus has been propagated across the nation. Although beset by problems (it has had extreme difficulty finding a tenable position on the race question), it is one of the fastest growing denominations in the country—at a time when elsewhere church membership is falling off. With contributions from their 34,340 churches, the Southern Baptists operate 6 theological seminaries, 43 senior colleges and universities, 12 junior colleges, 8 academies, 4 Bible schools and one of the country's most active publishing operations. Of all the Baptist groupings, this one has probably had the most influence on contemporary American life and thought.

United Baptists—A conservative group of Baptists which had its origin in Virginia and Kentucky starting in 1787. It observes three ordinances: baptism and the Lord's Supper, in common with other Baptists, and also the rite of footwashing. There are 32 associations with 568 churches and 63,641 members.

United Free Will Baptists—This group of Negro Baptists, similar in doctrine to the other free will movements, was organized in 1870 with headquarters in Kinston, N. C. It has 836 churches, primarily in North Carolina, Georgia, Florida, Mississippi, Louisiana and Texas. It claims about 100,000 members.

CHAPTER ONE: A "PECULIAR" PEOPLE

[1]The adjective is not the author's. A Nineteenth Century Baptist historian, J. M. Cramp, said that "if Baptist history is peculiar, it is because the Baptists have been a peculiar people." See Cramp's *Baptist History: from the Foundation of the Christian Church to the Present Time* (London, 1871), p. 11.

[2]H. Richard Niebuhr, cited by Anson Phelps Stokes, *Church and State in the United States* (New York, 1950), p. 112.

[3]In "The Years Ahead" for the fourth quarter of 1970, the Annuity Board of the Southern Baptist Convention reported that the average salary of Baptist ministers in the preceding year in churches with a membership of 1-399 had been $3,714. In churches in the 500-member range, the salary was $6,338; where there were 1,000 members, $8,302; in 2,000-member churches, $10,941, and where there were more than 3,000 on the rolls, $13,900. (Convention figures show the average church has 335 members.) The salary figures do not include parsonange, travel allowances or retirement contributions, which often are quite generous – and just as often are non-existent.

[4]George W. Paschal, *History of North Carolina Baptists* (Raleigh, N. C., 1930), pp. 7-9; Thomas Armitage, *A History of the Baptists* (New York, 1890), pp. 151-153.

[5]Witness, almost any Baptist baptismal ceremony.

[6]Henry F. Brown, *Baptism Through the Centuries* (Mountain View, Cal., 1965), pp. 3-4, 10, 12, 32.

[7]*Twin City Sentinel,* May 28, 1971.

[8]Sydnor L. Stealey, ed., *A Baptist Treasury* (New York, 1958), pp. 317-318.

[9]George W. Truett, *Baptists and Religious Liberty* (Nashville, 1920), p. 22.

[10]*Ibid.,* p.7.

[11]*Ibid..* p. 6.

[12]Cramp, p. 73.

CHAPTER TWO: BAPTIST HERALDS

[1]Armitage, pp. 115-125.

[2]See G. H. Orchard's *Baptist History* (Nashville, n. d.).

[3]Henry C. Vedder, *A Short History of the Baptists* (Philadelphia, 1891), pp. 44-45.

[4]Armitage, p. 6

[5]Cramp, pp. 79-80.

[6]*Ibid.,* pp. 89-90.

[7]*Ibid.,* pp. 100-101.

[8]Armitage, p. 291.

[9]Paschal, p. 10.

[10]Armitage, p. 285

[11]*Ibid.,* p. 277.

[12]Cramp, p. 121.

[13]Vedder, p. 71.

[14]A. H. Newman, *American Church History* (New York, 1894), II, 17.

[15]Paschal, pp. 11-12.

[16]Henry W. Clark, *History of English Nonconformity* (London, 1911), I, 45.

[17]K. B. McFarlane, *John Wycliffe and English Nonconformity* (London, 1953), pp. 10, 35.

[18]W. E. Lunt, *History of England* (New York, 1946), pp. 255-256.

[19]Cramp, p. 117.

[20]Armitage, p. 315.

[21]Newman, p. 15

[22]Ferdinand Schevill, *A History of Europe* (New York, 1941), p. 114.

[23]*Ibid.*, p. 116.

[24]William R. Estep, *The Anabaptist Story* (Nashville, 1963), p. 10.

[25]Armitage, p. 186

[26]E. Belfort Bax, *Rise and Fall of the Anabaptists* (New York, 1966), p. 18.

[27]*Ibid.*, pp. 30-32.

[28]Estep, pp. 15-16.

[29]Bax, pp. 53-54.

[30]Estep, pp. 26-28.

[31]*Ibid.*, p. 20.

[32]*Ibid.*, p. 37.

[33]*Ibid.*, pp.49-50.

[34]Quoted in Paschal, p. 27.

[35]Paschal, p. 14; a full account of the Munster Kingdom can be found in Leopold Ranke's *History of the Reformation in Germany* (Philadelphia, 1844), VI, pp. 431-443.

[36]Cramp, p. 231.

[37]Newman, p. 37.

[38]John Christian Wenger, ed., *The Complete Writings of Menno Simons* (Scottsdale, Pa., 1956), p. 16.

[39]*Ibid.*, p. 668.

[40]*Ibid.*

[41]Cramp, p. 194.

[42]Wenger, note, p. 405.

[43]*Ibid.*, p. 28

[44]*Ibid.*, p. 120.

CHAPTER THREE: RISE OF THE ENGLISH BAPTISTS

[1]Cramp, pp. 218-219.

[2]*Ibid.*, pp. 220-221.

[3]Armitage, p. 446

[4]Clark, p. 127.

[5]Torbet, p. 33.

[6]Quoted in Torbet, p. 33.

[7]Henry M. Dexter, quoted in Newman, p. 39.

[8]Torbet, pp. 36-37.

[9]Robert A. Baker, *The Baptist March in History* (Nashville, 1958), p. 41.

[10]Paschal, pp. 21-23.

[11]Baker, p. 44.

[12]Quoted in Torbet, p. 39.

[13]Torbet, pp. 39-40.

[14]*Ibid.*, pp. 40-41.

[15]Quoted in John T. Christian's *A History of the Baptists* (Nashville, 1922), p. 252.

[16]Paschal, p. 28

[17] Armitage, pp. 547-550.

[18] *Ibid.*, p. 474.

[19] George B. Woods and others, *The Literature of England* (New York, 1941), I, 675.

[20] Armitage, p. 476.

[21] *Ibid.*, p. 482.

CHAPTER FOUR: A BEGINNING IN NEW ENGLAND

[1] Armitage, p. 264.

[2] Joseph Martin Dawson, *Baptists and the American Republic* (Nashville, 1956), p. 3.

[3] Alvah Hovey, *A Memoir of the Life and Times of the Rev. Isaac Backus* (Boston, 1858), p. 158.

[4] *Ibid.*, pp. 158-159.

[5] Torbet, p. 202.

[6] One of the best accounts of Williams's early career can be found in Samuel Hugh Brockunier's *The Irrepressible Democrat, Roger Williams* (New York, 1940).

[7] Brockunier, p. 37.

[8] Armitage, pp. 627-628.

[9] Brockunier, p. 42.

[10] Nathaniel B. Shurtleff, ed., *Records of Massachusetts* (Boston, 1853), I, 160-161.

[11] Henry S. Burrage, *A History of the Baptists in New England* (Philadelphia, 1894), p. 20.

[12] Quoted in Brockunier, p. 87.

[13] Quoted in Armitage, p. 642.

[14] Armitage, p. 643.

[15] *Ibid.*, p. 642.

[16] Brockunier, p. 118.

[17] Jesse L. Boyd, *A History of Baptists in America Prior to 1845* (New York, 1957), p. 23.

[18] Brockunier, p. 125.

[19] James D. Knowles, *Memoir of Roger Williams* (Boston, 1834), p. 173.

[20] S. Adlam, *The First Baptist Church in America, Not Founded by Roger Williams* (Memphis, 1890), p. 36.

[21] Thomas W. Bicknell, *The Story of Dr. John Clarke* (Providence, 1915) p. 176.

[22] Knowles, p. 175.

[23] Cited in Cramp, pp. 477-478.

[24] Cramp, note, p. 175.

[25] Armitage, pp. 662-667.

[26] Newman, p. 108.

[27] For a careful biography see Wilbur Nelson, *The Hero of Aquidneck* (Bloomfield, N. J., 1938).

[28] Nelson, pp. 27-38.

[29] *Ibid.*, p. 70.

[30] Armitage, pp. 405-406.

[31] Nelson, p. 61.

[32] Armitage, p. 672.

[33] Nelson, p. 79.

CHAPTER FIVE: IN MASSACHUSETTS, A FIGHT FOR LIFE

[1] Newman, p. 123.

[2] Paschal, p. 39

[3] Hovey, pp. 157-158.

[4] John Winthrop, *The History of New England from 1630 to 1649 (Boston, 1853), II, 148-149.*

[5] Witter's case is treated in Newman, p. 125.

[6] Isaac Backus, *A History of New England, with Particular Reference to the Denomination of Christians Called Baptists* (Newton, Mass., 1871), I, 126.

[7] Burrage, pp. 36-37.

[8] Newman, p. 139.

[9] Quoted in Newman's account of Dunster's life, pp. 139-161.

[10] Newman, pp. 153-154.

[11] Burrage, p. 40.

[12] Newman, pp. 174-179.

[13] Paschal, p. 39.

[14] Newman, p. 194.

[15] Hovey, p. 168.

[16] Cramp, p. 528.

[17] Burrage, p. 106.

[18] Hovey, P. 39.

[19] *Ibid.,* p. 84. The account of Backus at this point leans heavily on Hovey and T. B. Maston's *Isaac Backus: Pioneer of Religious Liberty* (Rochester, 1962).

[20] Newman, p. 348.

[21] *Ibid.,* pp. 348-349.

[22] *Ibid.,* p. 349.

[23] *Ibid.,* p. 351.

[24] *Ibid.,* p. 353.

[25] *Ibid.,* p. 354.

[26] *Ibid.,* pp. 356-358.

[27] Maston, p. 90.

CHAPTER SIX: IN VIRGINIA, A FORMIDABLE CHALLENGE

[1] Paschal, p. 54.

[2] Charles F. James, *The Struggle for Religious Liberty in Virginia* (Lynchburg, Va., 1900), p. 19.

[3] William Peden, ed., *Notes on the State of Virginia,* by Thomas Jefferson (Chapel Hill, N. C., 1955), p. 157.

[4] Garnett Ryland, *The Baptists of Virginia, 1699-1926* (Richmond, Va., 1955), p. 37.

[5] Morgan Edwards, quoted in William L. Lumpkin's *Baptist Foundations in the South* (Nashville, 1961), p. 39.

[6] Cramp, p. 556.

[7] Newman, p. 293.

[8] Quoted in Cramp, p. 554.

[9] Wesley M. Gewehr, *The Great Awakening in Virginia* (Durham, N. C., 1930) , p. 114.

[10] Robert B. Semple, *History of the Rise and Progress of the Baptists in Virginia,* revised and extended by W. G. Beale (Richmond, 1894), p. 29.

[11] Gewehr, p. 115.

[12] Ryland, p. 41.

[13] *Ibid.*, p. 38.

[14] Cramp, p. 560.

[15] Quoted in Ryland, p. 60.

[16] Semple, pp. 31-32.

[17] William Henry Foote, *Sketches of Virginia* (Philadelphia, 1850), pp. 316-317.

[18] Virginius Dabney, *Liberalism in the South* (Chapel Hill, N. C., 1932), p. 30; Semple pp. 3-4.

[19] Francis L. Hawks, *Rise and Progress of the Protestant Episcopal Church in Virginia* (New York, 1836), pp. 121-122. The internal quote is from John Leland.

[20] Semple, p. 36.

[21] Lewis Peyton Little, *Imprisoned Preachers and Religious Liberty in Virginia* (Lynchburg, Va., 1938), pp. 233-234.

[22] Gewehr, p. 36.

[23] Newman, p. 367.

[24] Peden, p. 158.

[25] Hawks, p. 152.

[26] *Ibid.*, p. 138.

[27] Peden, p. 291.

[28] William Warren Sweet, *Religion in the Development of American Culture,* (New York, 1952), pp. 31-32.

[29] Newman, p. 367.

[30] *Ibid.*, p. 368.

[31] Peden, p. 224.

[32] Hawks, p. 173

[33] Newman, p. 372.

[34] *Ibid.*, pp. 373-374.

[35] James, pp. 151-155.

[36] William Cathcart, quoted in James, pp. 167-168.

[37] Armitage, p. 807.

CHAPTER SEVEN: THE SPREAD OF BAPTIST PRINCIPLES

[1] Newman, p. 201.

[2] Quoted in Cramp, p. 479.

[3] Henry C. Vedder, *A History of the Baptists in the Middle States,* (Philadelphia, 1898), p. 41.

[4] C. Edwin Barrows, ed., *The Diary of John Comer* (Philadelphia, 1892), pp. 114-118.

[5] *Ibid.*, pp. 54, 112-113.

[6] Norman H. Maring, *Baptists in New Jersey* (Valley Forge, Pa., 1964), p. 38.

[7] Burrage, p. 62.

[8] Vedder, *A History of the Baptists in the Middle States,* p. 21.

[9] *Ibid.*

[10] *Ibid.*, p. 25.

[11] *Ibid.*

[12] Paschal, p. 347.

[13] *Ibid.*, pp. 458-461.

[14] Riley, p. 20.

[15] *Ibid.*, p. 22.

[16] Armitage, p. 776.

[17] *Ibid.*, p. 789

[18] Maring, p. 73.

[19] *Ibid.*, pp. 72-73; Armitage, pp. 793-795.

[20] William Cathcart, *The Baptists and the American Revolution* (Philadelphia, 1876), pp. 62-63.

[21] David Benedict, *Fifty Years Among the Baptists* (Boston, 1860), pp. 93-94.

[22] Sweet, p. 57.

[23] W. W. Barnes, *The Southern Baptist Convention, 1845-1953* (Nashville, 1954), note, p. 12.

[24] Newman, p. 334.

[25] *Ibid.*, p. 303.

[26] William Warren Sweet, *Religion on the American Frontier: The Baptists, 1783-1830* (New York, 1831), p. 19.

[27] *Ibid.*, pp. 21-22.

[28] Newman, pp. 344-345.

[29] Quoted in Sweet, *Religion on the American Frontier*, p. 21.

[30] Both Furman and Leland are quoted in Benedict, p. 61.

[31] Sweet, *Religion on the American Frontier*, p. 37.

[32] Newman, p. 380.

[33] *Ibid.*

[34] Sweet, *Religion in the Development of American Culture*, pp. 141-142; Rufus Babcock, ed., *Memoir of John Mason Peck* (Carbondale, III., 1965), p. XLIV.

[35] Ryland, note, p. 173.

[36] Newman, p. 379.

CHAPTER EIGHT: THE GREAT(?) COMMISSION

[1] Quoted in Paschal, p. 37.

[2] *Dictionary of National Biography* (London, 1922), p. 986.

[3] Evelyn Wingo Thompson, *Luther Rice: Believer in Tomorrow* (Nashville, 1967), p. 45.

[4] William Cathcart, *Baptist Encyclopaedia* (Philadelphia, 1881), p. 979.

[5] Thompson, p. 77.

[6] *Dictionary of American Biography* (New York, 1933), XV, p. 543.

[7] Newman, p. 394.

[8] *Ibid.*, p. 404.

[9] *Ibid.*, p. 405.

[10] Babcock, pp. XIII-XV.

[11] Sweet, *Religion in the Development of American Culture*, p. 272.

[12] Newman, p. 420.

[13] *Dictionary of American Biography*, VII, p. 362.

[14] Sweet, *Religion in the Development of American Culture*, p. 273.

[15] Newman, pp. 422-423.

[16] *Ibid.*, p. 431.

[17] Sweet, *Religion on the American Frontier*, p. 61.

[18] Newman, p. 437.

[19] *Ibid.*, pp. 434-435.

[20] Sweet, *Religion on the American Frontier* pp. 72-75.

[21] Quoted in Newman, pp. 439-440.

[22] Sweet, *Religion on the American Frontier*, p. 75.

[23]Newman, p. 433.
[24]*Ibid.*, p. 442.

CHAPTER NINE: A PARTING OF THE WAYS

[1]Sweet, *Religion on the American Frontier*, p. 47.
[2]*Ibid.*, p. 79.
[3]Newman, p. 288.
[4]Sweet, *Religion on the American Frontier*, p. 79.
[5]Mary Burnham Putnam, *The Baptists and Slavery* (Ann Arbor, Mich., 1913), pp. 13-15.
[6]Newman, p. 306.
[7]Torbet, p. 285.
[8]*Ibid.*, p. 283.
[9]Putnam, p. 14.
[10]Torbet, p. 285.
[11]*Ibid.*, p. 284.
[12]Putnam, p. 15.
[13]Newman, p. 341; Barnes, p. 19.
[14]Robert Andrew Baker, *Relations Between Northern and Southern Baptists,* Second edition (p.p., 1954), pp. 44-45; Putnam, pp. 16,23.
[15]Baker, p. 45.
[16]Torbet, p. 285.
[17]Baker, p. 45.
[18]*Ibid.*, pp. 47-48.
[19]*Dictionary of American Biography*, pp. 558-559.
[20]Barnes, p. 24.
[21]Newman, pp. 443-444.
[22]Baker, pp. 49-50.
[23]Torbet, p. 290.
[24]Riley, pp. 200-201.
[25]Newman, pp. 444-445.
[26]Barnes, p. 23.
[27]Riley, p. 204.
[28]Newman, p. 447; Riley, p. 205.
[29]Putnam, pp. 67-68.
[30]*Ibid.*, p. 70.
[31]*Ibid.*, p. 46.
[32]*Ibid.*, pp. 46-47.
[33]B. D. Ragsdale, *Story of Georgia Baptists* (Atlanta, 1938), III, p. 63.
[34]Putnam, p. 61.
[35]*Ibid.*, p. 76.

CHAPTER TEN: BAPTISTS AT WAR

[1]Quoted by Lynn E. May, Jr., "Those Days in May, 1845," *The Baptist Program,* May, 1970, p. 4.
[2]Barnes, pp. 311-312.
[3]Putnam, p. 36.
[4]*Proceeding of the Southern Baptist Convention*, 1845, p. 6.
[5]*Ibid.*, p. 13.
[6]*Ibid.*, pp. 6,14.
[7]The full text is in the *Proceedings* for 1845 at pp. 17-20.

[8] Barnes, pp. 41-42.

[9] Newman, p. 455.

[10] William M. Pinson, Jr., "Others Have, Preacher. What About You?", *The Baptist Program,* January, 1971, p. 13.

[11] Torbet, pp. 294-295.

[12] *Proceedings,* 1861, pp. 62-63.

[13] *Proceedings,* 1863, pp. 54-55.

[14] Douglas Southall Freeman, *Lee's Lieutenants,* (New York, 1942), I, p. xlii.

[15] *Proceedings,* 1863, pp. 35-36.

[16] *Ibid.,* p. 39.

[17] Barnes, pp. 55-56.

[18] Ryland, p. 299.

[19] George Braxton Taylor, *Virginia Baptist Ministers, Fourth Series* (Lynchburg, Va., 1931), p. 331.

[20] Ryland, pp. 297-299; also, see individual biographies in the Third and Fourth Series of Taylor's *Virginia Baptist Ministers.*

[21] Taylor, Third Series (Lynchburg, 1912), p. 54.

[22] Quoted by Barnes, pp. 51-52.

[23] *Minutes of the American Baptist Home Missions Society,* 1864, p. 15.

[24] Barnes, p. 53; Baker, p. 89.

[25] *Minutes of the American Baptist Home Missions Society,* 1864, p. 21.

[26] *Proceeding of the Southern Baptist Convention,* 1866, pp. 50-51.

[27] *Ibid.,* p. 87.

[28] Barnes, p. 71.

[29] Mead, p. 35.

CHAPTER ELEVEN: GOD, MAN, AND THE LOWER ORDERS

[1] Sweet, *Religion in the Development of American Culture,* pp. 193-194.

[2] *Dictionary of American Biography,* XVIII, pp. 621-622.

[3] *Ibid.*

[4] *Ibid.,* XX, p. 170.

[5] Paschal, p. 25.

[6] *Dictionary of American Biography,* XX, p. 170.

[7] Herbert Asbury, *The Great Illusion* (New York, 1950), pp. 3-5.

[8] *Ibid.,* p. 16.

[9] Maring, p. 179.

[10] Quoted by Asbury, pp. 14-15.

[11] Quoted in Armitage, p. 845.

[12] Ryland, pp. 217-218.

[13] Maring, p. 180.

[14] Cited by Roland H. Bainton, *Alcohol, Science and Society* (New Haven, Conn., 1945), p. 194.

[15] Asbury, p. 15.

[16] Ryland, p. 287.

[17] Asbury, pp. 88-89.

[18] "Southern Baptist Convention Presidents," *The Baptist Program,* January, 1970, p. 17.

[19] D. Leigh Colvin, *Prohibition in the United States* (New York, 1926), pp. 267-268.

[20] *Ibid.,* p. 286.

[21] Dale Moody, "Whither the Winds of Doctrine?", *The Baptist Program,* January, 1970, p. 9.

[22] L. Sprague de Camp, *The Great Monkey Trial* (New York, 1968), p. 29.

[23] *Ibid.,* p. 27.

[24] Norman F. Furniss, *The Fundamentalist Controversy, 1918-1931* (New Haven, 1954), p. 12.

[25] *Ibid.,* pp. 15, 38-39.

[26] William Jennings Bryan, *In His Image* (New York, 1922), p. 40.

[27] *Proceedings of the Southern Baptist Convention,* 1921, p. 83.

[28] Ray Ginger, *Six Days or Forever,* (Boston, 1958), p. 63.

[29] Furniss, p. 36.

[30] *Ibid.,*

[31] *Ibid.,* p. 38.

[32] Virginius Dabney, *Liberalism in the South* (Chapel Hill, 1932), pp. 291-292, 299.

[33] Furniss, p. 40.

[34] De Camp, p. 32.

[35] *Ibid.,* pp. 32-33 and 478-479; also see Ginger, p. 64; Dabney, p. 299; and Furniss, pp. 86-87.

[36] Furniss, p. 42.

[37] *Ibid.,* pp. 104-111.

[38] *Ibid.,* p. 111.

[39] *Ibid.,* pp. 112-113.

[40] Cited by Howard K. Beale, *Are American Teachers Free?* (New York, 1936), pp. 243, 250.

[41] Furniss, p. 113.

[42] *Ibid.,* pp. 131-132, 181.

[43] Willard B. Gatewood, Jr., *Preachers, Pedagogues and Politicians* (Chapel Hill, 1966), p. 12.

[44] Harry Emerson Fosdick, "Farewell Sermon," (p.p.), pp. 19-21.

[45] *National Cyclopaedia of American Biography* (New York, 1940), 28, p. 132.

[46] Suzanne Cameron Linder, *William Louis Poteat* (Chapel Hill, 1966), p. viii.

[47] Quoted in Gatewood, pp. 30-31.

[48] Gatewood, pp. 31-34.

[49] *Biblical Recorder,* April 22, 1922, p. 3.

[50] William Louis Poteat, "Christianity and Enlightenment" (n.d., n.p.), pp. 1-2, 8-9.

[51] Gatewood, p. 74.

[52] *Ibid.*

[53] *National Cyclopaedia of American Biography,* 28, p. 132.

[54] Beale, p. 228.

[55] De Camp, pp. 50-52.

[56] Furniss, pp. 81-83.

[57] Dabney, pp. 305-306.

[58] Furniss, pp. 96-97.

[59] *Ibid.,* pp. 60-61.

[60] De Camp, p. 475.

[61] *Ibid.*

[62] *Ibid.,* p. 63.

[63] Quoted in Jerry R. Tompkins, ed., *D-Days at Dayton: Reflections on the Scopes Trial* (Baton Rouge, 1965), p. 3.

[64]Ginger, p. 4.

[65]*Ibid.*, pp. 5-7.

[66]De Camp, p. 134.

[67]Ginger, p. 99.

[68]*Ibid.*, p. 106.

[69]Arthur Garfield Hays, *Let Freedom Ring* (New York, 1928), p. 28.

[70]Walter Lippmann, *American Inquisitors* (New York, 1928), p. 9.

[71]Furniss, p. 177.

CHAPTER TWELVE: THE BLACK BAPTISTS

[1]Victor T. Glass, "Working with National Baptists," Home Mission Board of the Southern Baptist Convention, n.d., p. 3.

[2]Owen D. Pelt and Ralph Lee Smith, *The Story of the National Baptists* (New York, 1960), p. 27.

[3]*Ibid.*, p. 29.

[4]*Ibid.*, p. 30.

[5]*Ibid.*, p. 40.

[6]*Ibid.*, p. 37.

[7]Carter Godwin Woodson, *The History of the Negro Church* (Washington, 1921), pp. 43-47.

[8]Pelt and Smith, p. 32.

[9]Quoted by Woodson, pp. 49-50.

[10]James M. Simms, *The First Colored Baptist Church in North America* (Philadelphia, 1888), p. 48.

[11]*Ibid.*, p. 34.

[12]Woodson, p. 52.

[13]*Ibid.*, p. 53.

[14]Pelt and Smith, pp. 45-46.

[15]Woodson, pp. 55-56.

[16]*Ibid.*, pp. 54-55.

[17]Rev. George Sale in A. H. Newman, ed., *A Century of Baptist Achievement* (Philadelphia, 1901), p. 165.

[18]*Ibid.*, p. 164.

[19]William B. Sprague, *Annals of the American Baptist Pulpit* (New York, 1860), pp. 578-583.

[20]Pelt and Smith, pp. 65-66.

[23]Woodson, pp. 131-132.

[24]Pelt and Smith, p. 68.

[25]*Ibid.*, pp. 69-70.

[26]Newman, *A Century of Baptist Achievement*, p. 167.

[27]B. F. Riley, *A Memorial History of the Baptists of Alabama* (Philadelphia, 1923), p. 167.

[28]*Proceedings of the Southern Baptist Convention*, 1866, pp. 85-86.

[29]Newman, *A Century of Baptist Achievement*, p. 164.

[30]*Proceedings*, 1867, p. 79.

[31]*Ibid.*, 1868, p. 62.

[32]*Ibid.*, 1869, p. 20.

[33]Woodson, pp. 199-201; Newman, *A Century of Baptist Achievement* p. 168.

[34]Pelt and Smith, pp. 85-86.

[35]*Ibid.*, pp. 87-91.

[36]*Ibid.*, pp. 83 91-93.

[37] *Ibid.,* pp. 94-95.

[38] *Ibid.,* pp. 72, 96.

[39] Newman, *A Century of Baptist Achievement,* p. 167.

[40] Pelt and Smith, p. 96.

[41] *Ibid.,* pp. 102-104.

[42] Mead, p. 38.

[43] Torbet, p. 477.

[44] Glass, p. 3.

[45] Ploski and Brown, p. 469.

[46] Joseph R. Washington, Jr., *Black Religion* (Boston, 1964), p. 469.

[47] Murray S. Stedman, *Religion and Politics in America,* (New York, 1964), p. 17.

[48] The details of King's life are taken from Peter M. Bergman, *The Chronological History of the Negro in America* (New York, 1969), pp. 445-446.

[49] Ploski and Brown, p. 29.

[50] The author covered the march as a correspondent for the Baltimore *Sun.*

[51] Washington, p. 3.

CHAPTER THIRTEEN: BAPTIST SCHIZOPHRENIA

[1] Woodson, p. 306.

[2] "Racial Christianity," *Time* (December 9, 1946), p. 73.

[3] Frank S. Loescher, *The Protestant Church and the Negro* (New York, 1948), p. 121.

[4] *Ibid.,* pp. 123-125, 131.

[5] Adapted from a *Compiliation of American Baptist Convention Resolutions,* prepared by the Division of Christian Social Concern of the ABC, pp. 24-29.

[6] "Integration by Baptists Advances," *Twin City Sentinel,* May 13, 1971.

[7] Culbert G. Rutenberger, "American Baptists Respond to Black Power Challenge," *Christian Century* (July 3, 1968), p. 878.

[8] *Ibid.,* p. 879.

[9] Loescher, pp. 124, 128.

[10] *Ibid.,* pp. 139-140.

[11] *North Carolina Baptist Annual,* 1946, p. 92; "Racial Christianity," p. 73.

[12] "Racial Christianity," p. 73.

[13] *Annual of the Southern Baptist Convention,* 1945, p. 56.

[14] "Southern Baptists Approve Decision," *Christian Century* (June 9, 1954), pp. 691-692.

[15] *Ibid.,* p. 692.

[16] *Annual of the Southern Baptist Convention,* 1955, p. 333.

[17] "Evading the Issue," *Christian Century* (Nov. 6, 1963), pp. 1356-1357.

[18] "Baptists: Behind the Front," *Time* (May 29, 1964), pp. 68-69.

[19] *Annual of the Southern Baptist Convention,* 1965, pp. 246-247.

[20] "Southern Baptists: Toward Integration," *Time* (Nov. 26, 1965), p. 68.

[21] *Annual of the Baptist General Association of Virginia,* 1965, p. 64.

[22] Taken from · "A Statement Concerning the Crisis in Our Nation," circulated by the Christian Life Commission on June 20, 1968.

[23] "Baptists Applaud Racial Amity Plea," *Twin City Sentinel* (June 5, 1970).

[24] Edward B. Fiske, "Black Students Urge Baptists to Follow Principles of Jesus," *The New York Times,* June 3, 1970.

[25] Marshall Frady, "God and Man in the South," *Atlantic* (January, 1967), p. 39.

[26] *Ibid.*, p. 40.

[27] The story of this integrated church is told by Joseph Martin Dawson, "I Belong to a Southern Baptist Integrated Church," *Christian Century* (June 9, 1954), pp. 1303-1304.

[28] Quoted by Pinson, p. 14.

[29] Frady, p. 42.

[30] *Ibid.*, p. 39.

[31] The letter is quoted by Donald G. Shockley in "First Baptist, Birmingham: A Case of Old Wineskins Bursting," *Christian Century* (December 2, 1970), pp. 1462-1463; other details taken from "Birmingham First Defeats Membership Resolution," *The Alabama Baptist* (September 10, 1970), p. 7; "Birmingham Church Moves to Bar Negro Members," *Biblical Recorder* (September 12, 1970), p. 5, and "Breakaway Congregation is Formed," Winston-Salem *Journal,* November 6, 1970.

[32] "Chafin Calls for Realism on Racism in Baptist Churches," *The Alabama Baptist* (September 3, 1970), p. 5.

[33] "Writers Share Convictions on Birmingham Incidents," *Biblical Recorder,* (September 19, 1970), p. 6.

[34] Virtie Stroup, "Church Worker Says Racism Imbedded," *Twin City Sentinel,* September 9, 1970.

[35] Quoted by Dora Byron, "Courage in Action: Koinonia Revisited," *Nation* (March 16, 1957), p. 228.

[36] Robert Lee, "The Crisis at Koinonia," *Christian Century* (November 7, 1956), p. 1291.

[37] Byron, p. 227.

[38] Harold E. Fey, "Creative Church in Georgia," *Christian Century* (March 6, 1957), p. 287.

[39] *Ibid.*, p. 286.

CHAPTER FOURTEEN: QUO VADIS?

[1] W. C. Fields, "Baptists on the Edge of it," *The Baptist Faculty Paper* (Spring, 1970), p. 4.

[2] *Ibid.*

[3] *Ibid.*

[4] *Ibid.*, p. 5.

[5] "Churches Weak, Says Top Baptist," Winston-Salem *Journal,* June 3, 1971.

[6] "Southern Baptists Approve Abortion," *Twin City Sentinel,* June 3, 1971.

[7] "Carson-Newman Asked to Rescind Dancing Policy," *Biblical Recorder,* (November 21, 1970), pp. 16, 22.

[8] This account, involving the First Baptist Church of Newton, is based on interviews with members.

[9] "Storms Gather in Southern Baptist Convention," *Christian Century,* (March 21, 1962), p. 350; "Storm over Genesis," *Newsweek* (November 12, 1962), p. 68.

[10] "Southern Baptists Vote to Censor Book on Bible after Hot Dispute," Winston-Salem *Journal* June 4, 1971.

[11] Clifton J. Allen, ed., *Broadman Bible Commentary,* I (Nashville, 1969), p. 90.

[12] *Ibid.*, p. 198.

[13] "Baptists Uphold Tradition," Winston-Salem *Journal* June 4, 1971.

[14] Virtie Stroup, "Official Defends Book Withdrawal," Winston-Salem *Journal* ,July 6, 1970.

[15] William E. Hull, "Shall We Call the Bible Infallible," *Baptist Program,* (December, 1970), pp. 5, 6, 17-19.

[16] The letters quoted are from *The Baptist Program* (March, 1971), p. 10.

[17] " 'A Gathering Storm,' Minister Says of Southern Baptists' Conflicts," Winston-Salem *Journal* March 13, 1970.

[18] Toby Druin, "Seminar Plumbs Depths of 'Authentic Morality'," *Biblical Recorder,* (March 28, 1970), pp. 4-7.

[19] Virtie Stroup, "Baptist Minister Backs Immersion," *Twin City Sentinel,* April 12, 1971.

[20] "Protestants Feel Pinch of Inflation," Winston-Salem *Journal* April 16, 1970.

[21] Edward B. Fiske, "Baptists Seeking National Character," Winston-Salem *Journal,* June 5, 1970.

[22] *Proceedings of the 1968 Christian Citizenship Seminar on Christian Action in A Disordered Society,* pp. 52, 54.

[23] *Ibid.*, p. 51.

[24] "Book Ban May Split Baptists," *Twin City Sentinel,* June 4, 1970.

[25] David Dudley Field, quoted by Anson Phelps Stokes, *Church and State in the United States* (New York, 1950), p. 37.

[26] Written by an English Baptist minister, John Fawcett (1739-1817).

APPENDIX A

[1] Except where other wise shown, the information in this listing is adapted from Frank S. Mead, *Handbook of Denominations in the United States* (Nashville, 1970) and Constant H. Jacquet, ed., *Yearbook of American Churches* (New York, 1972).

[2] Additional material from Dale Moody, "Whither the Winds of Doctrine?", *The Baptist Program,* January, 1970, p. 9.

[3] Additional material from Frank a. Sharp, "The ABC," *The Baptist Program,* March, 1971, pp. 12-13.

[4] Robert G. Torbet, *A History of the Baptists* (Valley Forge, Pa., 1963), pp. 466-467.

[5] Some data from B. F. Riley, *A History of the Baptists in the Southern States East of the Mississippi* (Philadelphia, 1898), pp. 340-345.

[6] Ollie Latch, "The General Association of General Baptists," *The Baptist Program,* February, 1971, pp. 15-17.

[7] Material taken from Harry A. Ploski and Roscoe C. Brown, Jr., eds., *The Negro Almanac,* (New York, 1967), p. 801.

[8] Additional Material from John Binder, "The North American Baptist General Conference," *The Baptist Program,* May, 1971, pp. 7-8.

[9] Material supplemented by Alton L. Wheeler, "An Overview of Seventh Day Baptists," *The Baptist Program,* January, 1971, pp. 16-17.

BIBLIOGRAPHY

Adlam, S. *The First Baptist Church in America, Not Founded by Roger Williams.* Memphis, Tenn.: Baptist Book House, 1890.

Alcohol, Science and Society. New Haven, Conn: *Quarterly Journal of Studies on Alcohol,* 1945.

Allen, Clifton J., editor. *The Broadman Bible Commentary,* I, Nashville: Broadman Press, 1969.

Annual of the Baptist General Association of Virginia.

Annual of the Southern Baptist Convention, 1923-1970.

Armitage, Thomas. *A History of the Baptists.* New York: Bryan, Taylor, and Co., 1890.

Armstrong, O. K., and Marjorie M. Armstrong. *The Indomitable Baptists.* Garden City, N. Y.: Doubleday and Company, 1967.

Asbury, Herbert. *The Great Illusion.* Garden City, N. Y.: Doubleday and Company, 1950.

Babcock, Rufus, editor. *Memoir of John Mason Peck. Carbondale, Ill.: Southern Illinois University Press,* 1965.

Backus, Isaac. *A History of New England, with Particular Reference to the Denomination of Christians called Baptists,* Second Edition, with editorial notes by David Weston. Newton, Mass.: Backus Historical Society, 1871.

Baker, Robert A. *The Baptist March in History.* Nashville, Tenn.: Convention Press, 1958.

————. *Relations Between Northern and Southern Baptists,* Second Edition. P. p., 1954.

"Baptists Applaud Racial Amity Plea," *Twin City Sentinel,* June 5, 1970.

"Baptists: Behind the Front," *Time,* 83 (May 29, 1964), p. 68.

"Baptists: In a Spirit of Repentance," *Time,* 85 (June 11, 1965), p. 68.

"Baptists to Tighten Screening," *Twin City Sentinel,* Sept. 9, 1970.

"Baptists Uphold Tradition," Winston-Salem *Journal,* June 4, 1971.

Barnes, W. W. *The Southern Baptist Convention,* 1845-1953. Nashville, Tenn.: Broadman Press, 1954.

Barrows, C. E. *History of the First Baptist Church in Newport, R.I.* Newport, R.I.: John P. Sanborn and Company, 1876.

Barrows, E. Edwin, editor. *The Diary of John Comer.* Philadelphia: American Baptist Publication Society, 1892.

Bax, E. Belfort. *Rise and Fall of the Anabaptists.* New York: American Scholar Publications, 1966.

Beale, Howard K. *Are American Teachers Free?* New York: Charles Scribner's Sons, 1936.

"Belligerent Baptists," Christian Century, 85 (Sept. 4, 1968), p. 1096.

Bender, Harold S. *Conrad Grebel*. Goshen, Ind.: The Mennonite Historical Society, 1950.

Benedict, David. *A General History of the Baptist Denomination in America*. New York: Lewis Colby and Company, 1850.

————. *Fifty Years Among the Baptists*. Boston: Sheldon and Company, 1860.

Bicknell, Thomas W. *The Story of Dr. John Clarke*. Providence, R. I.: P.b.a., 1915.

Binder, John. "The North American Baptist General Conference," *The Baptist Program*, May, 1971, pp. 7-8.

"Birmingham Church Moves to Bar Negro Members," *Biblical Recorder*, 136 (Sept. 12, 1970), p. 5.

"Birmingham First Church Defeats Membership Resolution," *The Alabama Baptist*, 135 (Sept. 10, 1970), p. 7.

"Book Ban May Split Baptists," *Twin City Sentinel*, June 4, 1970.

Boyd, Jesse L. *A History of Baptists in America Prior to 1845*. New York: The American Press, 1957.

"Breakaway Congregation is Formed," Winston-Salem *Journal*, November 6, 1970.

Brockunier, Samuel Hugh. *The Irrepressible Democrat, Roger Williams*. New York: The Ronald Press, 1940.

"Brotherhood Limited," *Time*, 59 (June 2, 1952), p. 60.

Brown, Henry F. *Baptism Through the Centuries*. Mountain View, Cal.: Pacific Press Publishing Association, 1965.

Bryan, William Jennings. *In His Image*. New York: Fleming H. Revell Co., 1922.

Burgess, Walter H. *John Smith, the Se-Baptist, Thomas Helwys and the First Baptist Church in England*. London: James Clarke and Company, 1911.

Burrage, Henry S. *A History of the Baptists in New England*. Philadelphia: American Baptist Publication Society, 1894.

Burroughs, P. E. *The Spiritual Conquest of the Second Frontier*. Nashville, Tenn.: Broadman Press, 1942.

Byron, Dora. "Courage in Action: Koinonia Revisited," *Nation*, 184 (March 16, 1957), pp. 226-228.

de Camp, L. Sprague. *The Great Monkey Trial*. New York: Doubleday & Company, 1968.

Campion, Nardi Reeder. "Unforgettable Harry Emerson Fosdick," *The Reader's Digest* January, 1971, pp. 69-73.

"Carson-Newman Asked to Rescind Dancing Policy," *Biblical Recorder*, 136 (Nov. 21, 1970), pp. 16-22.

Cathcart, William. *The Baptists and the American Revolution*. Philadelphia: S.

A. George and Company, 1876.

—————. *Baptist Encyclopedia*. Philadelphia: Louis H. Everts, 1881.

"Chafin Calls for Realism on Racism in Baptist Churches," *The Alabama Baptist*, 135 (Sept. 3, 1970), p. 5.

Childers, James Saxon, editor. *A Way Home: The Baptists Tell Their Story*. Atlanta: Tupper and Love, 1964.

Christian, John T. *A History of the Baptists*. Nashville, Tenn.: Sunday School Board of the Southern Baptist Convention, 1922.

"Churches Weak, Top Baptist Says," Winston-Salem *Journal*, June 3, 1971.

Clark, Henry W. *History of English Nonconformity,* Vol. I. London: Chapman and Hall, Ltd., 1911.

"Clerics' Protest Ousts Two Books," *The New York Times*, December 27, 1970.

Colvin, D. Leigh. *Prohibition in the United States*. New York: George H. Doran Company, 1926.

Compilation of American Baptist Convention Resolutions, Division of Christian Social Concern, American Baptist Convention, n.d., n.p.

Cox, F. A., and J. Hoby. *The Baptists in America*. New York: Leavitt, Lord and Company, 1836.

Cox, Norman W. *Dreams, Dungeons, Diadems!* Nashville, Tenn.: Historical Commission of the Southern Baptist Convention, 1954.

Cramp, J. M. *Baptist History: From the Foundation of the Christian Church to the Present Time*. London: Elliott Stock, 1871.

Dabney, Virginius. *Liberalism in the South*. Chapel Hill, N. C.: The University of North Carolina Press, 1932.

Dawson, Joseph Martin. *Baptists and the American Republic*. Nashville, Tenn.: Broadman Press, 1956.

—————. "I Belong to a Southern Baptist Integrated Church," *Christian Century*, 75 (Nov. 12, 1958), pp. 1303-1304.

Dictionary of American Biography. New York: Charles Scribner's Sons, 1933.

Dictionary of National Biography. London: Oxford University Press, 1921-22.

Druin, Toby, "Seminar Plumbs Depths of 'Authentic Morality'," *Biblical Recorder*, 136 (March 28, 1970), pp. 4-7.

Estep, William R. *The Anabaptist Story*. Nashville, Tenn.: Broadman Press, 1963.

"Evading the Issue," *Christian Century*, 80 (Nov. 6, 1963), pp. 1356-1357.

Fearheily, Don M. *The John Leland Story*. Nashville, Tenn.: Broadman Press, 1964.

Fey, Harold E. "Creative Church in Georgia," *Christian Century*, 74 (March 6, 1957), pp. 285-287.

Fields, W. C. "Baptists on the Edge of It," *The Baptist Faculty Paper* (Spring, 1970), pp. 4-5.

Fiske, Edward B. "Baptists Seeking National Character," Winston-Salem *Journal*, June 5, 1970.

————. "Black Students Urge Baptists to Follow the Principles of Jesus," *The New York Times*, June 3, 1970.

Foote, William Henry. *Sketches of Virginia*. Philadelphia: William S. Martien, 1850.

Fosdick, Harry Emerson. "The Farewell Sermon of Dr. Harry Emerson Fosdick to the First Presbyterian Church of New York." New York, P.P., 1925.

Frady, Marshall. "God and Man in the South," *Atlantic*, 219 (Jan., 1967), pp. 37-42.

Freeman, Douglas Southall. *Lee's Lieutenants*, Volume I. New York: Charles Scribner's Sons, 1942.

Furniss, Norman F. *The Fundamentalist Controversy*, 1918-1931. New Haven, Conn: Yale University Press, 1954.

Gammell, William. *History of the First Baptist Church in Providence, 1639-1877*. Providence, R.I.: J. A. and R. A. Reid, 1877.

Gatewood, Willard B., Jr. *Preachers, Pedagogues and Politicians*. Chapel Hill, N. C.: The University of North Carolina Press, 1966.

" 'A Gathering Storm', Minister Says of Southern Baptists' Conflicts," Winston-Salem *Journal*, March 13, 1970.

Gewehr, Wesley M. *The Great Awakening in Virginia*. Durham, N. C., Duke University Press; 1930.

Ginger, Ray. *Six Days or Forever*. Boston: Beacon Press, 1958.

Glass, Victor T. *Working with National Baptists*. Nashville: Home Mission Board of the Southern Baptist Convention, n. d.

Goadby, J. Jackson. *Bye-Paths in Baptist History*. London: Elliot Stock, 1871.

Griffiths, Thomas S. *A History of Baptists in New Jersey*. Highstown, N.J.: Barr Press Publishing Company, 1904.

Hawks, Francis L. *Rise and Progress of the Protestant Episcopal Church in Virginia*. New York: Harper and Brothers, 1836.

Hays, Arthur Garfield. *Let Freedom Ring*. New York: Boni and Liveright, 1928.

Hordern, William E. *A Layman's Guide to Protestant Theology*. New York: The Macmillan Company, 1968.

Hovey, Alvah. *A Memoir of the Life and Times of the Rev. Isaac Backus*. Boston: Gould and Lincoln, 1858.

Howell, Robert Boyle C. *The Early Baptists of Virginia*. Philadelphia: The Bible and Publication Society, 1857.

Hull, William E. "Shall We Call the Bible Infallible," *The Baptist Program*, (Dec., 1970), pp. 5-6, 17-19.

"Integration by Baptists Advances," *Twin City Sentinel*, May 13, 1971.

Jacquet, Constant H., Jr., editor. *Yearbook of American Churches*. New York: Council Press, 1972.

James, Charles F. *The Struggle for Religious Liberty in Virginia*. Lynchburg, Va.: J. P. Bell Co., 1900.

Jarrel, W. A. *Baptist Church Perpetuity*. Dallas, Tex.: Published by the author, 1894.

Jefferson, Thomas. *Notes on the State of Virginia*. Edited by William Peden. Chapel Hill, N.C.: University of North Carolina Press, 1955.

Knowles, James D. *Memoir of Roger Williams*. Boston: Lincoln, Edmands and Company, 1834.

Latch, Ollie. "The General Association of General Baptists." *The Baptist Program* (Feb., 1971), pp. 15-17.

Lee, Robert. "The Crisis at Koinonia." *Christian Century*, 73 (Nov. 7, 1956), pp. 1290-1291.

Lewis, John. *A Brief History of the Rise and Progress of Anabaptism in England*. London: J. Roberts, 1738.

"Letters," *The Baptist Program* (March, 1971), p. 10.

Linder, Suzanne Cameron. *William Louis Poteat*. Chapel Hill: University of North Carolina Press, 1966.

Lippmann, Walter. *American Inquisitors*. New York: The Macmillan Company, 1928.

Little, Lewis Payton. *Imprisoned Preachers and Religious Liberty In Virginia*. Lynchburg, Va: J. P. Bell Company, 1938.

Loescher, Frank S. *The Protestant Church and the Negro*. New York: Association Press, 1948.

Lumpkin, William L. *Baptist Foundations in the South*. Nashville, Tenn: Broadman Press, 1961.

Lunt, W. E. *History of England*, third edition. New York: Harper and Brothers, 1946.

McFarlane, K. B. *John Wycliffe and English Nonconformity*. London: The Macmillan Company, 1953.

McLoughlin, William G. "Isaac Backus and the Separation of Church and State in America." American Historical Review, LXIII (June, 1968), 1392-1413.

Maston, T. B. *Isaac Backus: Pioneer of Religious Liberty*. Rochester, N.Y.: American Baptist Historical Society, 1962.

May, Lynn E., Jr. "Those Days in May, 1845," *The Baptist Program* (May, 1970), p. 4.

Maring, Norman H. *Baptists in New Jersey*. Valley Forge, Pa.: The Judson Press, 1964.

Marnell, William H. *The First Amendment*. New York: Doubleday & Company, 1964.

Mead, Frank S. *Handbook of Denominations in the United States*. Nashville, Tenn.: Abingdon Press, 1970.

Menno Simons' Life and Writings. Selected and translated from the Dutch by John Horsch. Scottsdale, Pa: Mennonite Publishing House, 1936.

Miller, John C. *Origins of the American Revolution*. Boston: Little, Brown and Company. 1943.

Minutes of the American Baptist Home Missions Society.

Moody, Dale. "Whither the Winds of Doctrine?" *The Baptist Program* (January, 1970), pp. 8-9.

National Cyclopaedia of American Biography. New York: James T. White and Co., 1940.

Nelson, Wilbur. *The Hero of Aquidneck*. Bloomfield, N.J.: Schaefer Enterprises, 1938.

Newman, A. H. *American Church History*, Volume II. New York: Christian Literature Co., 1894.

————, editor. *A Century of Baptist Achievement*. Philadelphia: American Baptist Publication Society, 1901.

————, *A History of Anti-Pedobaptism*. Philadelphia: American Baptist Publication Society, 1897.

————, *A History of the Baptist Churches in the United States*. Philadelphia: American Baptist Publication Society, 1898.

North Carolina Baptist Annual.

Orchard, G. H. *Baptist History*. Nashville, Tenn.: Graves, Marks and Rutland, n.d.

Paschal, George W. *History of North Carolina Baptists*. Raleigh, N.C.: General Board, North Carolina Baptist State Convention, 1930.

Patterson, W. Morgan. *Baptist Successionism, A Critical View*. Valley Forge, Pa.: The Judson Press, 1969.

Pelt, Owen D. and Ralph Lee Smith. *The Story of the National Baptists*. New York: Vantage Press, 1960.

Pinson, William M., Jr. "Others Have, Preacher. What About You?" *The Baptist Program* (January, 1971), p. 13.

Ploski, Harry A., and Roscoe C. Brown, Jr., editors. *The Negro Almanac*. New York: Bellwether Publishing Co., 1967.

Poteat, William Louis. "Christianity and Enlightenment." Printed at the direction of the North Carolina Baptist State Convention, n.d. n.p.

Proceedings at the 250th Anniversary of the Formation of the First Baptist Church in Providence, R.I., April 28, 1889. Providence, R.I.: The Providence Press, 1889.

Proceedings of the 1968 Christian Citizenship Seminar on Christian Action in a Disordered Society.

Proceedings of the Southern Baptist Convention, 1845-1922.

"Protestants Feel Pinch of Inflation," Winston-Salem *Journal*, April 16, 1970.

Putnam, Mary Burnham. *The Baptists and Slavery*, Ann Arbor, Mich: George Wahr, 1913.

"Racial Christianity," *Time*, 48 (Dec. 9, 1946), p. 73.

Ragsdale, B. D. *Story of Georgia Baptists*, Vol. III. Atlanta: Executive Committee of the Georgia Baptist Convention, 1938.

Ranke, Leopold. *History of the Reformation in Germany*. Translated by Sarah Austin. Philadelphia: Lea and Blanchard, 1844.

"Richmond Church Suit Dismissed," *Christian Century*, 83 (March 30, 1966), pp. 411-412.

Riley, B. F. *A History of the Baptists in the Southern States East of the Mississippi*. Philadelphia: American Baptist Publication Society, 1898.

————. *A Memorial History of the Baptists of Alabama*. Philadelphia: The Judson Press, 1923.

Robertson, Archie. *That Old-Time Religion*. Boston: Houghton Mifflin Co., 1950.

Ryland, Garnett. *The Baptists of Virginia, 1699-1926*. Richmond: The Virginia Board of Missions and Education, 1955.

Rutenberger, Culbert G. "American Baptists Respond to Black Power Challenge," *Christian Century*, 85 (July 3, 1968), pp. 878-880.

Schevill, Ferdinand. *A History of Europe*. New York: Harcourt, Brace and Company, 1941.

Semple, Robert B. *History of the Rise and Progress of the Baptists in Virginia*. Revised and extended by W. G. Beale. Richmond, Va.: Pitt and Dickinson, 1894.

Sharp, Frank A. "The ABC," *The Baptist Program* (March, 1971), pp. 12-13.

Shockley, Donald G. "First Baptist, Birmingham: A Case Study of Old Wineskins Bursting." *Christian Century*, 87 (Dec. 2, 1970), pp. 1462-1463.

Shurtleff, Nathaniel B., editor. *Records of Massachusetts*, Vol. I. Boston: William White Press, 1853.

Simms, James M. *The First Colored Baptist Church in North America*, Philadelphia: J. B. Lippincott, 1888.

"Southern Baptist Convention Presidents," *The Baptist Program* (January, 1970), pp. 16-19.

"Southern Baptists Approve Abortion," *Twin City Sentinel*, June 3, 1971.

"Southern Baptists Approve Decision," *Christian Century*, 71 (June 9, 1954), pp. 691-692.

"Southern Baptists Tackle Race Problem," *Christian Century*, 81 (Sept. 23, 1964), pp. 1164-1165.

"Southern Baptists: Toward Integration," *Time*, 86 (Nov. 26, 1965), p. 68.

"Southern Baptists Vote to Censor Book on Bible after Hot Debate," Winston-Salem *Journal*, June 4, 1971.

Sprague, William B. *Annals of the American Baptist Pulpit*. New York: Robert Carter and Brothers, 1860.

"A Statement Concerning the Crisis in Our Nation," Christian Life Commission of the Southern Baptist Convention, n.d., n.p.

Stealey, Sydnor L., editor. *A Baptist Treasury*. New York: Thomas Y. Crowell Co., 1958.

Stedman, Murray S., Jr. *Religion and Politics in America*. New York: Harcourt, Brace and World, 1964.

Stokes, Anson Phelps. *Church and State in the United States*. New York: Harper and Bros., 1950.

"Storm Over Genesis," *Newsweek*, 60 (Nov. 12, 1962), p. 68.

"Storms Gather in Southern Baptist Convention," *Christian Century*, 79 (Mar. 21, 1962), p. 350.

Stroup, Virtie. "Baptist Minister Backs Immersion," Twin City *Sentinel*, April 12, 1971.

————. "Church Worker Says Racism Imbedded, Winston-Salem *Journal*, Aug. 30, 1970.

————. "Official Defends Book Withdrawal," Winston-Salem *Journal*, July 6, 1970.

Sweet, William Warren. *Religion in the Development of American Culture*. New York: Charles Scribner's Sons, 1952.

————. *Religion on the American Frontier: The Baptists, 1783-1830*. New York: Henry Holt and Company, 1931.

Taylor, George Braxton. *Virginia Baptist Ministers*, Third and Fourth Series. Lynchburg, Va.: J. P. Bell Company, 1912, 1913.

Taylor, James B. *Lives of Virginia Baptist Ministers*, Vol. I Richmond, Va.: Yale and Wyatt, 1837.

Thom, W. T. *The Struggle for Religious Freedom in Virginia: The Baptists*. Baltimore: The Johns Hopkins Press, 1900.

Thompson, Evelyn Wingo. *Luther Rice: Believer in Tomorrow*. Nashville, Tenn.: Broadman Press, 1967.

Tompkins, Jerry R., editor. *D-Days at Dayton: Reflections on the Scopes Trial*. Baton Rouge, La.: Louisiana State University Press, 1965.

Torbet, Robert G. *A History of the Baptists*. Valley Forge, Pa.: The Judson Press, 1963.

Truett, George W. *Baptists and Religious Liberty*. Nashville, Tenn: Sunday School Board, Southern Baptist Convention, 1920.

Underhill, Edward B., editor. *A Martyrology of the Churches of Christ, Commonly Called Baptists*, Vols. I-II. London: The Hanserd Knollys Society, 1850, 1853.

Vedder, Henry C. *A History of the Baptists in the Middle States.* Philadelphia: American Baptist Publication Society, 1898.

——————. *A Short History of the Baptists.* Philadelphia: American Baptist Publication Society, 1891.

"Votes to Admit Negroes," *Christian Century*, 81 (Feb. 19, 1964), p. 229.

Warner, H. J. *The Albigensian Heresy.* New York: Russell & Russell, 1967.

Washington, Joseph R., Jr. *Black Religion.* Boston: Beacon Press, 1964.

Wenger, John Christian, editor. *The Complete Writings of Menno Simons.* Scottsdale, Pa.: Herald Press, 1956.

Wheeler, Alton L. "An Overview of Seventh Day Baptists." *The Baptist Program* (January, 1971), pp. 16-17.

Whitley, W. T. *A History of British Baptists.* London: Charles Griffin and Company, Ltd., 1923.

Whitsitt, William H. *A Question in Baptist History.* Louisville, Ky.: Charles T. Dearing, 1896.

Winthrop, John. *The History of New England from 1630 to 1649.* Boston: Little, Brown and Company, 1853.

Woolley, Davis C., editor. *Baptist Advance.* Nashville, Tenn.: Broadman Press, 1964.

Woods, George B., Homer A. Watt and George K. Anderson. *The Literature of England*, revised edition. New York: Scott, Foresman and Co., 1941.

Woodson, Carter Godwin. *The History of the Negro Church.* Washington: Associated Publishers, 1921.

"Writers Share Convictions on Birmingham Church Incidents," *Biblical Recorder*, 136 (Sept. 19, 1970), p. 6.

241

Bryan, William Jennings, 142, 156
Bryant, Twila, 193
Bryant, Mrs. Winifred, 193
Buell, Rev. John, 200
Bull, Henry, 44
Bull Run, Battles of, 126
Bunyan, John, 30, 31
Burma, 102, 103, 105
Bushyhead, John, 118
Butler Act, 156
Butler, Benjamin F., 129
Butler, John Washington, 155

Caesar, 30
Calcutta, India, 100, 102
Callender, Elisha, 57
Callender, Ellis, 55
Callender, John, 42
Calvin, John, 22, 27, 49
Cambridge, Mass., 65
Cambridge University, 25, 36
Campbell, Alexander, 109
Canada, 107
Cape Cod, 43
Carey, Edmund, 100
Carey, Lott, 166
Carpenter, William, 40
Carson Newman College, 200
Carter, Robert, 111
Carthaginian Council, 15
Cartwright, Rev. Peter, 138
Cathari, 10
Cathcart, William, 30, 82, 92
Catholicism, 1, 6, 9-14, 17, 19, 31, 34, 35, 49, 55, 56, 80, 90, 94, 95, 145
Chafin, Kenneth L., 193
Charles I, 37
Charles II, 54, 55
Charles V, 20
Charleston, S. C., 83, 104, 122
Charleston Association, 114
Charter of Liberties of the Colony of New York, 88
Chelcicky, Peter, 14
Childs, James, 74
China, 125, 147
Chrisman, Dr. Thomas, 97
Christian Century, 186
Christian Life Commission, 185, 187, 188, 203, 204

Christian Reflector, 115
Church of England, 26, 36, 49, 68, 78
Clark, Henry W., 24
Clarke, Elizabeth, 44
Clarke, Dr. John, 42, 43, 44, 45, 46, 51, 52
Clarke, Joseph, 44
Clarke, Thomas, 44
Clopton, Abner W., 139
Coddington, William, 44
Coggleshall, John, 44
Coke, Sir Edward, 36
Cole, Robert, 40
Colgate University, 147, 174
Coleman, Benjamin, 97
Colley, Rev. W. W., 171, 172
Columbian College, 105
Comer, Rev. John, 85
Committee on the Religious Instruction of the Colored People, 169
Cone, Spencer H., 115
Congregationalism, 1, 25, 34, 35-38, 40, 43, 48, 55, 56, 59, 63, 65, 66, 69, 80, 82, 87, 101, 102, 104, 105
Connecticut, 34, 55
Constitution, 80, 81, 89
Continental Congress, 64
Conventicle Act, 31
Cooley, Jim, 194
CORE, 174
Cornwallis, Lord, 91
Council of Verone, 12
Counsel, Samuel, 97
Courtney, John, 165
Cox, Nicholas, 92
Craig, Lewis, 73, 74, 94
Cramp, J. M., 12, 13, 20
Crandall, John, 51
Crane, James C., 123
Criswell, Dr. W. A., 191
Crozer Theological Seminary, 175
Cundiff, Bryce, 154
Curtis, Richard, Jr., 95

Danes, 100
Darrow, Clarence, 156
Darwin, Charles, 141, 144
Darwinism, 142, 144, 154, 178

242

247

248